THE GREAT
WRITERS
L I B R A R Y

DIARY

Front cover: View of Greenwich (detail) by
Hendrik Danckerts/National Maritime Museum, London.

This edition is the copyright © 1988 of Marshall Cavendish Ltd.

Published in 1988 for The Great Writers library by
Marshall Cavendish Ltd, 58 Old Compton Street, London W1V 5PA.

Printed and bound in Spain by Printer Industria Gráfica, Barcelona. D.L.B. 38918-1988

ISBN 0-86307-715-3

This is a facsimile reproduction of an edition published in 1933 by
Macmillan and Co., Limited, London.

"*I walked towards Whitehall, but, being wearied, turned into St. Dunstan's Church, where I heard an able sermon of the minister of the place; and stood by a pretty, modest maid, whom I did labour to take by the hand; but she would not, but got further and further from me; and, at last, I could perceive her to take pins out of her pocket to prick me if I should touch her again – which seeing, I did forebear, and was glad I did spy her design. And then I fell to gaze upon another pretty maid in a pew close to me, and she on me; and I did go about to take her by the hand, which she suffered a little, and then withdrew. So the sermon ended, and the church broke up, and my amours ended also.*"

DIARY

SELECTIONS

SAMUEL PEPYS

THE DIARY OF SAMUEL PEPYS

1659

BLESSED be God, at the end of the last year I was in very good health, without any sense of my old pain, but upon taking of cold. I lived in Axe Yard, having my wife, and servant Jane, and no other in family than us three.

The condition of the State was thus: viz., the Rump, after being disturbed by my Lord Lambert, was lately returned to sit again. The officers of the Army all forced to yield. Lawson lies still in the river, and Monk is with his army in Scotland. Only my Lord Lambert is not yet come into the Parliament, nor is it expected that he will, without being forced to it. The new Common Council of the City do speak very high; and had sent to Monk their sword-bearer to acquaint him with their desires for a free and full Parliament, which is at present the desires and the hopes and the expectations of all: twenty-two of the old secluded members having been at the House-door the last week to demand entrance, but it was denied them; and it is believed that neither they nor the people will be satisfied till the House be filled. My own private condition very handsome, and esteemed rich, but indeed very poor; besides my goods of my house, and my office, which at present is somewhat uncertain. Mr. Downing master of my office.

January 1660

January 1st. (Lord's day.) This morning (we living lately in the garret) I rose, put on my suit with great skirts, having not lately worn any other clothes but them. Went to Mr. Gunning's chapel at Exeter House, where he made a very good sermon. Dined at home in the garret, where my wife dressed the remains of a turkey; and in the doing of it she burned her hand. I stayed at home the whole afternoon, looking over my accounts; then went with my wife to my father's, and in going observed the great posts which the City workmen set up at the Conduit in Fleet Street.

2nd. Walked a great while in Westminster Hall, where I heard that Lambert was coming up to London; that my Lord Fairfax was in the head of the Irish brigade, but it was not certain what he would declare for. The House was to-day upon finishing the act for the Council of State, which they did; and for the indemnity to the soldiers; and were to sit again thereupon in the afternoon. Great talk that many places had declared for a free Parliament; and it is believed that they will be forced to fill up the House with the old members. From the Hall I called at home, and so went to Mr. Crewe's (my wife she was to go to her father's); and Mr. Moore and I and another gentleman went out and drank a cup of ale together in the new market, and there I ate some bread and cheese for my dinner.

16th. In the morning I went up to Mr. Crewe's, who did talk to me concerning things of state; and expressed his mind how just it was that the secluded members should come to sit again. From thence to my office, where nothing to do; but Mr. Downing came and found me all alone; and did mention to me his going back into Holland, and did ask me whether I would go or no, but gave me little encouragement, but bid me consider of it; and asked me whether I did not think that Mr. Hawley could perform the work of my office alone. I confess I was at a great loss all the day after to bethink myself how to carry this business. I staid up till the bell-man came by with his bell just under my window as I was writing of this very line, and cried, " Past one of the clock, and a cold, frosty, windy morning."

19th. This morning I was sent for to Mr. Downing, and at his bedside he told me that he had a kindness for me, and that he thought that he had done me one; and that was, that he had got me to be one of the Clerks of the Council; at which I was a little stumbled, and could not tell what to do, whether to thank him or no; but by and by I did; but not very heartily, for I feared that his doing of it was only to ease himself of the salary which he gives me.

26th. Home from my office to my Lord's lodgings, where my wife had got ready a very fine dinner —viz., a dish of marrow bones; a leg of mutton, a loin of veal; a dish of fowl, three pullets, and a dozen of larks all in a dish; a great tart, a neat's tongue, a dish of anchovies; a dish of prawns and cheese. My company was my father, my uncle Fenner, his two sons, Mr. Pierce, and all their wives, and my brother Tom. The news this day is a letter that speaks absolutely Monk's concurrence with this Parliament, and nothing else, which yet I hardly believe.

29th. Casting up my accounts, I do find myself to be worth £40 and more, which I did not think, but am afraid that I have forgot something.

30th This morning, before I was up, I fell a-singing of my song, " Great, good, and just," etc., and put myself thereby in mind that this was the fatal day, now ten years since, his Majesty died. There seems now to be a general cease of talk, it being taken for granted that Monk do resolve to stand to the Parliament, and nothing else. I took my £12 : 10s. due to me for my last quarter's salary.

February 1660

February 3rd. Drank my morning draught at Harper's, and was told there that the soldiers were all quiet upon promise of pay. Thence to St. James's Park, back to Whitehall, where in a guard-chamber I saw about thirty or forty 'prentices of the City, who were taken at twelve o'clock last night, and brought prisoners hither. Thence to my office. About noon, Mrs. Turner came to speak with me and Joyce, and I took them and showed them the manner of the Houses sitting, the doorkeeper very civilly opening the door for us. We went walking all over Whitehall, whither General Monk was newly come, and we saw all his forces march by in very good plight, and stout officers. After dinner I went to hear news, but only found that the Parliament House was most of them with Monk at Whitehall, and that in passing through the town he had many calls to him for a free Parliament, but little other welcome. I saw in the Palace Yard how unwilling some of the old soldiers were yet to go out of town without their money, and swore if they had it not in three days, as they were promised, they would do them more mischief in the country than if they had stayed here; and that is very likely, the country being all discontented. The town and guards are already full of Monk's soldiers. It growing dark, to take a turn in the Park, where Theoph. (she was sent for to us to dinner) outran my wife and another poor woman, that laid a pot of ale with me that she would outrun her.

14th. My wife, hearing Mr. Moore's voice in my dressing-chamber, got herself ready, and came down and challenged him for her Valentine.

21st. After dinner, to Westminster Hall. Here I met with Mr. Lock and Pursell, Master of Music, and went

with them to the Coffee-House, into a room next the
water, by ourselves, where we spent an hour or two.
Here we had variety of brave Italian and Spanish
songs, and a canon for eight voices, which Mr. Lock
had lately made on these words, " Domine salvum fac
Regem." Here out of the windows it was a most
pleasant sight to see the City from one end to the other
with a glory about it, so high was the light of the bonfires, and so thick round the City, and the bells rang
everywhere.

22nd. Mr. Pierce told me he would go with me
to Cambridge, where Colonel Ayres' regiment, to
which he is surgeon, lieth.

23rd. Thursday, my birthday, now twenty-seven
years. To Westminster Hall, where, after the House
rose, I met with Mr. Crewe, who told me that my
Lord was chosen by 73 voices to be one of the Council
of State. Mr. Pierpoint had the most, 101, and himself the next, 100.

24th. I rose very early, and taking horse at Scotland Yard, at Mr. Garthwayt's stable, I rode to Mr.
Pierce's; we both mounted, and so set forth about
seven of the clock; at Puckridge we baited, the way
exceeding bad from Ware thither. Then up again
and as far as Foulmer, within six miles of Cambridge,
my mare being almost tired; here we lay at the
Chequer. I lay with Mr. Pierce, who we left here the
next morning, upon his going to Hinchingbroke, to
speak with my Lord, before his going to London, and
we two came to Cambridge by eight o'clock in the
morning. I went to Magdalene College, to Mr. Hill,
with whom I found Mr. Zanchy, Burton, and Hollins,
and took leave on promise to sup with them. To the
Three Tuns, where we drank pretty hard and many
healths to the King, etc.; then we broke up, and I
and Mr. Zanchy went to Magdalene College, where
a very handsome supper at Mr. Hill's chambers, I

suppose upon a club among them, where I could find that there was nothing at all left of the old preciseness in their discourse, specially on Saturday nights; and Mr. Zanchy told me that there was no such thing nowadays among them at any time.

25th. My father, brother, and I to Mr. Widdrington, at Christ's College, who received us very civilly, and caused my brother to be admitted.

26th. (Sunday.) My brother went to the College Chapel. At St. Botolph's Church we heard Mr. Nicholas, of Queens' College, who I knew in my time to be Tripos with great applause, upon this text, " For thy commandments are broad." To Mr. Widdrington's to dinner, where he used us very courteously. Found Mr. Pierce at our Inn, who told us that he had lost his journey, for my Lord was gone from Hinchingbroke to London on Thursday last, at which I was a little put to a stand. I went to Magdalene College, to get the certificate of the College for my brother's entrance there that he might save his year.

27th. Up by four o'clock. Mr. Blayton and I took horse and straight to Saffron Walden, where, at the White Hart, we set up our horses, and took the master of the house to show us Audley End House, who took us on foot through the park, and so to the house, where the housekeeper showed us all the house, in which the stateliness of the ceilings, chimney-pieces, and form of the whole was exceedingly worth seeing. He took us into the cellar, where we drank most admirable drink, a health to the King. Here I played on my flageolet, there being an excellent echo. He showed us excellent pictures; two especially, those of the four Evangelists and Henry VIII. In our going, my landlord carried us through a very old hospital or almshouse, where forty poor people were maintained; a very old foundation; and over the chimney-piece was an inscription in brass: "Orate pro anima Thomae

6

Bird," etc. They brought me a draught of their drink
in a brown bowl, tipped with silver, which I drank off,
and at the bottom was a picture of the Virgin with the
child in her arms, done in silver. So we took leave,
the road pretty good, but the weather rainy to Epping.

28th. Up in the morning, and had some red
herrings to our breakfast, while my boot-heel was
a-mending; by the same token the boy left the hole
as big as it was before. Then to horse for London.

29th. To my office. Mr. Moore told me how my
Lord is chosen General at Sea by the Council, and that
it is thought that Monk will be joined with him therein.
This day my Lord came to the House, the first time
since he came to town; but he had been at the
Council before. My cousin Morton gave me a brave
cup of metheglin, the first I ever drank.

March 1660

March 2nd. Great is the dispute now in the House,
in whose name the writs shall run for the next Parliament; and it is said that Mr. Prin, in open House,
said, " In King Charles's."

5th. To Westminster by water, only seeing Mr.
Pinkney at his own house, where he showed me how he
had always kept the Lion and Unicorn, in the back of
his chimney, bright, in expectation of the King's
coming again. At home I found Mr. Hunt, who told
me how the Parliament had voted that the Covenant
be printed and hung in churches again. Great hopes
of the King's coming again.

6th. (Shrove Tuesday.) I called Mr. Shepley, and
we both went up to my Lord's lodgings at Mr. Crewe's,
where he bids us to go home again, and get a fire
against an hour after; which we did, at Whitehall,
whither he came, and after talking with him about our
going to sea, he called me by myself into the garden,

where he asked me how things were with me. He bid me look out now at this turn some good place, and he would use all his own, and all the interest of his friends that he had in England, to do me good; and asked me whether I could, without too much inconvenience, go to sea as his secretary, and bid me think of it. He also began to talk of things of State, and told me that he should want one in that capacity at sea, that he might trust in, and therefore he would have me to go. He told me also that he did believe the King would come in, and did discourse with me about it, and about the affection of the people and City, at which I was full glad. Mr. Hawley brought me a seaman that had promised £10 to him if he get him a purser's place, which I think to endeavour to do. My uncle Tom inquires about the Knights of Windsor, of which he desires to be one. To see Mrs. Jem, at whose chamber door I found a couple of ladies, but she not being there, we hunted her out, and found that she and another had hid themselves behind a door. Well, they all went down into the dining-room, where it was full of tag, rag, and bobtail, dancing, singing, and drinking, of which I was ashamed, and, after I had stayed a dance or two, I went away. Wrote by the post, by my Lord's command, for J. Goods to come up presently; for my Lord intends to go forthwith into the *Swiftsure* till the *Nazeby* be ready. This day I hear that the Lords do intend to sit: a great store of them are now in town, and, I see, in the Hall to-day. Overton at Hull do stand out, but can, it is thought, do nothing; and Lawson, it is said, is gone with some ships thither, but all that is nothing. My Lord told me that there was great endeavours to bring in the Protector again; but he told me, too, that he did believe it would not last long if he were brought in; no, nor the King neither (though he seems to think that he will come in), unless he carry himself very soberly and well.

8

Everybody now drinks the King's health without any fear, whereas before it was very private that a man dare do it. Monk this day is feasted at Mercers' Hall, and is invited one after another to the twelve Halls in London. Many think that he is honest yet, and some or more think him to be a fool that would raise himself, but think that he will undo himself by endeavouring it.

9th. To my Lord at his lodging, and came to Westminster with him in his coach; and Mr. Dudley and he in the Painted Chamber walked a good while; and I telling him that I was willing and ready to go with him to sea, he agreed that I should, and advised me what to write to Mr. Downing about it.

10th. To my father in his cutting-house, and told him my resolution to go to sea with my Lord, and we resolved of letting my wife be at Mr. Bowyer's.

12th. Rode to Huntsmore to Mr. Bowyer's, where I found him, and all well, and willing to have my wife come and board with them while I was at sea. Here I lay, and took a spoonful of honey and a nutmeg, scraped for my cold, by Mr. Bowyer's direction.

13th. At my Lord's lodgings, who told me that I was to be secretary, and Crewe deputy-treasurer to the Fleet; at which I was troubled, but I could not help it. This day the Parliament voted all that had been done by the former Rump against the House of Lords to be void, and to-night that the writs go out without any qualification. Things seem very doubtful what will be the end of all; for the Parliament seems to be strong for the King, while the soldiers do all talk against.

14th. To my Lord's, where infinity of applications to him and to me. To my great trouble, my Lord gives me all the papers that was given to him, to put in order and to give him an account of them. I went hence to St. James's, to speak with Mr. Clerke, Monk's secretary, about getting some soldiers removed out of Huntingdon to Oundle, which my Lord told me he did to do a courtesy to the town, that he might have the greater interest in them, in the choice of the next Parliament; not that he intends to be chosen himself, but that he might have Mr. G. Montagu and my Lord Mandeville chose there in spite of the Bernards. This done, I saw General Monk, and methought he seemed a dull, heavy man. I did promise to give my wife all that I have in the world, but my books, in case I should die at sea. After supper I went to Westminster Hall, and the Parliament sat till ten at night, thinking and being expected to dissolve themselves to-day, but they did not. Great talk to-night that the discontented officers did think this night to make a stir, but prevented.

15th. Early packing up my things to be sent by cart with the rest of my Lord's. At Will's I met Tom Alcock, one that went to school with me at Huntingdon, but I had not seen him these sixteen years.

16th. To Westminster Hall, where I heard how the Parliament had this day dissolved themselves, and did pass very cheerfully through the Hall, and the Speaker without his mace. The whole Hall was joyful thereat, as well as themselves, and now they begin to talk loud of the King. To-night I am told that yesterday, about five o'clock in the afternoon, one came with a ladder to the Great Exchange, and wiped with a brush the inscription that was on King Charles, and that there was a great bonfire made in the Exchange, and people called out, " God bless King Charles the Second! "

17th. This day, before I went out with my wife, I did seal my will to her, whereby I did give her all that I have in the world, but my books, which I give to my brother John, excepting only French books, which my wife is to have.

20th. I took a short melancholy leave of my father and mother, without having them to drink, or say anything of business one to another. At Westminster, by reason of rain and an easterly wind, the water was so high that there was boats rowed in King Street, and all our yards was drowned, that one could not go to my house, so as no man has seen the like almost, and most houses full of water.

24th. At work hard all the day writing letters to the Council, etc.; Mr. Creed came on board, and dined very boldly with my Lord. The boy Eliezer flung down a can of beer upon my papers, which made me give him a box of the ear, it having cost me a great deal of work.

25th. (Lord's day.) About two o'clock in the morning, letters from London by our coxswain; so they waked me, but I bid him stay till morning, which he did, and then I rose and carried them into my Lord, who read them a-bed. Among the rest, there was the writ and mandate for him to dispose to the Cinque Ports for choice of Parliament-men. There was also one for me from Mr. Blackburne, who with his own hand superscribes it to S. P., Esq., of which God knows I was not a little proud.

26th. This day it is two years since it pleased God that I was cut for the stone at Mrs. Turner's in Salisbury Court; and did resolve while I live to keep it a festival, as I did the last year at my house, and for ever to have Mrs. Turner and her company with me. But now it pleased God that I am prevented to do it openly; only within my soul I can and do rejoice, and bless God, being at this time, blessed be his holy name, in as good health as ever I was in my life.

April 1660

April 29th. (Sunday.) After sermon in the morning Mr. Cooke came from London with a packet, bringing news how all the young lords that were not in arms against the Parliament do now sit. That a letter is come from the King to the House, which is locked up by the Council till next Thursday, that it may be read in the open House when they meet again, they having adjourned till then to keep a fast to-morrow. And so the contents are not yet known.

30th. Mr. Shepley and I got my Lord's leave to go on shore, it being very pleasant in the fields, but a very pitiful town Deal is.

May 1660

May 2nd. Mr. Donne from London, with letters that tell us the welcome news of the Parliament's votes yesterday, which will be remembered for the happiest May-day that hath been many a year to England. The King's letter was read in the House, wherein he submits himself and all things to them, as to an Act of Oblivion to all, unless they shall please to except any; as to the confirming of the sales of the King's and Church lands, if they see good. The House, upon reading the letter, ordered £50,000 to be forthwith provided to send to His Majesty for his present supply; and a committee chosen to return an answer of thanks to His Majesty for his gracious letter; and that the letter be kept among the records of the Parliament; and in all this not so much as one No. The City of London have put out a Declaration, wherein they do disclaim their owning any other government but that of a King, Lords, and

Commons. Great joy all yesterday at London, and at night more bonfires than ever, and ringing of bells, and drinking of the King's health upon their knees in the streets, which methinks is a little too much. But everybody seems to be very joyful in the business, insomuch that our sea-commanders now begin to say so too, which a week ago they would not do. And our seamen, as many as had money or credit for drink, did do nothing else this evening.

3rd. This morning my Lord showed me the King's declaration and his letter to the two Generals to be communicated to the fleet. The contents of the letter are his offer of grace to all that will come in within forty days, only excepting them that the Parliament shall hereafter except. That the sales of lands during these troubles, and all other things, shall be left to the Parliament, by which he will stand. The letter dated at Breda, April $\frac{4}{14}$, 1660, in the twelfth year of his reign. Upon the receipt of it this morning by an express, Mr. Philips, one of the messengers of the Council from General Monk, my Lord summoned a council of war, and in the meantime did dictate to me how he would have the vote ordered which he would have pass this council. Which done, the Commanders all came on board, and the council sat in the coach (the first council of war that had been in my time), where I read the letter and declaration; and while they were discoursing upon it, I seemed to draw up a vote, which, being offered, they passed. Not one man seemed to say No to it, though I am confident many in their hearts were against it. After this was done, I went up to the quarter-deck with my Lord and the Commanders, and there read both the papers and the vote; which done, and demanding their opinion, the seamen did all of them cry out, " God bless King Charles ! " with the greatest joy imaginable. After dinner, to the rest of the ships quite through the fleet, which was a very brave sight to visit all the ships, and to be received with the respect and honour that I was on board them all; and much more to see the great joy that I brought to all men; not one through the whole fleet showing me the least dislike of the business. In the evening as I was going on board the Vice-Admiral, the General began to fire his guns, which he did all that he had in the ship, and so did all the rest of the Commanders, which was very gallant, and to hear the bullets go hissing over our heads as we were in the boats. This done, and finished my Proclamation, I returned to the *Nazeby*, where my Lord was much pleased to hear how all the fleet took it in a transport of joy, showed me a private letter of the King's to him, and another from the Duke of York, in such familiar style as their common friend, with all kindness imaginable. And I found by the letters, and so my Lord told me too, that there had been many letters passed between them for a great while, and I perceive unknown to Monk. The King speaks of his being courted to come to the Hague, but do desire my Lord's advice where to come to take ship; and the Duke offers to learn the seaman's trade of him, in such familiar words as if Jack Cole and I had writ them. This was very strange to me, that my Lord should carry all things so wisely and prudently as he do, and I was over-joyful to see him in so good condition, and he did not a little please himself to tell me how he had provided for himself so great a hold on the King. After this to supper, and then to writing of letters till twelve at night, and so up again at three in the morning. My Lord seemed to put great confidence in me, and would take my advice in many things. I perceive his being willing to do all the honour in the world to Monk, and to let him have all the honour of doing the business, though he will many times express his thoughts of him to be but a thick-skulled fool. So that I do believe there is some agreement more than ordinary between the King and my Lord to let Monk carry on the business, for it is he that must do the business, or at least that can hinder it, if he be not flattered and observed. This my Lord will hint himself sometimes.

4th. I wrote this morning many letters, and to all the copies of the vote of the council of war I put my name, that if it should come in print my name may be to it.

8th. After dinner came several persons of honour, as my Lord St. John and others, for convoy to Flushing, and great giving of them salutes. My Lord and we at ninepins: I lost 9s. Mr. Cooke brings me news of my wife. He went to Huntsmore to see her, and brought her and my father Bowyer to London, where he left her at my father's very well, and speaks very well of her love to me. My letters to-day tell me how it was intended that the King should be proclaimed to-day in London, with a great deal of pomp. I had also news who they are that are chosen of the Lords and Commons to attend the King; and also the whole story of what we did the other day in the fleet, at reading of the King's declaration, and my name at the bottom of it.

11th. This morning we began to pull down all the State's arms in the fleet, having first sent to Dover for painters and others to come to set up the King's.

14th. Mr. North and Dr. Clerke went to kiss the Queen of Bohemia's hands, from my Lord, with twelve attendants from on board to wait on them, among which I sent my boy. After noon they came back again, after having kissed the Queen of Bohemia's hand, and were sent again by my Lord to do the same to the Prince of Orange. So I got the Captain to ask leave for me to go, which my Lord did give, and I, taking my boy and Judge Advocate with me, went in company with them. The weather bad; we were sadly washed when we came near the shore, it being very hard to land there. The shore is, as all the country between that and the Hague, all sand. The Hague is a most neat place in all respects. The houses so neat in all places and things as is possible. Here we walked up and down a great while, the town being now very full of Englishmen, for that the Londoners were come on shore to-day. But going to see the Prince, he was gone forth with his governor, and so we walked up and down the town and court to see the place; and by the help of a stranger, an Englishman, we saw a great many places, and were made to understand many things, as the intention of maypoles, which we saw there standing at every great man's door, of different greatness according to the quality of the person. About ten at night the Prince comes home, and we found an easy admission. His attendance very inconsiderable as for a Prince; but yet handsome, and his tutor a fine man, and himself a very pretty boy. This done, we went to a place we had taken to sup in, where a sallet and two or three bones of mutton were provided for a matter of ten of us, which was very strange. The Judge and I lay in one press bed, there being two more in the same room; my boy sleeping on a bench by me.

16th. This afternoon Mr. Edward Pickering told me in what a sad poor condition for clothes and money the King was, and all his attendants, when he came to him first from my Lord, their clothes not being worth forty shillings the best of them. And how overjoyed the King was when Sir J. Greenville brought him some money; so joyful, that he called

the Princess Royal and Duke of York to look upon
it, as it lay in the portmanteau, before it was taken
out. My Lord told me, too, that the Duke of York
is made High Admiral of England.

17th. Dr. Clerke came to tell me that he heard
this morning, by some Dutch that are come on board
already to see the ships, that there was a Portuguese
taken yesterday at the Hague, that had a design to
kill the King. But this I heard afterwards was only
the mistake upon one being observed to walk with
his sword naked, he having lost his scabbard. Before
dinner Mr. Edward Pickering and I, W. Howe, Pim,
and my boy, to Scheveling, where we took coach;
and so to the Hague, where walking, intending to
find one that might show us the King incognito, I
met with Captain Whittington (that had formerly
brought a letter to my Lord from the Mayor of
London), and he did promise me to do it, but first
we went and dined at a French house, but paid 16s.
for our part of the club. At dinner in came Dr. Cade,
a merry mad parson of the King's. And they two
got the child and me (the others not being able to
crowd in) to see the King, who kissed the child very
affectionately. Then we kissed his, and the Duke of
York's, and the Princess Royal's hands. The King
seemed to be a very sober man; and a very splendid
Court he hath in the number of persons of quality
that are about him, English, very rich in habit.
From the King to the Lord Chancellor, who did lie
bedrid of the gout, he spoke very merrily to the child
and me. After that, going to see the Queen of
Bohemia, I met Dr. Fuller, whom I sent to a tavern
with Mr. Edward Pickering, while I and the rest
went to see the Queen, who used us very respectfully:
her hand we all kissed. She seems a very debonair,
but a plain lady.

21st. The weather foul all this day also. After

dinner, about writing one thing or other all day, and setting my papers in order, hearing, by letters that came hither in my absence, that the Parliament had ordered all persons to be secured, in order to a trial, that did sit as judges in the late King's death, and all the officers attending the Court. Sir John Lenthall moving in the House that all that had borne arms against the King should be exempted from pardon, he was called to the bar of the House, and after a severe reproof, he was degraded his knighthood. At Court I find that all things grow high. The old clergy talk as being sure of their lands again, and laugh at the Presbytery; and it is believed that the sales of the King's and Bishops' lands will never be confirmed by Parliament, there being nothing now in any man's power to hinder them and the King from doing what they had a mind, but everybody willing to submit to anything. We expect every day to have the King and Duke on board as soon as it is fair. My Lord does nothing now, but offers all things to the pleasure of the Duke as Lord High Admiral, so that I am at a loss what to do.

22nd. Up, and trimmed by a barber that has not trimmed me yet, my Spaniard being on shore. News brought that the two Dukes are coming on board; which, by and by, they did, in a Dutch boat, the Duke of York in yellow trimmings, the Duke of Gloucester in grey and red. My Lord went in a boat to meet them; the Captain, myself, and others, standing at the entering port. So soon as they were entered, we shot the guns off round the fleet. After that, they went to view the ship all over, and were most exceedingly pleased with it. They seem to be very fine gentlemen. After that done, upon the quarter-deck table, under the awning, the Duke of York and my Lord, Mr. Coventry, and I, spent an hour at allotting to every ship their service, in their return to

England; which being done, they went to dinner, where the table was very full; the two Dukes at the upper end, my Lord Opdam next on one side, and my Lord on the other. Two guns given to every man while he was drinking the King's health, and so likewise to the Duke's health. By the time we came on board again, news is sent us that the King is on shore; so my Lord fired all his guns round twice, and all the fleet after him, which, in the end, fell into disorder, which seemed very handsome. The gun over against my cabin I fired myself to the King, which was the first time that he had been saluted by his own ships since this change; but, holding my head too much over the gun, I had almost spoiled my right eye. Nothing in the world but going of guns almost all this day. In the evening we began to remove cabins; I to the carpenter's cabin, and Dr. Clerke with me, who came on board this afternoon, having been twice ducked in the sea to-day, and Mr. North and John Pickering the like. Many of the King's servants came on board to-night; and so many Dutch of all sorts came to see the ship till it was quite dark, that we could not pass by one another, which was a great trouble to us all. This afternoon Mr. Downing (who was knighted yesterday by the King) was here on board, and had a ship for his passage into England with his lady and servants. By the same token he called me to him when I was going to write the order, to tell me that I must write him Sir G. Downing. My Lord lay in the round house to-night. This evening I was late writing a French letter by my Lord's order to Monsieur Kragh, Ambassadeur de D[a]n[e]mark à la Haye, which my Lord signed in bed.

23rd. In the morning came infinity of people on board from the King to go along with him. My Lord, Mr. Crewe, and others go on shore to meet the

King as he comes off from shore, where, Sir R. Stayner bringing his Majesty into the boat, I hear that his Majesty did with a great deal of affection kiss my Lord upon his first meeting. The King, with the two Dukes and Queen of Bohemia, Princess Royal, and Prince of Orange, came on board, where I, in their coming in, kissed the King's, Queen's, and Princess's hands, having done the other before. Infinite shooting off of the guns, and that in a disorder on purpose, which was better than if it had been otherwise. All day nothing but Lords and persons of honour on board, that we were exceeding full. Dined in a great deal of state, the royal company by themselves in the coach, which was a blessed sight to see. After dinner the King and Duke altered the name of some of the ships, viz., the *Nazeby* into *Charles*; the *Richard, James*; the *Speaker, Mary*; the *Dunbar* (which was not in company with us), the *Henry*; *Winsly, Happy Return*; *Wakefield, Richmond*; *Lambert*, the *Henrietta*; *Cheriton*, the *Speedwell*; *Bradford*, the *Success*. That done, the Queen, Princess Royal, and Prince of Orange took leave of the King, and the Duke of York went on board the *London*, and the Duke of Gloucester, the *Swiftsure*. Which done, we weighed anchor, and with a fresh gale and most happy weather we set sail for England. All the afternoon the King walked here and there, up and down, (quite contrary to what I thought him to have been) very active and stirring. Upon the quarterdeck he fell into discourse of his escape from Worcester, where it made me ready to weep to hear the stories that he told of his difficulties that he had passed through, as his travelling four days and three nights on foot, every step up to his knees in dirt, with nothing but a green coat and a pair of country breeches on, and a pair of country shoes that made him so sore all over his feet, that he could scarce stir. Yet he was forced to run away from a miller and other company, that took them for rogues. His sitting at table at one place, where the master of the house, that had not seen him in eight years, did know him, but kept it private; when at the same table there was one, that had been of his own regiment at Worcester, could not know him, but made him drink the King's health, and said that the King was at least four fingers higher than he. At another place he was by some servants of the house made to drink, that they might know that he was not a Roundhead, which they swore he was. In another place, at his inn, the master of the house, as the King was standing with his hands upon the back of a chair by the fireside, kneeled down and kissed his hand privately, saying that he would not ask him who he was, but bid God bless him whither he was going. Then the difficulties in getting a boat to get into France, where he was fain to plot with the master thereof to keep his design from the foreman and a boy (which was all the ship's company), and so get to Fécamp in France. At Rouen he looked so poorly that the people went into the rooms before he went away, to see whether he had not stole something or other. In the evening I went up to my Lord to write letters for England, which we sent away with word of our coming, by Mr. Edward Pickering. The King supped alone in the coach; after that I got a dish, and we four supped in my cabin, as at noon. About bedtime my Lord Bartlett (who I had offered my service to before) sent for me to get him a bed, who with much ado I did get to bed to my Lord Middlesex, in the great cabin below; but I was cruelly troubled before I could dispose of him, and quit myself of him. So to my cabin again, where the company still was, and were talking more of the King's difficulties; as how he was fain to eat a piece of bread and cheese out of a poor boy's pocket; how, at a Catholic house, he was fain to lie in the priest's hole a good while in the house for his privacy. After that, our company broke up. We have all the Lords Commissioners on board us, and many others. Under sail all night, and most glorious weather.

24th. Up, and made myself as fine as I could, with the linen stockings on and wide canons that I bought the other day at Hague. Extraordinary press of noble company, and great mirth all the day.

25th. By the morning we were come close to the land, and everybody made ready to get on shore. The King and the two Dukes did eat their breakfast before they went; and there being set some ship's diet before them, only to show them the manner of the ship's diet, they ate of nothing else but pease and pork, and boiled beef. I spoke to the Duke of York about business, who called me Pepys by name, and upon my desire did promise me his future favour. Great expectation of the King's making some knights, but there was none. About noon (though the brigantine that Beale made was there ready to carry him) yet he would go in my Lord's barge with the two Dukes. Our Captain steered, and my Lord went along bare with them. I went, and Mr. Mansell, and one of the King's footmen, and a dog that the King loved, in a boat by ourselves, and so got on shore when the King did, who was received by General Monk with all imaginable love and respect at his entrance upon the land at Dover. Infinite the crowd of people and the gallantry of the horsemen, citizens, and noblemen of all sorts. The Mayor of the town came and give him his white staff, the badge of his place, which the King did give him again. The Mayor also presented him from the town a very rich Bible, which he took, and said it was the thing that he loved above all things in the world. A canopy was provided for him to stand under, which he did, and talked awhile with General Monk and others, and so into a stately coach there set for him, and so away through the town towards Canterbury, without making any stay at Dover. The shouting and joy expressed by all is past imagination. Seeing that my Lord did not stir out of his barge, I got into a boat, and so into his barge, and we back to the ship, seeing a man almost drowned that fell into the sea. My Lord almost transported with joy that he had done all this without any the least blur or obstruction in the world, that could give offence to any, and with the great honour he thought it would be to him. Being overtook by the brigantine, my Lord and we went out of our barge into it, and so went on board with Sir W. Batten and the Vice- and Rear-Admirals. At night I supped with the Captain, who told me what the King had given us. My Lord returned late, and at his coming did give me order to cause the mark to be gilded, and a Crown and C.R. to be made at the head of the coach table, where the King to-day with his own hand did mark his height; which accordingly I caused the painter to do, and is now done, as is to be seen.

27th. (Lord's day.) Called up by John Goods to see the Garter and Herald's coat, which lay in the coach, brought by Sir Edward Walker, King-at-Arms, this morning, for my Lord. My Lord had summoned all the Commanders on board him to see the ceremony, which was thus: Sir Edward, putting on his coat, and having laid the George and Garter, and the King's letter to my Lord, upon a crimson cushion (in the coach, all the Commanders standing by), makes three congees to him, holding the cushion in his arms. Then, laying it down with the things upon it upon a chair, he takes the letter, and delivers it to my Lord, which my Lord breaks open and gives him to read. It was directed to our trusty and well

23

beloved Sir Edward Montagu, Knight, one of our Generals at sea, and our Companion elect of our Noble Order of the Garter. The contents of the letter are to show that the Kings of England have for many years made use of this honour, as a special mark of favour, to persons of good extraction and virtue, and that many Emperors, Kings, and Princes of other countries have borne this honour; and that whereas my Lord is of a noble family, and hath now done the King such service by sea, at this time, as he hath done, he do send him this George and Garter to wear as Knight of the Order, with a dispensation for the other ceremonies of the habit of the Order and other things, till hereafter, when it can be done. So the herald putting the ribbon about his neck, and the Garter on his left leg, he saluted him with joy as Knight of the Garter. And after that was done, he took his leave of my Lord, and so to shore again to the King at Canterbury, where he yesterday gave the like honour to General Monk, who are the only two for many years that have had the Garter given them, before they had honours of Earldom, or the like, excepting only the Duke of Buckingham, who was only Sir George Villiers when he was made Knight of the Garter. The officers being all on board, there was no room for me at table, so I dined in my cabin, where Mr. Drum brought me a lobster and a bottle of oil, instead of vinegar, whereby I spoiled my dinner. Late to a sermon.

31st. This day the month ends. I in very good health, and all the world in a merry mood, because of the King's coming.

June 1660

June 1st. At night Mr. Cooke comes from London with letters, leaving all things there very gallant and joyful; and brought us word that the Parliament had ordered the 29th of May, the King's birthday, to be for ever kept as a day of thanksgiving for our redemption from tyranny, and the King's return to his government, he entering London that day. My poor wife has not been well; she would fain see me and be at her house again, but we must be content. She writes how there was a talk that I should be knighted by the King, which they (the Joyces) laugh at; but I think myself happier in my wife and estate than they are. The Captain came on board quite fuddled; the Vice-Admiral, Rear-Admiral, and he had been drinking all day. My Lord being now to sit in the House of Peers, he endeavours to get Mr. Edward Montagu for Weymouth, and Mr. George for Dover.

2nd. Being with my Lord in the morning about business in his cabin, I took occasion to give thanks for his love to me in the share that he had given me of his Majesty's money, and the Duke's. He told me he hoped to do me a more lasting kindness, if all things stand as they are now between him and the King; but, says he, "We must have a little patience, and we will rise together; in the meantime, I will do you all the good jobs I can." Which was great content for me to hear from my Lord.

3rd. At sermon in the morning; after dinner into my cabin, to cast my accounts up, and find myself to be worth near £100, for which I bless Almighty God, it being more than I hoped for so soon, being, I believe, not clearly worth £25 when I came to sea, besides my house and goods.

8th. Out early, took horses at Deal. Dined at Canterbury. I saw the minster, and the remains of Becket's tomb. To Sittingborne and Rochester: the ships and bridge. Came to Gravesend.

9th. Landed at the Temple. To Whitehall with my Lord and Mr. Edward Montagu. Found the

King in the Park. There walked. Gallantly great.

10th. (Lord's day.) At my father's found my wife, and to walk with her in Lincoln's Inn walks.

18th. By barge to Stepney with my Lord, where at Trinity House we had great entertainment. With my Lord there went Sir W. Pen, Sir H. Wright, Hetly, Pierce, Creed, Hill, I, and other servants. Back again to the Admiralty, and so to my Lord's lodgings, where he told me that he did look after the place of the Clerk of the Acts for me. Murford showed me five pieces to get a business done for him, and I am resolved to do it.

19th. My wife and the girl and dog came home to-day. I found a quantity of chocolate left for me, I know not from whom.

22nd. To bed the first time since my coming from sea, in my own house, for which God be praised.

23rd. To my Lord's lodgings, where Tom Guy came to me, and there stayed to see the King touch people for the King's evil. But he did not come at all, it rained so; and the poor people were forced to stand all the morning in the rain in the garden. Afterward he touched them in the Banqueting House. With my Lord to my Lord Frezendorfe's, where he dined to-day. He told me that he had obtained a promise of the Clerk of the Acts place for me, at which I was glad.

28th. To Sir G. Downing, the first visit I have made him since he came. He is so stingy a fellow I care not to see him; I quite cleared myself of his office, and did give him liberty to take anybody in. After this to my Lord, who lay a-bed till eleven o'clock; it being almost five before he went to bed, they supped so late last night with the King.

29th. Up and to Whitehall, where I got my warrant from the Duke to be Clerk of the Acts.

Then to Whitehall, where I was told by Mr. Hutchinson at the Admiralty, that Mr. Barlow, my predecessor, Clerk of the Acts, is yet alive, and coming up to town to look after his place, which made my heart sad a little. At night told my Lord thereof, and he bad me get possession of my Patent; and he would do all that could be done to keep him out. This night my Lord and I looked over the list of the Captains, and marked some that my Lord had a mind to put out.

July 1660

July 1st. (Lord's day.) This morning came home my fine camlet cloak, with gold buttons, and a silk suit, which cost me much money, and I pray God to make me able to pay for it. In the afternoon to the Abbey, where a good sermon by a stranger, but no Common Prayer yet.

2nd. Infinite of business; my heart and head full. Met with Purser Washington, with whom and a lady, a friend of his, I dined at the Bell Tavern in King Street, but the rogue had no more manners than to invite me, and to let me pay my club.

5th. This morning my brother Tom brought me my jackanapes coat with silver buttons. It rained this morning, which makes us fear that the glory of this day will be lost; the King and Parliament being to be entertained by the City to-day with great pomp. Mr. Hater was with me to-day, and I agreed with him to be my clerk. Being at Whitehall, I saw the King, the Dukes, and all their attendants go forth in the rain to the City, and it bedraggled many a fine suit of clothes. I was forced to walk all the morning in Whitehall, not knowing how to get out because of the rain. Met with Mr. Cooling, my Lord Chamberlain's secretary, who took me to dinner among the gentlemen waiters, and after dinner into the wine-cellar. He told me how he had a project for all us Secretaries to join together and get money by bringing all business into our hands. Thence to the Admiralty, where Mr. Blackburne and I (it beginning to hold up) went and walked an hour or two in the Park, he giving of me light in many things in my way in this office that I go about. At my Lord's at night comes Dr. Petty to me, to tell me that Barlow was come to town, and other things, which put me into a despair, and I went to bed very sad.

7th. I took an order for the advance of the salaries of the officers of the Navy, and mine is raised to £350 per annum.

8th. (Lord's day.) To Whitehall chapel, where I got in with ease by going before the Lord Chancellor with Mr. Kipps. Here I heard very good music, the first time that ever I remember to have heard the organs and singing-men in surplices in my life. The Bishop of Chichester preached before the King, and made a great flattering sermon, which I did not like that the clergy should meddle with matters of State. Dined with Mr. Luellin and Salisbury at a cook's shop. Home, and stayed all the afternoon with my wife till after sermon. There till Mr. Fairbrother came to call us out to my father's to supper. He told me how he had perfectly procured me to be made Master in Arts by proxy, which did somewhat please me, though I remember my cousin Roger Pepys was the other day persuading me from it.

9th. To the Navy Office, where in the afternoon we met and sat; and there I began to sign bills in the Office the first time.

13th. Up early, the first day that I put on my black camlet coat with silver buttons. To Mr. Spong, whom I found in his nightgown writing of my patent. It being done, we carried it to Worcester

28

House, to the Chancellor, where Mr. Kipps (a strange providence that he should now be in a condition to do me a kindness) got me the Chancellor's "recipe" to my bill; and so carried it to Mr. Beale for a docket; but he was very angry, and unwilling to do it, because he said it was ill writ (because I had got it writ by another hand, and not by him); but by much importunity I got Mr. Spong to go to his office and make an end of my patent; and in the meantime Mr. Beale to be preparing my docket, which being done, I did give him two pieces, after which it was strange how civil and tractable he was to me. To my wife, whom I had left in a coach, and presented her with my patent, at which she was overjoyed; so to the Navy Board, and showed her my house and both mightily pleased.

17th. This morning (as indeed all the mornings nowadays) much business at my Lord's. There came to my house before I went out Mr. Barlow, an old consumptive man, and fair conditioned. After much talk, I did grant him what he asked, viz. £50 per annum if my salary be not increased, and £100 per annum in case it be £350, at which he was very well pleased to be paid as I received my money, and not otherwise; so I brought him to my Lord's bedside, and he and I did agree together. Will, Mr. Blackburne's nephew, is so obedient, that I am greatly glad of him.

31st. To Whitehall, where my Lord and the principal officers met, and had a great discourse about raising of money for the Navy, which is in very sad condition; and money must be raised for it. Mr. Blackburne, Dr. Clerke, and I to the Quaker, and dined there. I back to the Admiralty, and there was doing things in order to the calculating of the debts of the Navy and other business, all the afternoon.

August 1660

August 1st. In the afternoon at the office, where we had many things to sign; and I went to the Council Chamber, and there got my Lord to sign the first bill, and the rest all myself; but received no money to-day.

2nd. To Westminster by water with Sir W. Batten and Sir W. Pen (our servants in another boat) to the Admiralty; and from thence I went to my Lord's to fetch him thither, where we stayed in the morning about ordering of money for the victuallers, and advising how to get a sum of money to carry on the business of the Navy. From thence W. Hewer and I to the office of Privy Seal, where I stayed all the afternoon, and received about £40 for yesterday and to-day, at which my heart rejoiced for God's blessing to me, to give me this advantage by chance, there being of this £40 about £10 due to me for this day's work. So great is the present profit of this office, above what it was in the King's time; there being the last month about 300 bills, whereas in the late King's time it was much to have 40.

10th. With Mr. Moore and Creed to Hyde Park by coach, and saw a fine foot-race three times round the Park, between an Irishman and Crow, that was once my Lord Claypoole's footman. (By the way, I cannot forget that my Lord Claypoole did the other day make inquiry of Mrs. Hunt concerning my house in Axe Yard, and did set her on work to get it of me for him; which methinks is a very great change.) Crow beat the other by above two miles. Unable to think of anything, because of my constant business, not having read a new book or inquiring after any news. Many people look after my house in Axe Yard, to hire it, so that I am troubled with them.

But blessed be God for my good chance of the Privy Seal, where I get every day I believe about £3. This place my Lord did give me by chance, neither he nor I thinking it to be of the worth that he and I find it to be.

14th. I did make even with Mr. Fairbrother for my degree of Master of Arts, which cost me about £9 : 16s. At night good sport, having the girl and boy to comb my head.

15th. To the office, and after dinner by water to Whitehall, where I found the King gone this morning by five of the clock to see a Dutch pleasure-boat below bridge, where he dines, and my Lord with him. The King do tire all his people that are about him with early rising since he came.

17th. At the Half Moon I saw Mr. Creed show the strangest emotions to shift off his drink I ever saw.

18th. Towards Westminster by water. I landed my wife at Whitefriars, with £5 to buy her a petticoat, and my father persuaded her to buy a most fine cloth, of 26s. a yard, and a rich lace, that the petticoat will come to £5 : but she doing it very innocently, I could not be angry. Captain Ferrers took me and Creed to the Cockpit play, the first that I have had time to see since my coming from sea, *The Loyal Subject*, where one Kinaston, a boy, acted the Duke's sister, but made the loveliest lady that ever I saw in my life. After the play done, we went to drink, and, by Captain Ferrers' means, Kinaston and another (that acted Archas the General) came and drank with us.

19th. (Lord's day.) This morning Sir William Batten, Pen, and myself went to church to the church-wardens to demand a pew, which at present could not be given us; but we are resolved to have one built. So we stayed, and heard Mr. Mills, a very good minister. Home to dinner, where my wife had on her new petticoat that she bought yesterday, which indeed is a very fine cloth and a fine lace; but that being of a light colour, and the lace all silver, it makes no great show.

20th. This afternoon at the Privy Seal, where reckoning with Mr. Moore, he had got £100 for me together, which I was glad of, guessing that the profit of this month would come to £100. With W. Hewer by coach to Worcester House, where I light, sending him home with the £100 that I received to-day. Here I stayed, and saw my Lord Chancellor come into his Great Hall, where wonderful how much company there was to expect him. Before he would begin any business, he took my papers of the state of the debts of the Fleet, and there viewed them before all the people, and did give me his advice privately how to order things to get as much money as we can of the Parliament.

27th. Came a vessel of Northdown ale from Mr. Pierce, the purser, to me, and a brave Turkey-carpet and a jar of olives from Captain Cuttance, and a pair of fine turtle-doves from John Burr to my wife. Major Hart came to me, whom I did receive with wine and anchovies, which made me so dry, that I was ill with them all night, and was fain to have the girl rise and fetch me some drink.

September 1660

September 16th. To the Park, where I saw how far they had proceeded in the Pell-mell, and in making a river through the Park, which I had never seen before since it was begun. Thence to Whitehall Garden, where I saw the King in purple mourning for his brother.

21st. Upon the water saw the corpse of the Duke of Gloucester brought down Somerset House stairs, to

go by water to Westminster, to be buried to-night.
To the Hope Tavern, and sent for Mr. Chaplin, who
with Nicholas Osborne and one Daniel came to us,
and we drank off two or three quarts of wine, which
was very good; the drawing of our wine causing a great
quarrel in the house between the two drawers which
should draw us the best, which caused a great deal of
noise and falling-out till the master parted them, and
came up to us, and did give a long account of the
liberty that he gives his servants, all alike, to draw
what wine they will to please his customers; and ate
above 200 walnuts.   Nicholas Osborne did give me a
barrel of samphire, and showed me the keys of
Mardyke Fort, which he that was commander of the
fort sent him as a token when the fort was demolished;
and I will get them of him if I can.

24th.   I arose from table and went to the Temple
church, where I had appointed Sir W. Batten to meet
him; and there at Sir Heneage Finch Solicitor-
General's chambers, before him and Sir W. Wilde,
Recorder of London (whom we sent for from his
chamber), we were sworn justices of peace for
Middlesex, Essex, Kent, and Southampton; with
which honour I did find myself mightily pleased,
though I am wholly ignorant in the duties of a justice
of peace.

25th.   I did send for a cup of tea (a China drink) of
which I never had drunk before.

October 1660

October 3rd.   To my Lord's, who sent a great
iron chest to Whitehall; and I saw it carried into
the King's closet, where I saw most incomparable
pictures.   Among the rest a book open upon a desk,
which I durst have sworn was a real book.   Back
again to my Lord, and dined all alone with him, who

did treat me with a great deal of respect; and after dinner did discourse an hour with me, and advise about some way to get himself some money to make up for his great expenses, saying that he believed that he might have anything that he would ask of the King. This day I heard the Duke speak of a great design that he and my Lord of Pembroke have, and a great many others, of sending a venture to some parts of Africa to dig for gold ore there. They intend to admit as many as will venture their money, and so make themselves a company. £250 is the lowest share for every man. But I do not find that my Lord do much like it.

4th. I and Lieutenant Lambert to Westminster Abbey, where we saw Dr. Frewen translated to the Archbishopric of York. Here I saw the Bishops of Winchester, Bangor, Rochester, Bath and Wells, and Salisbury, all in their habits, in King Henry Seventh's chapel. But, Lord! at their going out, how people did most of them look upon them as strange creatures, and few with any kind of love or respect!

11th. To walk in St. James's Park, where we observed the several engines at work to draw up water, with which sight I was very much pleased. Above all the rest, I liked that which Mr. Greatorex brought, which do carry up the water with a great deal of ease. Here, in the Park, we met with Mr. Salisbury, who took Mr. Creed and me to the Cockpit to see *The Moor of Venice*, which was well done. Burt acted the Moor; by the same token, a very pretty lady that sat by me called out, to see Desdemona smothered.

12th. My Lady Sandwich came to town, and showed me most extraordinary love and kindness.

13th. I went out to Charing Cross, to see Major-General Harrison hanged, drawn, and quartered; which was done there, he looking as cheerful as any man could do in that condition. He was presently cut down, and his head and heart shown to the people, at which there was great shouts of joy. It is said that he said that he was sure to come shortly at the right hand of Christ to judge them that now had judged him; and that his wife do expect his coming again. Thus it was my chance to see the King beheaded at Whitehall, and to see the first blood shed in revenge for the King at Charing Cross. Setting up shelves in my study.

21st. (Lord's day.) George Vine carried me up to the top of his turret, where there is Cooke's head set up for a traitor, and Harrison's set up on the other side of Westminster Hall. Here I could see them plainly, as also a very fair prospect about London.

23rd. One of Mr. Shepley's pistols, charged with bullets, flew off, and it pleased God that the mouth of the gun being downwards, it did us no hurt; but I think I never was in more danger in my life.

29th. I up early, it being my Lord Mayor's day (Sir Richard Browne), and neglecting my office, I went to the Wardrobe, where I met my Lady Sandwich and all the children; and after drinking of some strange and incomparable good claret of Mr. Rumball's, he and Mr. Townsend did take us, and set the young Lords at one Mr. Nevill's, a draper in Paul's Churchyard; and my Lady, and my Lady Pickering and I to one Mr. Isaacson's, a linen-draper at the Key in Cheapside; where there was a company of fine ladies, and we were very civilly treated, and had a very good place to see the pageants, which were many, and I believe good for such kind of things, but in themselves but poor and absurd.

November 1660

November 1st. This morning Sir W. Pen and I were mounted early, and had very merry discourse

35

all the way, he being very good company. We came
to Sir W. Batten's, where he lives like a prince, and
we were made very welcome. Among other things,
he showed me my Lady's closet, wherein was great
store of rarities; as also a chair, which he calls King
Harry's chair, where he that sits down is catched with
two irons, that come round about him, which makes
good sport. Here dined with us two or three more
country gentlemen; among the rest, Mr. Christmas,
my old schoolfellow, with whom I had much talk.
He did remember that I was a great Roundhead when
I was a boy, and I was much afraid that he would
have remembered the words that I said the day the
King was beheaded (that, were I to preach upon him,
my text should be—" The memory of the wicked
shall rot "); but I found afterwards that he did go
away from school before that time. He did make us
good sport in imitating Mr. Case, Ash, and Nye, the
ministers; but a deadly drinker he is, and grown
very fat.

2nd. To Whitehall, where I saw the boats coming
very thick to Lambeth, and all the stairs to be full of
people. I was told the Queen was a-coming; so I
got a sculler for sixpence to carry me thither and back
again, but I could not get to see the Queen : so came
back, and to my Lord's, where he was come; and I
supped with him, he being very merry, telling merry
stories of the country mayors; how they entertained
the King all the way as he came along; and how the
country gentlewomen did hold up their heads to be
kissed by the King, not taking his hand to kiss, as they
should do. I took leave of my Lord and Lady, and
so took coach at Whitehall, and carried Mr. Childe as
far as the Strand, and myself got as far as Ludgate by
all the bonfires, but with a great deal of trouble; and
there the coachman desired that I would release him,
for he durst not go further for the fires. In Paul's

Churchyard I called at Kirton's, and there they had got a mass-book for me, which I bought, and cost me twelve shillings; and, when I came home, sat up late and read in it with great pleasure to my wife, to hear that she was long ago acquainted with it. I observed this night very few bonfires in the City, not above three in all London, for the Queen's coming; whereby I guess that (as I believed before) her coming do please but very few.

4th. (Lord's day.) In the morn to our own church, where Mr. Mills did begin to nibble at the Common Prayer, by saying "Glory be to the Father," etc., after he had read the two psalms: but the people had been so little used to it that they could not tell what to answer. This declaration of the King's do give the Presbyterians some satisfaction, and a pretence to read the Common Prayer, which they would not do before because of their former preaching against it. After dinner to Westminster. In our way we called at the Bell, to see the seven Flanders mares that my Lord has bought lately. Then I went to my Lord's, and, having spoken with him, I went to the Abbey, where the first time that ever I heard the organs in a cathedral. My wife seemed very pretty to-day, it being the first time I had given her leave to wear a black patch.

12th. To the Comptroller's house in Lime Street, a fine house, where I never was before. Agreed with Jack Spicer to help me to tell money this afternoon. My father and I discoursed seriously about my sister's coming to live with me, and yet I am much afraid of her ill-nature. I told her plainly my mind was to have her come not as a sister but as a servant, which she promised me that she would, and with many thanks did weep for joy.

13th. Found my wife making of pies and tarts to try her oven with; but, not knowing the nature of it, did heat it too hot, and so did a little overbake her things; but knows how to do better another time.

15th. To Sir W. Batten's to dinner, he having a couple of servants married to-day; and so there was a great number of merchants, and others of good quality, on purpose after dinner to make an offering, which, when dinner was done, we did; and I did give ten shillings and no more, though I believe most of the rest did give more, and did believe that I did so too.

20th. Mr. Shepley and I to the new playhouse near Lincoln's-Inn-Fields (which was formerly Gibbon's tennis-court) where the play of *Beggar's Bush* was newly begun; and so we went in, and saw it well acted: and here I saw the first time one Moone, who is said to be the best actor in the world, lately come over with the King, and indeed it is the finest playhouse, I believe, that ever was in England. This morning I found my Lord in bed late, he having been with the King, Queen, and Princess at the Cockpit all night, where General Monk treated them; and after supper a play, where the King did put a great affront upon Singleton's music, he bidding them stop, and bade the French music play, which my Lord says, do much outdo all ours.

21st. This morning my cousin, Thos. Pepys, the turner, sent me a cup of lignum vitæ for a token. My wife and I went to Paternoster Row, and there we bought some green-watered moyre for a morning waistcoat. And after that we went to Mr. Cade's to choose some pictures for our house. I to Pope's Head, and bought me an agate-hafted knife, which cost me 5s. At night to my violin (the first time that I have played on it since I came to this house) in my dining-room, and afterwards to my lute there, and I took much pleasure to have the neighbours come forth into the yard to hear me.

22nd. This morning came the carpenters to make

me a door at the other side of the house, going into the entry. My wife and I walked to the Old Exchange, and there she bought her a white whisk, and put it on, and I a pair of gloves. To Mr. Fox's, where we found Mrs. Fox within, and an alderman of London paying £1000 or £1400 in gold upon the table for the King. Mr. Fox came in presently, and did receive us with a great deal of respect; and then did take my wife and I to the Queen's presence-chamber, where he got my wife placed behind the Queen's chair, and the two Princesses came to dinner. The Queen a very little, plain, old woman, and nothing more in her presence in any respect nor garb than any ordinary woman. The Princess of Orange I had often seen before. The Princess Henrietta is very pretty, but much below my expectation; and her dressing of herself with her hair frizzed short up to her ears did make her seem so much the less to me. But my wife standing near her with two or three black patches on, and well dressed, did seem to me much handsomer than she.

26th. My father came and dined with me, who seems to take much pleasure to have a son that is neat in his house. I heard that my Lady Batten had given my wife a visit (the first that ever she made her), which pleased me exceedingly. Mr. Moore told me how the House had this day voted the King to have all the Excise for ever. This day I do also hear that the Queen's going to France is stopped, which do like me well, because then the King will be in town the next month, which is my month again at the Privy Seal.

December 1660

December 1st. This morning observing some things to be laid up not as they should be by my girl,

I took a broom and basted her till she cried extremely, which made me vexed; but, before I went out, I left her appeased.

4th. To the Duke of York, and he took us into his closet, and we did open to him our project of stopping the growing charge of the fleet, by paying them in hand one moiety, and the other four months hence. This he do like. This day the Parliament voted that the bodies of Oliver, Ireton, Bradshaw, and Thomas Pride, should be taken up out of their graves in the Abbey, and drawn to the gallows, and there hanged and buried under it: which (methinks) do trouble me that a man of so great courage as he was should have that dishonour, though otherwise he might deserve it enough.

5th. After dinner went to the New Theatre, and there I saw *The Merry Wives of Windsor* acted—the humours of the country gentleman and the French doctor very well done, but the rest but very poorly, and Sir J. Falstaff as bad as any.

12th. To the Exchequer, and did give my mother Bowyer a visit, and her daughters, the first time that I did see them since I went last to sea. My father did offer me six pieces of gold, in lieu of six pounds that he borrowed of me the other day, but it went against me to take it of him, and therefore did not. Home and to bed, reading myself asleep, while the wench sat mending my breeches by my bedside.

20th. This day I hear that the Princess Royal has the smallpox.

21st. They told me that this is St. Thomas's, and that, by an old custom, this day the Exchequer men had formerly, and do intend this night, to have a supper; which, if I could, I promised to come to, but did not. To my Lady's and dined with her: but told me how dangerously ill the Princess Royal is: and that this morning she was said to be dead. But she hears that she hath married herself to young Jermyn, which is worse than the Duke of York's marrying the Chancellor's daughter, which is now publicly owned.

22nd. Went to the Sun Tavern on Fish Street hill, to a dinner of Captain Teddiman's, where was my Lord Inchiquin (who seems to be a very fine person), Sir W. Pen, Captain Cuttance, and one Mr. Lawrence (a fine gentleman, now going to Algiers), and other good company, where we had a very fine dinner, good music, and a great deal of wine. I very merry. Went to bed: my head aching all night.

31st. In Paul's Churchyard I bought the play of *Henry the Fourth*, and so went to the new Theatre and saw it acted; but my expectation being too great, it did not please me, as otherwise I believe it would; and my having a book I believe did spoil it a little. That being done, I went to my Lord's, where I found him private at cards with my Lord Lauderdale and some persons of honour, my boy taking a cat home with him from my Lord's, which Sarah had given him for my wife, we being much troubled with mice. At Whitehall we inquiring for a coach, there was a Frenchman with one eye that was going my way, so he and I hired the coach between us, and he set me down in Fenchurch Street. Strange how the fellow, without asking, did tell me all what he was, and how he had run away from his father, and come into England to serve the King, and now going back again, etc.

1661

At the end of the last and the beginning of this year I do live in one of the houses belonging to the Navy Office, as one of the principal officers, and have

done now about half-a-year; my family being myself,
my wife, Jane, Will. Hewer, and Wayneman, my
girl's brother. Myself in constant good health, and
in a most handsome and thriving condition. Blessed
be Almighty God for it! As to things of State—The
King settled, and loved of all. The Duke of York
matched to my Lord Chancellor's daughter, which
do not please many. The Queen upon her return to
France with the Princess Henrietta. The Princess of
Orange lately dead, and we into new mourning for
her. We have been lately frighted with a great plot,
and many taken up on it, and the fright not quite
over. The Parliament, which had done all this
great good to the King, beginning to grow factious,
the King did dissolve it December 29th last, and
another likely to be chosen speedily. I take myself
now to be worth £300 clear in money, and all my
goods, and all manner of debts paid, which are none
at all.

January 1661

January 1st. Comes in my brother Thomas, and
after him my father, Dr. Thomas Pepys, my uncle
Fenner and his two sons (Anthony's only child dying
this morning, yet he was so civil to come, and was
pretty merry) to breakfast; and I had for them a
barrel of oysters, a dish of neat's tongues, and a dish
of anchovies, wine of all sorts, and Northdown ale.
We were very merry till about eleven o'clock, and
then they went away. At noon I carried my wife
by coach to my cousin Thomas Pepys, where we, with
my father, Dr. Thomas, cousin Stradwick, Scott,
and their wives dined. Here I saw first his second
wife, which is a very respectful woman; but his
dinner a sorry, poor dinner for a man of his estate,
there being nothing but ordinary meat in it. To-day

the King dined at a lord's two doors from us. Mr. Moore and I went to Mr. Pierce's; in our way seeing the Duke of York bring his Lady to-day to wait upon the Queen, the first time that ever she did since that business; and the Queen is said to receive her now with much respect and love; and there he cast up the fees, and I told the money, by the same token the £100 bag, after I had told it, fell all about the room, and I fear I have lost some of it. Supped with them and Mr. Pierce, the purser, and his wife and mine, where we had a calf's head carboned, but it was raw—we could not eat it—and a good hen. But she is such a slut that I do not love her victuals.

2nd. My Lord did give me many commands in his business: as about taking care to write to my uncle that Mr. Barnewell's papers should be locked up, in case he should die, he being now suspected to be very ill. Also about consulting with Mr. W. Montagu for the settling of the £4000 a year that the King had promised my Lord; as also about getting Mr. George Montagu to be chosen at Hunting-don this next Parliament, etc. That done, he to Whitehall Stairs with much company, and I with him; where we took water for Lambeth, and there coach for Portsmouth. The Queen's things were all in Whitehall Court, ready to be sent away, and her Majesty ready to be gone an hour after to Hampton Court to-night, and so to be at Portsmouth on Saturday next. Home to dinner, where I found Pall (my sister) was come; but I do not let her sit down at table with me, which I do at first that she may not expect it hereafter from me. To Mr. George Montagu about the business of election, and he did give me a piece in gold; so to my Lord's, and got the chest of plate brought to the Exchequer, and my brother Spicer put it into his treasury. I took a turn in the Hall, and bought the King and Chancellor's speeches at the dissolving the Parliament last Saturday. This day I lent Sir W. Batten and Captain Rider my chine of beef for to serve to-morrow at Trinity House, the Duke of Albemarle being to be there, and all the rest of the Brethren, it being a great day for the reading over of their new charter, which the King hath newly given them.

3rd. To the theatre, where was acted *Beggar's Bush*, it being very well done; and here the first time that ever I saw women come upon the stage.

6th. (Lord's day.) My wife and I to church this morning. To church again, where, before sermon, a long Psalm was set that lasted an hour, while the sexton gathered his year's contribution through the whole church. After sermon home, and there I went to my chamber, and wrote a letter to send to Mr. Coventry with a piece of plate along with it, which I do preserve among my other letters.

7th. This morning news was brought to me to my bedside that there had been a great stir in the City this night by the Fanatics, who had been up and killed six or seven men, but all are fled. My Lord Mayor and the whole City had been in arms, about 40,000. Tom and I and my wife to the theatre, and there saw *The Silent Woman*. Among other things here, Kinaston, the boy, had the good turn to appear in three shapes: first, as a poor woman in ordinary clothes, to please Morose; then in fine clothes, as a gallant; and in them was clearly the prettiest woman in the whole house; and lastly, as a man; and then likewise did appear the handsomest man in the house.

9th. Waked in the morning about six o'clock by people running up and down in Mr. Davis's house, talking that the Fanatics were up in arms in the City. And so I rose and went forth; where in the street I found everybody in arms at the doors. So I returned (though with no good courage at all, but that I might not seem to be afraid) and got my sword and pistol, which, however, I had no powder to charge; and went to the door, where I found Sir R. Ford, and with him I walked up and down as far as the Exchange, and there I left him. In our way the streets full of train-bands, and great stories what mischief these rogues have done; and I think near a dozen had been killed this morning on both sides. The shops shut, and all things in trouble. Home to my lute till late, and then to bed, there being strict guards all night in the city, though most of the enemies, they say, are killed or taken.

12th. With Colonel Slingsby and a friend of his, Major Waters (a deaf and most amorous melancholy gentleman, who is under a despair in love, as the Colonel told me, which makes him bad company, though a most good-natured man), by water to Redriffe, and so on foot to Deptford. We fell to choosing four captains to command the guards, and choosing the place where to keep them, and other things in order thereunto. Never till now did I see the great authority of my place, all the captains of the fleet coming cap in hand to us. I went home with Mr. Davis, storekeeper (whose wife is ill, and so I could not see her), and was there most prince-like lodged, with so much respect and honour, that I was at a loss how to behave myself.

19th. To the Comptroller's, and with him by coach to Whitehall, in our way meeting Venner and Pritchard upon a sledge, who with two more Fifth-Monarchy men were hanged to-day, and the two first drawn and quartered. Went to the theatre, where I saw *The Lost Lady*, which do not please me much. Here I was troubled to be seen by four of our office clerks, which sat in the half-crown box, and I in the 1s. 6d. From thence by link, and bought two mouse-traps of Thomas Pepys, the turner.

21st. To Westminster Hall, to the Commissioners for paying off the Army and Navy, where the Duke of Albemarle was; and we sat with our hats on, and did discourse about paying off the ships, and do find that they do intend to undertake it without our help; and we are glad of it, for it is a work that will much displease the poor seamen, and so we are glad to have no hand in it. It is strange what weather we have had all this winter; no cold at all; but the ways are dusty, and the flies fly up and down, and the rose-bushes are full of leaves; such a time of the year as was never known in this world before here. This day many more of the Fifth-Monarchy men were hanged.

22nd. I met with Dr. Thomas Fuller; he tells me of his last and great book that is coming out: that is, the History of all the Families in England; and could tell me more of my own than I knew myself. And also to what perfection he hath now brought the art of memory; that he did lately to four eminently great scholars dictate together in Latin, upon different subjects of their proposing, faster than they were able to write, till they were tired; and that the best way of beginning a sentence, if a man should be out and forget his last sentence (which he never was), that then his last refuge is to begin with an "Utcunque."

29th. To Mr. Turner's house, where the Comptroller, Sir William Batten, and Mr. Davis, and their ladies; and here we had a most neat little but costly and genteel supper. After that, a great deal of impertinent mirth by Mr. Davis, and some catches, and so broke up, and going away, Mr. Davis's eldest son took up my old Lady Slingsby in his arms, and carried her to the coach, and is said to be able to carry three of the biggest men that were in the company, which I wonder at.

February 1661

February 4th. To the tavern, where Sir William Pen, and the Comptroller, and several others were, men and women; and we had a very great and merry dinner; and after dinner the Comptroller began some sports, among others, the naming of people round, and afterwards demanding questions of them that they are forced to answer their names to, which do make very good sport. And here I took pleasure to take forfeits of the ladies who would not do their duty by kissing of them; among others a pretty lady, who I found afterwards to be wife to Sir William Batten's son. We sat late, talking with my Lady and others, and Dr. Whistler, who I found good company and a very ingenious man; so home and to bed.

10th. (Lord's day.) Took physic all day, and, God forgive me, did spend it in reading of some little French romances. At night my wife and I did please ourselves talking of our going into France, which I hope to effect this summer.

14th. (Valentine's day.) Up early, and to Sir W. Batten's, but could not go in till I asked whether they that opened the door was a man or a woman; and Mingo, who was there, answered a woman, which, with his tone, made me laugh; so up I went, and took Mrs. Martha for my Valentine (which I do only for complacency), and Sir W. Batten he go in the same manner to my wife, and so we were very merry. About ten o'clock we with a great deal of company went down by our barge to Deptford, and there only went to see how forward Mr. Pett's yacht is; and so all into the barge again, and so to Woolwich, on board the *Rosebush*, Captain Brown's ship, that is brother-in-law to Sir W. Batten, where we had a very fine dinner, dressed on shore, and great mirth, and all things successful; the first time I ever carried my wife a-shipboard, as also my boy Wayneman, who hath all this day been called young Pepys, as Sir W. Pen's boy young Pen. The talk of the town now is, who the King is like to have for his Queen; and whether Lent shall be kept with the strictness of the King's proclamation; which is thought cannot be, because of the poor, who cannot buy fish. And also the great preparation for the King's crowning is now much thought upon and talked of.

15th. Making up my accounts for my Lord to-morrow; and that being done, I found myself to be clear (as I think) £350 in the world, besides my goods in my house, and all things paid for.

18th. In the afternoon my wife and I and Mrs. Martha Batten, my Valentine, to the Exchange, and there upon a pair of embroidered and six pair of plain white gloves I laid out 40s. upon her. Then we went to a mercer's at the end of Lombard Street, and there she bought a suit of lutestring for herself; and so home. It is much talked that the King is already married to the niece of the Prince de Ligne, and that he hath two sons already by her; which I am sorry to hear; but yet am gladder that it should be so than that the Duke of York and his family should come to the Crown, he being a professed friend to the Catholics.

23rd. To the playhouse, and there saw *The Changeling*, the first time it hath been acted these twenty years, and it takes exceedingly. Besides, I see the gallants do begin to be tired with the vanity and pride of the theatre actors, who are indeed grown very proud and rich. I also met with the Comptroller, who told me how it was easy for us all, the principal officers, and proper for us, to labour to get into the next Parliament; and would have me to ask the

Duke's letter, but I shall not endeavour it. This is now 28 years that I am born. And blessed be God, in a state of full content, and a great hope to be a happy man in all respects, both to myself and friends.

April 1661

April 2nd. To St. James's Park, where I saw the Duke of York playing at Pelemele, the first time that ever I saw the sport. Then to my Lord's, where I dined with my Lady, and, after we had dined, in comes my Lord and Ned Pickering hungry, and there was not a bit of meat left in the house, the servants having ate up all, at which my Lord was very angry, and at last got something dressed. So to White-friars, and saw *The Little Thief*, which is a very merry and pretty play, and the little boy do very well. Then to the Dolphin to Sir W. Batten, and Pen, and other company; among others Mr. Delabar; where strange how these men, who at other times are all wise men, do now, in their drink, betwit and reproach one another with their former conditions, and their actions as in public concerns, till I was ashamed to see it.

3rd. Up among my workmen, my head aching all day from last night's debauch. At noon dined with Sir W. Batten and Pen, who would have me drink two good draughts of sack to-day, to cure me of my last night's disease, which I thought strange, but I think find it true. I hear that the Dutch have sent the King a great present of money, which we think will stop the match with Portugal; and judge this to be the reason that our so great haste in sending the two ships to the East Indies is also stayed.

6th. Among other things met with Mr. Townsend, who told of his mistake the other day, to put both his legs through one of his knees of his breeches, and went so all day.

8th. About eight o'clock we took barge at the Tower, Sir William Batten and his Lady, Mrs. Turner, Mr. Fowler and I. A very pleasant passage, and so to Gravesend, where we dined; and from thence a coach took them, and me, and Mr. Fowler, with some others come from Rochester to meet us on horseback. At Rochester, where alight at Mr. Alcock's, and there drank, and had good sport with his bringing out so many sorts of cheese. Then to the Hill-house at Chatham, where I never was before, and I found a pretty pleasant house, and am pleased with the arms that hang up there. Here we supped very merry, and late to bed; Sir William telling me that old Edgeborrow, his predecessor, did die and walk in my chamber, did make me somewhat afraid, but not so much as, for mirth sake, I did seem. So to bed in the Treasurer's chamber.

9th. Lay and slept well till three in the morning, and then waking, and by the light of the moon I saw my pillow (which overnight I flung from me) stand upright; but, not bethinking myself what it might be, I was a little afraid, but sleep overcame all, and so lay till nigh morning, at which time I had a candle brought me, and a good fire made, and in general it was a great pleasure all the time I stayed here to see how I am respected and honoured by all people; and I find that I begin to know now how to receive so much reverence, which, at the beginning, I could not tell how to do.

11th. I met two little schoolboys going with pitchers of ale to their schoolmaster to break up against Easter, and I did drink of some of one of them, and give him two-pence. By and by, we came to two little girls keeping cows, and I saw one of them very pretty, so I had a mind to make her ask my blessing; and, telling her that I was her godfather, she asked me innocently whether I was not Ned Wooding, and I said that I was; so she kneeled down, and very simply called, " Pray, godfather, pray to God to bless me," which made us very merry, and I gave her twopence. In several places I asked women whether they would sell me their children, but they denied me all, but said they would give me one to keep for them, if I would. Mrs. Anne and I rode under the man that hangs upon Shooter's Hill, and a filthy sight it was to see how his flesh is shrunk to his bones. So home, and I found all well, and a good deal of work done since I went. So to bed very sleepy for last night's work, concluding that it is the pleasantest journey in all respects that ever I had in my life.

20th. Comes my boy to tell me that the Duke of York had sent for all the principal officers, etc., to come to him to-day. We went up and saw the Duke dress himself, and in his night habit he is a very plain man.

22nd. The King's going from the Tower to Whitehall. Up early, and made myself as fine as I could, and put on my velvet coat, the first day that I put it on, though made half a year ago. And being ready, Sir W. Batten, my Lady, and his two daughters, and his son and wife, and Sir W. Pen and his son and I went to Mr. Young's, the flagmaker in Cornhill; and there we had a good room to ourselves, with wine and good cake, and saw the show very well. In which it is impossible to relate the glory of this day, expressed in the clothes of them that rode, and their horses and horse-clothes. Among others, my Lord Sandwich's embroidery and diamonds were not ordinary among them. The Knights of the Bath was a brave sight of itself; and their Esquires, among which Mr. Armiger was an Esquire to one of the Knights. Remarkable were the two men that represent the Dukes of Normandy and Aquitaine. The Bishops came next after Barons, which is the higher place; which makes me think that the next Parliament they will be called to the House of Lords. My Lord Monk rode bare after the King, and led in his hand a spare horse, as being Master of the Horse. The King, in a most rich embroidered suit and cloak, looked most noble. Wadlow, the vintner, at the Devil in Fleet Street, did lead a fine company of soldiers, all young, comely men, in white doublets. There followed the Vice-Chamberlain, Sir G. Carteret, a company of men all like Turks; but I know not yet what they are for. The streets all gravelled, and the houses hung with carpets before them, made brave show, and the ladies out of the windows. So glorious was the show with gold and silver, that we were not able to look at it, our eyes at last being so much overcome. Both the King and the Duke of York took notice of us, as they saw us at the window. In the evening, by water to Whitehall to my Lord's, and there I spoke with my Lord. He talked with me about his suit, which was made in France, and cost him £200, and very rich it is with embroidery. The show being ended, Mr. Young did give us a dinner, at which we very merry, and pleased above imagination at what we have seen. Sir W. Batten going home, he and I called, and drank some mum, and laid our wager about my Lady Faulconbridge's name, which he says not to be Mary, and so I won above 20s. So home, where Will and the boy stayed, and saw the show upon Tower Hill, and Jane at T. Pepys's the turner, and my wife at Charles Glassecocke's in Fleet Street.

CORONATION DAY

23rd. About four I rose and got to the Abbey, where I followed Sir J. Denham, the surveyor, with some company he was leading in. And with much ado, by the favour of Mr. Cooper, his man, did get

up into a great scaffold across the north end of the
Abbey, where with a great deal of patience I sat from
past four till eleven before the King came in. And a
great pleasure it was to see the Abbey raised in the
middle, all covered with red, and a throne (that is, a
chair) and footstool on the top of it; and all the officers
of all kinds, so much as the very fiddlers, in red vests.
At last comes in the Dean and Prebendaries of
Westminster, with the Bishops (many of them in cloth
of gold copes), and after them the Nobility, all in
their Parliament robes, which was a most magnificent
sight. Then the Duke and the King with a sceptre
(carried by my Lord Sandwich) and sword and mond
before him, and the crown too. The King in his
robes, bareheaded, which was very fine. And after
all had placed themselves, there was a sermon and
the service; and then in the choir at the high altar
the King passed through all the ceremonies of the
Coronation, which to my great grief I and most in the
Abbey could not see. The crown being put upon
his head, a great shout began, and he came forth to
the throne, and there passed through more ceremonies: as taking the oath, and having things read
to him by the Bishop; and his lords (who put on
their caps as soon as the King put on his crown) and
bishops came, and kneeled before him. And three
times the King-at-Arms went to the three open
places on the scaffold, and proclaimed, that if any
one could show any reason why Charles Stewart
should not be King of England, that now he should
come and speak. And a General Pardon also was
read by the Lord Chancellor, and medals flung up
and down by my Lord Cornwallis, of silver, but I
could not come by any. But so great a noise that I
could make but little of the music; and indeed, it
was lost to everybody. I went out a little while
before the King had done all his ceremonies, and went

53

round the Abbey to Westminster Hall, all the way within rails, and 10,000 people with the ground covered with blue cloth; and scaffolds all the way. Into the Hall I got, where it was very fine with hangings and scaffolds one upon another, full of brave ladies; and my wife in one little one, on the right hand. Here I stayed walking up and down, and at last upon one of the side stalls I stood and saw the King come in with all the persons (but the soldiers) that were yesterday in the cavalcade; and a most pleasant sight it was to see them in their several robes. And the King came in with his crown on, and his sceptre in his hand, under a canopy borne up by six silver staves, carried by Barons of the Cinque Ports, and little bells at every end. And after a long time he got up to the farther end, and all set themselves down at their several tables; and that was also a brave sight: and the King's first course carried up by the Knights of the Bath. And many fine ceremonies there was of the Herald's leading up people before him, and bowing; and my Lord of Albemarle's going to the kitchen and eating a bit of the first dish that was to go to the King's table. But, above all, was these three Lords, Northumberland, and Suffolk, and the Duke of Ormond, coming before the courses on horseback, and staying so all dinner-time, and at last bringing up (Dymock) the King's Champion, all in armour on horseback, with his spear and target carried before him. And a Herald proclaims " That if any dare deny Charles Stewart to be lawful King of England, here was a Champion that would fight with him "; and with these words, the Champion flings down his gauntlet, and all this he do three times in his going up towards the King's table. At last, when he is come, the King drinks to him, and then sends him the cup, which is of gold, and he drinks it off, and then rides back again with the cup in his hand. I went from table to table to see the Bishops and all others at their dinner, and was infinitely pleased with it. And at the Lord's table I met with William Howe, and he spoke to my Lord for me, and he did give him four rabbits and a pullet, and so Mr. Creed and I got Mr. Minshell to give us some bread, and so we at a stall ate it, as everybody else did what they could get. I took a great deal of pleasure to go up and down, and look upon the ladies, and to hear the music of all sorts, but above all the 24 violins. About six at night they had dined, and I went up to my wife. And strange it is to think that these two days have held up fair till now that all is done, and the King gone out of the Hall; and then it fell a-raining and thundering and lightening as I have not seen it do for some years; which people did take great notice of; God's blessing of the work of these two days, which is a foolery to take too much notice of such things. I observed little disorder in all this, only the King's footmen had got hold of the canopy, and would keep it from the Barons of the Cinque Ports, which they endeavoured to force from them again, but could not do it till my Lord Duke of Albemarle caused it to be put into Sir R. Pye's hand till to-morrow to be decided. At Mr. Bowyer's; a great deal of company, some I knew, others I did not. Here we stayed upon the leads and below till it was late, expecting to see the fireworks, but they were not performed to-night; only the City had a light like a glory round about it, with bonfires. At last I went to King Street, and there sent Crockford to my father's and my house, to tell them I could not come home to-night, because of the dirt, and a coach could not be had. And so I took my wife and Mrs. Frankleyn (who I proffered the civility of lying with my wife at Mrs. Hunt's to-night) to Axe Yard, in which, at the further end, there were three great bonfires, and a great

many gallants, men and women; and they laid hold
of us, and would have us drink the King's health
upon our knees, kneeling upon a faggot, which we all
did, they drinking to us one after another, which we
thought a strange frolic; but these gallants continued
there a great while, and I wondered to see how the ladies
did tipple. At last I sent my wife and her bedfellow
to bed, and Mr. Hunt and I went in with Mr. Thorn-
bury (who did give the company all their wine, he
being yeoman of the wine-cellar to the King); and
there, with his wife and two of his sisters, and some
gallant sparks that were there, we drank the King's
health, and nothing else, till one of the gentlemen fell
down stark drunk, and there lay; and I went to my
Lord's pretty well. But no sooner a-bed with Mr.
Shepley but my head began to turn, and I to vomit,
and if ever I was foxed, it was now, which I cannot
say yet, because I fell asleep, and slept till morning.
Thus did the day end with joy everywhere; and
blessed be God, I have not heard of any mischance to
anybody through it all, but only to Serjeant Glynne,
whose horse fell upon him yesterday, and is like to kill
him, which people do please themselves to see how
just God is to punish the rogue at such a time as this;
he being now one of the King's Serjeants, and rode
in the cavalcade with Maynard, to whom people wish
the same fortune. There was also this night, in King
Street, a woman had her eye put out by a boy's
flinging a firebrand into the coach. Now, after all
this, I can say, that, besides the pleasure of the sight
of these glorious things, I may now shut my eyes
against any other objects, nor for the future trouble
myself to see things of state and show, as being sure
never to see the like again in this world.

24th. Waked in the morning, with my head in a
sad taking through the last night's drink, which I am
very sorry for; so rose, and went out with Mr.

Creed to drink our morning draught, which he did give me in chocolate to settle my stomach. At night set myself to write down these three days' diary, and, while I am about it, I hear the noise of the chambers, and other things of the fireworks, which are now playing upon the Thames before the King; and I wish myself with them, being sorry not to see them.

May 1661

May 8th. Came my brother John to take his leave of me, he being to return to Cambridge. I did give him some good counsel and 20s. in money, and so he went away. At night comes my wife not well, from my father's, having had a foretooth drawn out to-day, which do trouble me. To-day I received a letter from my uncle, to beg an old fiddle of me for Perkin, the miller, whose mill the wind hath lately broke down, and now he hath nothing to live by but fiddling, and he must needs have it against Whitsuntide to play to the country-girls; but it vexed me to see how my uncle writes to me, as if he were not able to buy him one. But I intend to-morrow to send him one.

23rd. To the Rhenish wine-house, and there Mr. Jonas Moore, the mathematician, to us, and there he did by discourse make us fully believe that England and France were once the same continent, by very good arguments, and spoke very many things not so much to prove the Scripture false, as that the time therein is not well computed nor understood. In my black silk suit, the first day I have put it on this year, to my Lord Mayor's by coach, with a great deal of honourable company, and great entertainment. At table I had very good discourse with Mr. Ashmole, wherein he did assure me that frogs and many insects do often fall from the sky, ready formed. Dr. Bates's singularity in not rising up nor drinking the King's nor other healths at the table was very much observed. From thence we all took coach, and to our office, and there sat till it was late; and so I home and to bed by daylight. This day was kept a holy-day through the town; and it pleased me to see the little boys walk up and down in procession with their broom-staffs in their hands, as I had myself long ago done.

June 1661

June 5th. This morning did give my wife £4 to lay out upon lace and other things for herself. Sir W. Pen and I went out with Sir R. Slingsby to bowls in his alley, and there had good sport. I took my flageolet, and played upon the leads in the garden, where Sir W. Pen came out in his shirt into his leads, and there we stayed talking and singing and drinking great draughts of claret, and eating botargo, and bread and butter, till twelve at night, it being moonshine; and so to bed, very near fuddled.

6th. My head hath ached all night, and all this morning, with my last night's debauch. Called up this morning by Lieutenant Lambert, who is now made Captain of the *Norwich*, and he and I went down by water to Greenwich, and ate and drank and heard music at the Globe, and saw the simple motion that is there of a woman with a rod in her hand keeping time to the music while it plays, which is simple, methinks. Back again by water, calling at Captain Lambert's house, which is very handsome and neat, and a fine prospect at top. So to the office. The weather very hot, this night I left off my waistcoat.

11th. At the office this morning, Sir G. Carteret with us; and we agreed upon a letter to the Duke of York, to tell him the sad condition of this office for want of money; how men are not able to serve us more without some money; and that now the credit of the office is brought so low, that none will sell us anything without our personal security given for the same.

18th. All this morning at home vexing about the delay of my painters; and about four in the afternoon my wife and I by water to Captain Lambert's, where we took great pleasure in their turret-garden, and seeing the fine needlework of his wife, the best I ever saw in my life, and afterwards had a very handsome treat and good music that she made upon the harpsichon.

19th. One thing I must observe here, while I think of it, that I am now become the most negligent man in the world as to matters of news, insomuch that, nowadays, I neither can tell any, nor ask any of others.

28th. Went to Moorfields, and there walked, and stood and saw the wrestling, which I never saw so much of before, between the north and west countrymen. This night had our bed set up in our room, that we called the Nursery, where we lay, and I am very much pleased with the room.

29th. By a letter from the Duke, complaining of the delay of the ships that are to be got ready, Sir Williams both and I went to Deptford, and there examined into the delays, and were satisfied. Mr. Chetwind fell commending of *Hooker's Ecclesiastical Polity*, as the best book, and the only one that made him a Christian, which puts me upon the buying of it, which I will do shortly.

30th. I to Gray's Inn Walks all alone, and with great pleasure, seeing the fine ladies walk there. Myself humming to myself (which nowadays is my constant practice since I began to learn to sing) the trillo, and found by use that it do come upon me.

July 1661

July 6th.   Waked this morning with news, brought me by a messenger on purpose, that my uncle Robert is dead; so I rose sorry in some respect, glad in my expectations in another respect; so I bought me a pair of boots in St. Martin's, and got myself ready, and then to the Post-house, and set out about eleven and twelve o'clock, taking the messenger with me that came to me, and so we rode, and got well by nine o'clock to Brampton, where I found my father well. My uncle's corpse in a coffin standing upon joint-stools in the chimney in the hall; but it began to smell, and so I caused it to be set forth in the yard all night, and watched by two men.   My father and I lay together to-night, I greedy to see the will; but did not ask to see it till to-morrow.

7th.   (Lord's day.)   In the morning my father and I read the will; where, though he gives me nothing at present till my father's death, or at least very little, yet I am glad to see that he hath done so well for us all, and well to the rest of his kindred.   After that done, we went about getting things, as ribbons and gloves, ready for the burial, which in the afternoon was done; where, it being Sunday, all people far and near came in; and, in the greatest disorder that ever I saw, we made shift to serve them with what we had of wine and other things; and then to carry him to the church, where Mr. Taylor buried him, and Mr. Turner preached a funeral sermon, where he spoke not particularly of him anything, but that he was one so well known for his honesty, that it spoke for itself above all that he could say for it.   And so made a very good sermon.

8th, 9th, 10th, 11th, 12th, 13th.   I fell to work, and my father to look over my uncle's papers and clothes, and continued all this week upon that business, much troubled with my aunt's base ugly humours. We had news of Tom Trice putting in a caveat against us, in behalf of his mother, to whom my uncle hath not given anything, and for good reason therein expressed, which troubled us also. But above all our trouble is to find that his estate appears nothing as we expected, and all the world believes; nor his papers so well sorted as I would have had them, but all in confusion, that break my brains to understand them. We missed also the surrenders of his copyhold land, without which the land would not come to us, but to the heir-at-law, so that what with this, and the badness of the drink, and the ill opinion I have of the meat, and the biting of the gnats by night, and my disappointment in getting home this week, and the trouble of sorting all the papers, I am almost out of my wits with trouble, only I appear the more contented, because I would not have my father troubled.

23rd. Put on my mourning; I went to the theatre, and saw *Brenoralt*, I never saw before. It seemed a good play, but ill acted; only I sat before Mrs. Palmer, the King's mistress, and filled my eyes with her, which much pleased me. Troubled to hear how proud and idle Pall is grown, that I am resolved not to keep her.

24th. This morning my wife in bed tells me of our being robbed of our silver tankard, which vexed me all day for the negligence of my people to leave the door open. To the Wardrobe, but came too late, and dined with the servants. And then to my Lady, who do show my wife and me the greatest favour in the world, in which I take great content. To the office all the afternoon, which is a great pleasure to me again, to talk with persons of quality, and to be in command, and I give it out among them that the estate left me is £200 a year in land, besides moneys, because I would put an esteem upon myself. I hear that my man Will hath lost his clock with my tankard, at which I am very glad.

August 1661

August 11th. (Lord's day.) To our own church in the forenoon, and in the afternoon to Clerkenwell church, only to see the two fair Botelers; and I happened to be placed in the pew where they afterwards came to sit, but the pew by their coming being too full, I went out into the next, and there sat, and had my full view of them both, but I am out of conceit now with them, Colonel Dillon being come back from Ireland again, and do still court them, and comes to church with them, which makes me think they are not honest. Hence to Gray's Inn Walks, and there stayed a good while; where I met with Ned Pickering, who told me what a great match of hunting of a stag the King had yesterday; and how the King tired all their horses, and come home with not above two or three able to keep pace with him.

24th. Called to Sir W. Batten's, to see the strange creature that Captain Holmes hath brought with him from Guinea; it is a great baboon, but so much like a man in most things, that, though they say there is a species of them, yet I cannot believe but that it is a monster. I do believe that it already understands much English, and I am of the mind that it might be taught to speak or make signs. To the opera, and there saw *Hamlet, Prince of Denmark*, done with scenes very well, but above all, Betterton did the Prince's part beyond imagination.

25th. (Lord's day.) Home ; and found my Lady Batten and her daughter to look something askew upon my wife, because my wife do not buckle to them, and is not solicitous of their acquaintance.

26th. Casting up my father's accounts, and upon the whole I find that all he hath in money of his own due to him in the world is about £45, and he owes about the same sum: so that I cannot but think in what a condition had he left my mother, if he should have died before my uncle Robert.

31st. Thus ends the month. My maid Jane newly gone, and Pall left now to do all the work till another maid comes, which shall not be till she goes away into the country with my mother. No money comes in, so that I have been forced to borrow a great deal for my own expenses, and to furnish my father, to leave things in order. I have some trouble about my brother Tom, who is now left to keep my father's trade, in which I have great fears that he will miscarry for want of brains and care. At Court things are in very ill condition, there being so much emulation, poverty, and the vices of drinking, swearing, and loose amours, that I know not what will be the end of it, but confusion. And the Clergy so high, that all people that I meet with do protest against their practice. In short, I see no content or satisfaction anywhere, in any one sort of people. The Benevolence proves so little, and an occasion of so much discontent everywhere, that it had better it had never been set up. I think to subscribe £20. We are at our Office quiet, only for lack of money all things go to rack. Our very bills offered to be sold upon the Exchange at 10 per cent. loss. We are upon getting Sir R. Ford's house added to our office; but I see so many difficulties will follow in pleasing of one another in the dividing of it, and in becoming bound personally to pay the rent of £200 per annum, that I do believe it will yet scarce come to pass. The season very sickly everywhere of strange and fatal fevers.

September 1661

September 2nd. Mr. Pickering and I to Westminster Hall again, and there walked an hour or two talking; and, though he be a fool, yet he keeps much company, and will tell all he sees or hears, and so a man may understand what the common talk of the town is. And I find that there are endeavours to get my Lord out of play at sea, which I believe Mr. Coventry and the Duke do think will make them more absolute; but I hope for all this, they will not be able to do it. My wife tells me that she met at Change with my young ladies of the Wardrobe, and there helped them to buy things, and also with Mr. Somerset, who did give her a bracelet of rings which did a little trouble me, though I know there is no hurt yet in it, but only for fear of further acquaintance.

7th. Having appointed the young ladies at the Wardrobe to go with them to the play to-day, my wife and I took them to the theatre, where we seated ourselves close by the King, the Duke of York, and Madame Palmer, which was great content; and, indeed, I can never enough admire her beauty. And here was *Bartholomew Fair*, with the puppet-show, acted to-day, which had not been these forty years, it being so satirical against Puritanism, they durst not till now, which is strange they should already dare to do it, and the King to countenance it; but I do never a whit like it the better for the puppets, but rather the worse. Thence home with the ladies, it being by reason of our staying a great while for the King's coming, and the length of the play, near nine o'clock before it was done.

8th. (Lord's day.) To church, and coming home again, found our new maid Doll asleep, that she could not hear to let us in, so that we were fain to send a boy in at a window to open the door to us. Began to look over my accounts, and, upon the whole, I do find myself, by what I can yet see, worth near £600, for which God be blessed.

11th. Home to my house to dinner, where I found my wife's brother Balty as fine as hands could make him, and his servant, a Frenchman, to wait on him, and come to have my wife visit a young lady which he is a servant to, and have hope to trepan, and get for his wife. I did give way for my wife to go with him. Walking through Lincoln's Inn Fields, observed at the Opera a new play, *Twelfth Night*, was acted there, and the King there; so I, against my own mind and resolution, could not forbear to go in, which did make the play seem a burden to me; and I took no pleasure at all in it; and so, after it was done, went home with my mind troubled for my going thither, after my swearing to my wife that I would never go to a play without her. My wife was with her brother to see his mistress to-day, and says she is young, rich, and handsome, but not likely for him to get.

29th. (Lord's day.) What at dinner and supper I drank I know not how, of my own accord, so much wine, that I was even almost foxed, and my head ached all night; so home and to bed, without prayers, which I never did yet, since I came to the house, of a Sunday night; I being now so out of order that I durst not read prayers, for fear of being perceived by my servants in what case I was.

October 1661

October 19th. We had a very good and handsome dinner and excellent wine. I not being neat in clothes, which I find a great fault in me, could not be so merry as otherwise, and at all times I am, and can be, when I am in good habit, which makes me remember my father Osborne's rule for a gentleman, to spare in all things rather than that.

20th. (Lord's day.) Much offended in mind at a proud trick my man Will hath got, to keep his hat on in the house, but I will not speak of it to him to-day, but I fear I shall be troubled with his pride and laziness, though in other things he is good enough. To church in the afternoon, where a sleepy Presbyter preached, and then to Sir W. Batten, who is to go to Portsmouth to-morrow to wait upon the Duke of York, who goes to take possession, and to set in order the garrison there.

November 1661

November 3rd. (Lord's day.) At night my wife and I had a good supper by ourselves of a pullet hashed, which pleased me much to see my condition come to allow ourselves a dish like that.

11th. Captain Ferrers carried me the first time that ever I saw any gaming-house, to one, entering into Lincoln's Inn Fields, at the end of Bell Yard, where strange the folly of men to lay and lose so much money, and very glad I was to see the manner of a gamester's life, which I see is very miserable, and poor, and unmanly. And thence he took me to a dancing school in Fleet Street, where we saw a company of pretty girls dance, but I do not in myself like to have young girls exposed to so much vanity. So to the Wardrobe, where I found my Lady had agreed upon a lace for my wife at £6, which I seemed much glad of that it was no more, though in my mind I think it too much, and I pray God to keep me so to order myself, and my wife's expenses, that no inconvenience in purse or honour follow this my prodigality.

17th. (Lord's day.) To our own church, and at noon, by invitation, Sir W. Pen dined with me, and I took Mrs. Hester, my Lady Batten's kinswoman, to dinner from church with me, and we were very merry. To church; and heard a simple fellow upon the praise of church music, and exclaiming against men's wearing their hats on in the church; but slept part of the sermon.

December 1661

December 13th. With my wife to the painter's, and there she sat the first time to be drawn, while I all the while stood looking on a pretty lady's picture, whose face did please me extremely. At last, he having done, I found that the dead colour of my wife is good, above what I expected, which pleased me exceedingly.

23rd. Lighting at my bookseller's in St. Paul's Churchyard, I met there with Mr. Crumlum, and the second master of Paul's School, and thence I took them to the Star, and there we sat and talked, and I had great pleasure in their company, and very glad I was of meeting him so accidentally, I have omitted too long to go to see him. Here in discourse of books I did offer to give the school what book he would choose of £5. So we parted.

31st. My wife and I this morning to the painter's, and there she sat the last time, and I stood by, and did tell him some little things to do, that now her picture I think will please me very well; and after her, her little black dog sat in her lap, and was drawn, which made us very merry; so home to dinner. To the office; and there late finishing our estimate of the debts of the Navy to this day; and it come to near £374,000. So home, and after supper and my barber had trimmed me, I sat down to end my journal for this year. And my condition at this time, by God's blessing, is that my health is very good, and so my wife's, in all respects; my servants, W. Hewer, Sarah, Nell, and Wayneman; my house at the Navy Office. I suppose myself to be worth about £500 clear in the world, and my goods of my house my own, and what is coming to me from Brampton, when my father dies, which God defer. But, by my uncle's death, the whole care and trouble and settling of all lies upon me, which is very great, because of lawsuits, especially that with T. Trice, about the interest of £200, which will, I hope, be ended soon. My chiefest thought is now to get a good wife for Tom, there being one offered by the Joyces, a cousin of theirs, worth £200 in ready money. I am upon writing a little treatise to present to the Duke, about our privilege in the seas as to other nations striking their flags to us. But my greatest trouble is that I have for this last half year been a very great spendthrift in all manner of respects, that I am afraid to cast up my accounts, though I hope I am worth what I say above. But I will cast them up very shortly. I have newly taken a solemn oath about abstaining from plays and wine, which I am resolved to keep, according to the letter of the oath which I keep by me. The fleet hath been ready to sail for Portugal, but hath lacked wind this fortnight, and by that means my Lord is forced to keep at sea all this winter, till he brings home the Queen, which is the expectation of all now, and the greatest matter of public talk.

January 1662

January 1st. Waking this morning out of my sleep on a sudden, I did with my elbow hit my wife a great blow over her face and nose, which waked her with pain, at which I was sorry, and to sleep again.

13th. Before twelve o'clock comes, by appointment, Mr. Peter and the Dean, and Colonel Honiwood, brothers, to dine with me; but so soon, that I was troubled at it. Mr. Peter did show us the experiment, which I had heard talk of, of the chemical glasses, which break all to dust by breaking off a little small end; which is a great mystery to me. My aunt Wight and my wife and I to cards, she teaching us to play at gleek, which is a pretty game; but I have not my head so free as to be troubled with it.

14th. This day, my brave vellum covers to keep pictures in, came in, which pleases me very much.

16th. Towards Cheapside; and in Paul's Church-yard saw the funeral of my Lord Cornwallis, late Steward of the King's House, go by. And thence I to the painter's, and there paid him £6 for the two pictures, and 36s. for the two frames. Stokes told us that notwithstanding the country of Gambo is so unhealthy, yet the people of the place live very long, so as the present King there is 150 years old, which they count by rains; because every year it rains continually four months together. He also told us that the kings there have above 100 wives a-piece.

February 1662

February 3rd. After music-practice I dined with Sir W. Batten with many friends more, it being his wedding-day, and among other frolics, it being their third year, they had three pies, whereof the middle-most was made of an oval form in an oval hole within the other two, which made much mirth, and was called the middle piece; and above all the rest, we had great striving to steal a spoonful out of it; and I remember Mrs. Mills, the minister's wife, did steal one for me, and did give it me; and to end all, Mrs. Shippman did fill the pie full of white wine, it holding at least a pint and a half, and did drink it off for a health to Sir William and my Lady—it being the greatest draught that ever I did see a woman drink in my life. I went along with my Lady and the rest of the gentlewomen to Major Holmes's, and there we had a fine supper—among others, excellent lobsters, which I never ate at this time of the year before. The Major had good lodgings at the Trinity House. At last home, and, being in my chamber, we do hear great noise of mirth at Sir William Batten's, tearing the ribbons from my Lady and him.

4th. To Westminster Hall, where it was full term. Here all the morning, and at noon to my Lord Crewe's, where one Mr. Templer, an ingenious man and a person of honour he seems to be, dined; and, discoursing of the nature of serpents, he told us some in the waste places of Lancashire do grow to a great bigness, and do feed upon larks, which they take thus:—They observe when the lark is soared to the highest, and do crawl till they come to be just underneath them; and there they place themselves with their mouth uppermost, and there, as is conceived, they do eject poison up to the bird; for the bird do suddenly come down again in its course of a circle, and falls directly into the mouth of the serpent; which is very strange.

9th. (Lord's day.) I took physic this day, and was all day in my chamber, talking with my wife about her laying out of £20, which I had long since promised her to lay out in clothes against Easter, for herself, and composing some airs, God forgive me! At night to prayers and to bed.

10th. To Paul's Churchyard, and there I met with Dr. Fuller's *England's Worthies*, the first time that I ever saw it; and so I sat down reading in it; being much troubled that, though he had some discourse with me about my family and arms, he says nothing at all, nor mentions us either in Cambridgeshire or

Norfolk. But I believe, indeed, our family were never considerable.

11th. At the office in the afternoon; so home to music; my mind being full of our alterations in the garden. At night began to compose songs, and begin with "Gaze not on swans."

12th. This morning till four in the afternoon I spent abroad, doing of many and very considerable businesses; so home, with my mind very highly contented with my day's work, wishing I could do so every day.

15th. With the two Sir Williams to the Trinity House; and there, in their society, had the business debated of Sir Nicholas Crisp's sasse at Deptford. After dinner I was sworn a Younger Brother, Sir W. Rider being Deputy-Master for my Lord of Sandwich; and after I was sworn all the Elder Brothers shake me by the hand; it is their custom, it seems. No news yet of our fleet gone to Tangier, which we now begin to think long.

24th. Long with Mr. Berkenshaw in the morning at my music practice, finishing my song of "Gaze not on swans," in two parts, which pleases me well; and I did give him £5 for this month or five weeks that he hath taught me, which is a great deal of money, and troubled me to part with it. Thence to the painter's, and sat again for my picture in little. Called Will up, and chid him before my wife, for refusing to go to church with the maids yesterday, and telling his mistress that he would not be made a slave of.

27th. Came Mr. Berkenshaw, and in our discourse we fell to angry words, so that in a pet he flung out of my chamber, and I never stopped him, having intended to put him off to-day, whether this had happened or no, because I think I have all the rules that he hath to give.

28th. The boy failing to call us up as I commanded, I was angry, and resolved to whip him for that and many other faults, to-day. Early with Sir W. Pen by coach to Whitehall, to the Duke of York's chamber, and there I presented him from my Lord a fine map of Tangier, done by one Captain Beckman, a Swede, that is with my Lord. We stayed looking it over a great while with the Duke after he was ready. I bade Will get me a rod, and he and I called the boy up to one of the upper rooms of the Comptroller's house towards the garden, and there I reckoned all his faults, and whipped him soundly, but the rods was so small that I fear they did not much hurt to him, but only to my arm, which I am already, within a quarter of an hour, not able to stir almost.

March 1662

March 1st. My wife and I by coach, first to see my little picture that is a-drawing, and thence to the Opera, and there saw *Romeo and Juliet*, the first time it was ever acted; but it is a play of itself the worst that ever I heard, and the worst acted that ever I saw these people do, and I am resolved to go no more to see the first time of acting, for they were all of them out more or less. I do find that I am £500 beforehand in the world, which I was afraid I was not; but I find that I had spent above £250 this last half-year.

2nd. (Lord's day.) Talking long in bed with my wife about our frugal life for the time to come, proposing to her what I could and would do if I were worth £2000, that is, be a knight and keep my coach, which pleased her. To church in the morning; none in the pew but myself.

23rd. (Lord's day.) This morning was brought me my boy's fine livery, which is very handsome, and I do think to keep the black and gold lace upon grey, being the colour of my arms, for ever.

26th. Up early. This being, by God's great blessing, the fourth solemn day of my cutting for the stone this day four years, and am, by God's mercy, in very good health, and like to do well; the Lord's name be praised for it! At noon came my good guest, Madam Turner, The., and cousin Norton, and a gentleman, one Mr. Lewin, of the King's Life-Guard; by the same token he told us of one of his fellows killed this morning in a duel. I had a pretty dinner for them, viz., a brace of stewed carps, six roasted chickens, and a jowl of salmon, hot, for the first course; a tanzy, and two neats' tongues, and cheese, the second. Merry all the afternoon, talking, and singing, and piping on the flageolet. We had a man-cook to dress dinner to-day, and sent for Jane to help us.

April 1662

April 1st. To the Wardrobe, and dined. Here was Mr. Harbord, son to Sir Charles Harbord, that lately came with letters from my Lord Sandwich to the King. He and I, and the two young ladies and my wife to the playhouse, the Opera, and saw *The Maid in the Mill*, a pretty good play; and, that being done, in their coach I took them to Islington, and then, after a walk in the fields, I took them to the great cheesecake house, and entertained them, and so home; and after an hour's stay with my Lady, their coach carried us home, and so weary to bed.

4th. I was much troubled to-day to see a dead man lie floating upon the waters, and had done (they say) these four days, and nobody takes him up to bury him, which is very barbarous.

11th. With Sir W. Pen by water to Deptford; and among the ships now going to Portugal with men and horse, to see them dispatched. So to Greenwich; and had a fine pleasant walk to Woolwich, having in our company Captain Minnes, whom I was much pleased to hear talk. Among other things, he and the Captains that were with us tell me that negroes drowned look white, and lose their blackness, which I never heard before. At Woolwich, up and down to do the same business; and so back to Greenwich by water. Sir William and I walked into the Park, where the King hath planted trees and made steps in the hill up to the Castle, which is very magnificent. So up and down the house, which is now repairing in the Queen's lodgings.

30th. After dinner comes Mr. Stephenson, one of the burgesses of the town, to tell me that the Mayor and burgesses did desire my acceptance of a burgess-ship, and were ready at the Mayor's to make me one. So I went, and there they were all ready, and did with much civility give me my oath, and after the oath, did by custom shake me all by the hand; so I took them to a tavern, and made them drink, and, paying the reckoning, went away. It cost me a piece in gold to the Town Clerk, and 10s. to the Bailiffs; and spent 5s.

May 1662

May 3rd. To the Duke's chamber, who had been a-hunting this morning, and is come back again. To dinner to my Lady Sandwich; and Sir Thomas Crewe's children coming thither, I took them and all my Ladies to the Tower, and showed them the lions, and all that was to be shown; Sir Thomas Crewe's children being as pretty and the best behaved that ever I saw of their age. Thence, at the goldsmith's, took my picture in little, which is now done, home with me; and pleases me exceedingly, and my wife.

4th. (Lord's day.) Mr. Holliard came to me, and let me blood, about sixteen ounces, I being exceeding

74

full of blood and very good. I began to be sick; but, lying upon my back, I was presently well again, and did give him 5s. for his pains. After dinner, my arm tied up with a black ribbon, I walked with my wife to my brother Tom's; our boy waiting on us with his sword, which this day he begins to wear, to outdo Sir W. Pen's boy, who this day, and Sir W. Batten's, do begin to wear new liveries; but I do take mine to be the neatest of them all. I led my wife to Mrs. Turner's pew, the church being full, it being to hear a Doctor who is to preach a probation sermon. When church was done, my wife and I walked to Gray's Inn to observe fashions of the ladies, because of my wife's making some clothes.

15th. To Westminster; and at the Privy Seal I saw Mr. Coventry's seal for his being Commissioner with us, at which I know not yet whether to be glad or otherwise. At night all the bells of the town rang, and bonfires were made for the joy of the Queen's arrival, who landed at Portsmouth last night. But I do not see much true joy, but only an indifferent one, in the hearts of people, who are much discontented at the pride and luxury of the Court, and running in debt.

June 1662

June 14th. Up by four o'clock in the morning, and upon business at my office. Then we sat down to business, and about eleven o'clock, having a room got ready for us, we all went out to the Tower-hill; and there, over against the scaffold, made on purpose this day, saw Sir Henry Vane brought. A very great press of people. He made a long speech, many times interrupted by the Sheriff and others there; and they would have taken his paper out of his hand, but he would not let it go. But they caused all the books of those that writ after him to be given the Sheriff; and the trumpets were brought under the scaffold that he might not be heard. Then he prayed, and so fitted himself, and received the blow; but the scaffold was so crowded that we could not see it done. But Boreman, who had been upon the scaffold, told us that first he began to speak of the irregular proceeding against him; that he was, against Magna Charta, denied to have his exceptions against the indictment allowed; and that there he was stopped by the Sheriff. Then he drew out his paper of notes, and began to tell them first of his life; that he was born a gentleman; he had been, till he was seventeen years old, a good fellow, but then it pleased God to lay a foundation of grace in his heart, by which he was persuaded, against his worldly interest, to leave all preferment and go abroad, where he might serve God with more freedom. Then he was called home, and made a member of the Long Parliament; where he never did, to this day, anything against his conscience, but all for the glory of God. Here he would have given them an account of the proceedings of the Long Parliament, but they so often interrupted him, that at last he was forced to give over; and so fell into prayer for England in general, then for the churches in England, and then for the City of London; and so fitted himself for the block, and received the blow. He had a blister, or issue, upon his neck, which he desired them not to hurt: he changed not his colour or speech to the last, but died justifying himself and the cause he had stood for; and spoke very confidently of his being presently at the right hand of Christ; and in all things appeared the most resolved man that ever died in that manner, and showed more of heat than cowardice, but yet with all humility and gravity. One asked him why he did not pray for the King. He answered, " You shall see I can pray for the King: I pray God bless him!" The

King had given his body to his friends; and, therefore, he told them that he hoped they would be civil to
his body when dead; and desired they would let him
die like a gentleman and a Christian, and not crowded
and pressed as he was. So to the office a little, and to
the Trinity House, and there all of us to dinner; and
to the office again all the afternoon till night.

21st. At noon Sir W. Pen and I to the Trinity
House, where was a feast made by the wardens. Great
good cheer, and much, but ordinary, company. The
Lieutenant of the Tower, upon my demanding how
Sir H. Vane died, told me that he died in a passion,
but all confess with so much courage as never man did.

OBSERVATIONS

30th. This I take to be as bad a juncture as ever I
observed. The King and his new Queen minding
their pleasures at Hampton Court. All people discontented; some that the King do not gratify them
enough; and the others, Fanatics of all sorts, that the
King do take away their liberty of conscience; and
the height of the Bishops, who I fear will ruin all again.
They do much cry up the manner of Sir H. Vane's
death, and he deserves it. Much clamour against the
chimney-money; and the people say they will not pay
it without force. And, in the meantime, like to have
war abroad; and Portugal to assist, when we have not
money to pay for any ordinary layings-out at home.
All in dirt about building of my house and Sir W.
Batten's a storey higher. Into a good way, fallen on
minding my business and saving money, which God
increase; and I do take great delight in it, and see the
benefit of it. In a longing mind of going to see
Brampton, but cannot get three days time, do what I
can. In very good health, my wife and myself.

July 1662

July 4th.   Up by five o'clock, and after my journal put in order, to my office about my business, which I am resolved to follow.   Comes Mr. Cooper, mate of the *Royal Charles*, of whom I intend to learn mathematics, and do begin with him to-day, he being a very able man; and no great matter, I suppose, will content him.   After an hour's being with him at arithmetic (my first attempt being to learn the multiplication-table); then we parted till to-morrow.

5th.   At noon had Sir W. Pen, who I hate with all my heart for his base treacherous tricks, but yet I think it not policy to declare it yet, and his son William to my house to dinner, where was also Mr. Creed and my cousin Harry Alcocke.   I having some venison given me a day or two ago, and so I had a shoulder roasted, another baked, and the umbles baked in a pie, and all very well done.   We were merry as I could be in that company.

21st.   Up early.   I did take boat and down to Greenwich, to Captain Cocke's, who hath a most pleasant seat, and neat.   Here I drank wine, and ate some fruit off the trees; and he showed a great rarity, which was, two or three of a great number of silver dishes and plates, which he bought of an ambassador that did lack money, in the edge or rim of which was placed silver and gold medals very ancient.   To Woolwich to the Ropeyard; and there looked over several sorts of hemp, and did fall upon my great survey of seeing the working and experiments of the strength and the charge in the dressing of every sort; and I do think have brought it to so great a certainty, as I have done the King great service in it; and do purpose to get it ready against the Duke's coming to town to present to him.   I see it is impossible for the King to have things done as cheap as other men.

August 1662

August 17th. (Lord's day.) This being the last Sunday that the Presbyterians are to preach, unless they read the new Common Prayer, and renounce the Covenant, I had a mind to hear Dr. Bates's farewell sermon; and walked to St. Dunstan's, where, it not being seven o'clock yet, the doors were not open; and so I walked an hour in Temple Gardens, reading my vows, which it is a great content to me to see how I am a changed man in all respects for the better, since I took them, which the God of Heaven continue to me, and make me thankful for. At eight o'clock I went, and crowded in at a back door among others, the church being half full almost before any doors were open publicly, which is the first time that I have done so these many years; and so got into the gallery, beside the pulpit, and heard very well. His text was, " Now the God of Peace——"; the last Hebrews, and the 20th verse; he making a very good sermon, and very little reflections in it to anything of the times.

20th. To my Lord Sandwich, whom I found in bed. Among other talk, he do tell me that he hath put me into the commission with a great many great persons in the business of Tangier, which is a very great honour to me, and may be of good concernment to me. By and by comes in Mr. Coventry to us, whom my Lord tells that he is also put into the commission, and that I am there, of which he said he was glad; and did tell my Lord that I was indeed the life of this office, and much more to my commendation beyond measure. And that, whereas before he did bear me respect for his sake, so he do it now much more for my own; which is a great blessing to me : Sir G. Carteret having told me what he did yesterday concerning his speaking to my Lord Chancellor about me: so that on all hands, by God's blessing, I find myself a very rising man. By and by comes my Lord Peterborough in, with whom we talked a good while, and he is going to-morrow towards Tangier again. I perceive there is yet good hopes of peace with Guyland, which is of great concernment to Tangier. Meeting Mr. Townsend, he would needs take me to Fleet Street, to one Mr. Barwell, squire sadler to the King, and there we and several other Wardrobe-men dined. We had a venison pasty, and other good, plain, and handsome dishes; the mistress of the house, a pretty well-carriaged woman, and a fine hand she hath; and her maid a pretty brown lass.

23rd. Mr. Coventry and I did walk together a great while in the garden, where he did tell me his mind about Sir G. Carteret's having so much the command of the money, which must be removed; and indeed it is the bane of all our business. He observed to me also how Sir W. Batten begins to struggle and to look after his business. I also put him upon getting an order from the Duke for our inquiries into the Chest, which he will see done. Mr. Creed and I walked down to the Styll Yard, and so all along Thames Street, but could not get a boat: I offered eight shillings for a boat to attend me this afternoon, and they would not, it being the day of the Queen's coming to town from Hampton Court. So we fairly walked it to Whitehall, and through my Lord's lodgings we got into Whitehall garden, and so to the Bowling Green, and up to the top of the new Banqueting House there, over the Thames, which was a most pleasant place as any I could have got; and all the show consisted chiefly in the number of boats and barges; and two pageants, one of a King, and another of a Queen, with her Maids of Honour sitting at her feet very prettily: and they tell me the Queen is Sir Richard Ford's daughter. Anon came the King and Queen in a barge, under a canopy, with 10,000 barges and boats I know, for we could see no water for them, nor discern the King nor Queen. And so they landed at Whitehall Bridge, and the great guns on the other side went off. But that which pleased me best was that my Lady Castlemaine stood over against us upon a piece of Whitehall. But methought it was strange to see her Lord and her upon the same place walking up and down without taking notice one of another, only at first entry he put off his hat, and she made him a very civil salute, but afterwards took no notice one of another; but both of them now and then would take their child, which the nurse held in her arms, and dandle it. One thing more; there happened a scaffold below to fall, and we feared some hurt, but there was none, but she of all great ladies only ran down among the common rabble to see what hurt was done, and did take care of a child that received some little hurt, which methought was so noble. Anon there came one there booted and spurred, that she talked long with; and by and by, she being in her hair, she put on his hat, which was but an ordinary one, to keep the wind off; but it became her mightily, as everything else do. I went away, not weary with looking on her, and to my Lord's lodgings, where my brother Tom and Dr. Thomas Pepys were to speak with me: so I walked with them in the garden, and was very angry with them both for their going out of town without my knowledge; and they told me the business, which was to see a gentlewoman for a wife for Tom, of Mr. Cooke's providing, worth £500, of good education, her name Hobell, and lives near Banbury; demands £40 per annum jointure. Tom likes her, and, they say, had a very good reception, and that Cooke hath been very serviceable therein, and that she is committed to old Mr. Young of the Wardrobe's

81

tuition. My Lord and I had half an hour's private discourse about the discontents of the times, which we concluded would not come to anything of difference, though the Presbyters would be glad enough of it; but we do not think religion will so soon cause another war. Then we fell to talk of Navy business; and he concludes, as I do, that he needs not put himself upon any more voyages abroad to spend money, unless a war comes; and that by keeping his family a while in the country, he shall be able to gather money. Here we broke off, and I bid him goodnight, and so, with much ado, the streets being at nine o'clock at night crammed with people going home to the city, for all the borders of the river had been full of people, as the King had come, to a miracle got to the Palace Yard, and there took boat, and so to the Old Swan; and so walked home, and to bed very weary.

September 1662

September 3rd. After dinner we met and sold the *Weymouth*, *Success*, and *Fellowship* hulks; where pleasant to see how backward men are at first to bid; and yet, when the candle is going out, how they bawl, and dispute afterwards who bid the most first. And here I observed one man cunninger than the rest, that was sure to bid the last man, and to carry it; and enquiring the reason, he told me that, just as the flame goes out, the smoke descends, which is a thing I never observed before, and by that he do know the instant when to bid last.

7th. (Lord's day.) To Whitehall Chapel, where I heard a good sermon of the Dean of Ely's, upon returning to the old ways. Home with Mr. Fox and his lady; and there dined with them, where much company came to them. Most of our discourse was

what ministers are flung out of that will not conform;
and the care of the Bishop of London that we are
here supplied with very good men. Meeting Mr.
Pierce, the surgeon, he took me into Somerset House;
and there carried me into the Queen-mother's
presence-chamber, where she was, with our Queen
sitting on her left hand, whom I never did see before;
and though she be not very charming, yet she
hath a good, modest, and innocent look, which is
pleasing. Here I also saw Madame Castlemaine,
and, which pleased me most, Mr. Crofts, a most
pretty spark of about fifteen years old, who, I
perceive, do hang much upon my Lady Castlemaine,
and is always with her; and, I hear, the Queens both
are mighty kind to him. By and by in comes the
King, and anon the Duke and his Duchess; so that,
they being all together, was such a sight as I never
could almost have happened to see with so much
ease and leisure. They stayed till it was dark, and
then went away; the King and his Queen, and my
Lady Castlemaine and young Crofts, in one coach,
and the rest in other coaches. Here were great store
of great ladies, but very few handsome.

29th. (Michaelmas day.) This day my oaths for
drinking of wine and going to plays are out; and so
I do resolve to take a liberty to-day, and then to fall
to them again. To the King's Theatre, where we
saw *Midsummer's Night's Dream*, which I had never
seen before, nor shall ever again, for it is the most
insipid ridiculous play that ever I saw in my life.

30th. To the Duke's play-house, where we saw
The Duchess of Malfi well performed, but Betterton
and Ianthe to admiration. Strange to see how easily
my mind do revert to its former practice of loving
plays and wine; but this night I have again bound
myself to Christmas next. My condition at present
is this: I have long been building, and my house,

to my great content, is now almost done. My Lord Sandwich has lately been in the country, and very civil to my wife, and hath himself spent some pains in drawing a plot of some alterations in our house there, which I shall follow as I get money. As for the office, my late industry hath been such, as I am become as high in reputation as any man there, and good hold I have of Mr. Coventry and Sir G. Carteret, which I am resolved, and it is necessary for me, to maintain, by all fair means. Things are all quiet. The late outing of the Presbyterian clergy, by their not renouncing the Covenant as the Act of Parliament commands, is the greatest piece of state now in discourse. But, for aught I see, they are gone out very peaceably, and the people not so much concerned therein as was expected.

October 1662

October 5th. (Lord's day.) I to church; and this day the parson has got one to read with a surplice on. I suppose himself will take it up hereafter, for a cunning fellow he is as any of his coat.

8th. To my Lord Sandwich's, and, among other things, to my extraordinary joy, he did tell me how much I was beholding to the Duke of York, who did yesterday of his own accord tell him that he did thank him for one person brought into the Navy, naming myself, and much more to my commendation, which is the greatest comfort and encouragement that ever I had in my life, and do owe it all to Mr. Coventry's goodness and ingenuity.

10th. Up, and between eight and nine mounted again; but my feet so swelled with yesterday's pain, that I could not get on my boots, which vexed me to the blood, but was forced to pay 4s. for a pair of old shoes of my landlord's, and so ride in shoes to Cambridge; the way so good that I got very well thither, and set up at the Bear: and there my cousin Angier came to me, and I must needs to his house; and there found Dr. Fairbrother, with a good dinner. But, above all, he telling me that this day there is a Congregation for the choice of some officers in the University, he after dinner gets me a gown, cap, and hood, and carries me to the Schools, where Mr. Pepper, my brother's tutor, and this day chosen Proctor, did appoint a M.A. to lead me into the Regent House, where I sat with them, and did vote by subscribing papers thus: "Ego Samuel Pepys eligo Magistrum Bernardum Skelton (and, which was more strange, my old schoolfellow and acquaintance, and who afterwards did take notice of me, and we spoke together) alterum e taxatoribus hujus Academiae in annum sequentem." The like I did for one Briggs, for the other Taxor, and for other officers, as the Vice-Proctor (Mr. Covell), for Mr. Pepper, and which was the gentleman that did carry me into the Regent House. This being done, I did with much content return to my cousin Angier's. Thence to Trinity Hall with Dr. John Pepys, who tells me that his brother Roger has gone out of town to keep a Court; and so I was forced to go to Impington, to take such advice as my old uncle and his son Claxton could give me. By and by after supper comes in, unlooked for, my cousin Roger, with whom I discoursed largely.

14th. My father and I admitted to all the lands; he for life, and I for myself and heirs in reversion. I did with most complete joy of mind go from the Court with my father home, and in a quarter of an hour did get on horseback, with my brother Tom, Cooke, and Will, all mounted, and, without eating or drinking, take leave of my father, mother, Pall, to whom I did give 10s., but have shown no kind of kindness since I came, for I find her so very ill-natured that I cannot love her, and she so cruel an hypocrite that she can cry when she pleases, and John and I away, calling in at Hinchingbroke, and taking leave in three words of my Lady and the young ladies; and so by moonlight to Cambridge, whither we came at about nine o'clock, and took up at the Bear.

November 1662

November 25th. Great talk among people how some of the Fanatics do say that the end of the world is at hand, and that next Tuesday is to be the day. Against which, whenever it shall be, good God fit us all!

27th. At my waking I found the tops of the houses covered with snow, which is a rare sight, which I have not seen these three years. To the office, where we sat till noon; when we all went to the next house upon Tower Hill, to see the coming by of the Russian Ambassador; for whose reception all the City trained bands do attend in the streets, and the King's lifeguards, and most of the wealthy citizens in their black velvet coats, and gold chains (which remain of their gallantry at the King's coming in), but they stayed so long that we went down again to dinner. And after I had dined I walked to the Conduit in the Quarrefowr, at the end of Gracious Street and Cornhill; and there (the spouts thereof running very near me upon all the people that were under it), I saw them pretty well go by. I could not see the Ambassador in his coach: but his attendants in their habits and fur caps very handsome comely men, and most of them with hawks upon their fists to present to the King. But, Lord! to see the absurd nature of Englishmen that cannot forbear laughing and jeering at everything that looks strange!

A POOR CHRISTMAS SERMON

December 1662

December 1st. To my Lord Sandwich's, to Mr. Moore; and then over the Park, where I first in my life, it being a great frost, did see people sliding with their skates, which is a very pretty art.

7th. After a drowsy sermon, to my aunt Wight's, where great store of her usual company, and here we stayed a pretty good while talking—I differing from my aunt, as I commonly do, in our opinion of the handsomeness of the Queen, which I oppose mightily, saying, that if my nose be handsome, then is hers, and such like: and so with my wife only to see Sir W. Pen, who is now got out of his bed, and sits by the fireside.

25th. (Christmas day.) Had a pleasant walk to Whitehall, where I intended to have received the Communion with the family, but I came a little too late. So I walked up into the house, and spent my time looking over pictures, particularly the ships in King Henry the VIII.'s voyage to Bullen; marking the great difference between their build then and now. By and by down to the chapel again, where Bishop Morley preached upon the song of the Angels, " Glory to God on high, on earth peace, and good will towards men." Methought he made but a poor sermon, but long; and, reprehending the mistaken jollity of the Court for the true joy that shall and ought to be on these days, he particularised concerning their excess in plays and gaming, saying that he whose office it is to keep the gamesters in order and within bounds serves but for a second rather in a duel, meaning the groom-porter. Upon which it was worth observing how far they are come from taking the reprehensions of a bishop seriously, that they all laugh in the chapel when he reflected on their ill actions and courses. He did much press us to joy in these public days of joy, and to hospitality; but one that stood by whispered in my ear that the Bishop do not spend one groat to the poor himself. The sermon done, a good anthem followed with viols, and the King came down to receive the sacrament. But I stayed not, but calling my boy from my Lord's lodgings, and giving Sarah some good advice by my Lord's order to be sober, and look after the house, I walked home again with great pleasure, and there dined by my wife's bedside with great content, having a mess of brave plum-porridge and a roasted pullet for dinner; and I sent for a mince-pie abroad, my wife not being well to make any herself yet.

26th. To the Wardrobe. Hither came Mr. Battersby; and we falling into discourse of a new book of drollery in verse called *Hudibras*, I would needs go find it out, and met with it at the Temple: cost me 2s. 6d. But when I came to read it, it is so silly an abuse of the Presbyter Knight going to the wars, that I am ashamed of it; and by and by meeting at Mr. Townsend's at dinner, I sold it to him for 18d.

31st. Thus ends this year, with great mirth to me and my wife. Our condition being thus:—we are at present spending a night or two at my Lord's lodgings at Whitehall. Our home at the Navy Office, which is and hath a pretty while been in good condition, finished and made very convenient. By my last year's diligence in my office, blessed be God! I am come to a good degree of knowledge therein; and am acknowledged so by all the world, even the Duke himself, to whom I have a good access: and by that, and by my being Commissioner for Tangier, he takes much notice of me; and I doubt not but, by the continuance of the same endeavours, I shall in a little time come to be a man much taken notice of in the world, specially being come to so great an esteem with

Mr. Coventry. Public matters stand thus: The King is bringing, it is said, his family, and Navy, and all other his charges, to a less expense. In the meantime, himself following his pleasures more than with good advice he would do; at least, to be seen to all the world to do so. His dalliance with my Lady Castlemaine being public, every day, to his great reproach; and his favouring of none at Court so much as those that are the confidants of his pleasure, as Sir H. Bennet and Sir Charles Barkeley; which, good God, put it into his heart to mend, before he makes himself too much contemned by his people for it! The Duke of Monmouth is in so great splendour at Court, and so dandled by the King, that some doubt that, if the King should have no child by the Queen, which there is yet no appearance of, whether he would not be acknowledged for a lawful son; and that there will be a difference follow between the Duke of York and him; which God prevent! My Lord Chancellor is threatened by people to be questioned, the next sitting of the Parliament, by some spirits that do not love to see him so great: but certainly he is a good servant to the King. The Queen-mother is said to keep too great a Court now; and her being married to my Lord St. Albans is commonly talked of; and that they had a daughter between them in France; how true, God knows. The Bishops are high, and go on without any diffidence in pressing uniformity; and the Presbyters seem silent in it, and either conform or lay down, though without doubt they expect a turn, and would be glad these endeavours of the other Fanatics would take effect; there having been a plot lately found out, for which four have been publicly tried at the Old Bailey and hanged. My Lord Sandwich is still in good esteem, and now keeping his Christmas in the country; and I in good esteem, I think, as any man can be, with him. Mr. Moore is very sickly, and I doubt will hardly get over his late fit of sickness, that still hangs on him. In fine, for the good condition of myself, wife, family, and estate, in the great degree that it is, and for the public state of the nation, so quiet as it is, the Lord God be praised!

January 1663

January 6th. (Twelfth day.) Into St. Paul's church, and there finding Elborough, my old school-fellow at Paul's, now a parson, whom I know to be a silly fellow, he tells me, and so do others, that Dr. Calamy is this day sent to Newgate for preaching, Sunday was sennight, without leave, though he did it only to supply the place; otherwise the people must have gone away without ever a sermon, they being disappointed of a minister: but the Bishop of London will not take that as an excuse. Thence into Wood Street, and there bought a fine table for my dining-room, cost me 50s.; and while we were buying it, there was a scare-fire in an alley over against us, but they quenched it. To the Duke's house, and there saw *Twelfth Night* acted well, though it be but a silly play, and not relating at all to the name or day. Home, and found all well, only myself somewhat vexed at my wife's neglect in leaving of her scarf, waistcoat, and night-dressings in the coach to-day, that brought us from Westminster; though, I confess, she did give them to me to look after. It might be as good as 25s. loss.

8th. Dined at home; and there being the famous new play acted the first time to-day, which is called *The Adventures of Five Hours*, at the Duke's house, being, they say, made or translated by Colonel Tuke, I did long to see it; and so we went; and, though early, were forced to sit, almost out of sight, at the end of one of the lower forms, so full was the house. And the play, in one word, is the best, for the variety and the most excellent continuance of the plot to the very end, that ever I saw, or think ever shall, and all possible, not only to be done in the time, but in most other respects very admittable, and without one word of ribaldry; and the house, by its frequent plaudits, did show their sufficient approbation. So home; with much ado in an hour getting a coach home, and now resolving to set up my rest as to plays till Easter, if not Whitsuntide next, excepting plays at Court.

13th. My poor wife rose by five o'clock in the morning, before day, and went to market and bought fowls and many other things for dinner, with which I was highly pleased, and the chine of beef was down also before six o'clock, and my own jack, of which I was doubtful, do carry it very well; things being put in order, and the cook come. By and by comes Dr. Clerke, and his lady, his sister, and a she-cousin, and Mr. Pierce and his wife, which was all my guests. I had for them, after oysters, at first course, a hash of rabbits and lamb, and a rare chine of beef. Next, a great dish of roasted fowl, cost me about 30s., and a tart, and then fruit and cheese. My dinner was noble, and enough. I had my house mighty clean and neat; my room below with a good fire in it; my dining-room above, and my chamber being made a with-drawing-chamber; and my wife's a good fire, also. I find my new table very proper, and will hold nine or ten people well, but eight with great room. At supper had a good sack posset and cold meat, and sent my guests away about ten o'clock at night, both them and myself highly pleased with our management of this day; and indeed their company was very fine, and Mrs. Clerke a very witty fine lady, though a little conceited and proud. I believe this day's feast will cost me near £5.

February 1663

February 4th.   To Paul's School, it being Apposition-day there.   I heard some of their speeches (and they were just as schoolboys used to be) of the seven liberal sciences, but I think not so good as ours were in our time.   Went up to see the head forms posed in Latin, Greek, and Hebrew; but I think they do not answer in any so well as we did; only in geography they did pretty well.   Dr. Wilkins and Outram were examiners.   So down to the school, where Mr. Crumlum did me much honour by telling many what a present I had made to the school, showing my Stephanus in four volumes.   He also showed us upon my desire an old edition of the grammar of Colet's, where his epistle to the children is very pretty.

5th.   To dinner and found it so well done, above what I did expect from my maid Susan, now Jane is gone, that I did call her in and give her sixpence.

March 1663

March 18th.   This day my triangle, which was put in tune yesterday, did please me very well—Ashwell playing upon it pretty well.

April 1663

April 3rd.   I met Captain Grove, who did give me a letter directed to myself from himself.   I discerned money to be in it, and took it, knowing, as I found it to be, the proceed of the place I have got him to be, the taking up of vessels for Tangier.   But I did not open it till I came home—not looking into it till all the money was out, that I might say I saw no money in the paper, if ever I should be questioned about it. There was a piece in gold, and £4 in silver.

4th. This being my feast, in lieu of what I should have had a few days ago, for the cutting of the stone, very merry at, before, and after dinner, and the more for that my dinner was great, and most neatly dressed by our own only maid. We had a fricassee of rabbits and chickens, a leg of mutton boiled, three carps in a dish, a great dish of a side of lamb, a dish of roasted pigeons, a dish of four lobsters, three tarts, a lamprey pie (a most rare pie), a dish of anchovies, good wine of several sorts, and all things mighty noble, and to my great content. After dinner to Hyde Park.

30th. To dinner, where Mrs. Hunt, my father, and W. Stankes; but, Lord! what a stir Stankes makes, with his being crowded in the streets, and wearied in walking in London, and would not be wooed by my wife and Ashwell to go to a play, nor to Whitehall, or to see the lions, though he was carried in a coach. I never could have thought there had been upon earth a man so little curious in the world as he is.

May 1663

May 1st. After dinner I got my father, brother Tom, and myself together, and I advised my father to good husbandry, and to be living within the compass of £50 a year, and all in such kind words, as not only made both them but myself to weep. That being done, we all took horse, and I, upon a horse hired of Mr. Game, saw him out of London, at the end of Bishopsgate Street, and so I turned, and rode, with some trouble, through the fields, and then Holborn, etc., towards Hyde Park, whither all the world, I think, are going; and in my going, almost thither, met W. Howe coming, galloping upon a little crop black nag; it seems one that was taken in some ground of my Lord's, by some mischance being left by his master, a thief—this horse being found with black cloth ears on, and a false mane, having none of his own; and I back again with him to the Chequer, at Charing Cross, and there put up my own dull jade, and by his advice saddled a delicate stone-horse of Captain Ferrers's, and with that rid in state to the Park, where none better mounted than I almost; but being in a throng of horses, seeing the King's riders showing tricks with their managed horses, which were very strange, my stone-horse was very troublesome, and began to fight with other horses, to the dangering him and myself; and with much ado I got out, and kept myself out of harm's way. Here I saw nothing good, neither the King, nor my Lady Castlemaine, nor any great ladies or beauties being there, there being more pleasure a great deal at an ordinary day; or else those few good faces that there were choked up with the many bad ones, there being people of all sorts in coaches there, to some thousands. Going thither in the highway again, by the Park gate, I met a boy in a sculler-boat, carried by a dozen people at least, rowing as hard as he could drive—it seems upon some wager. By and by, about seven o'clock, homeward; and changing my horse again, I rode home, coaches going in great crowds to the further end of the town almost. In my way, in Leadenhall Street, there was morris-dancing, which I have not seen a great while. So set my horse up at Game's, paying 5s. for him, and went to hear Mrs. Turner's daughter play on the harpsichon; but, Lord! it was enough to make any man sick to hear her; yet was I forced to commend her highly. This day Captain Grove sent me a side of pork, which was the oddest present, sure, that was ever made any man; and the next, I remember I told my wife, I believed would be a pound of candles, or a shoulder of mutton; but the fellow do it in kindness, and is one I am beholden to. So to bed, very weary, and a little

galled, for lack of riding, praying to God for a good
journey to my father, of whom I am afraid, he being
so lately ill.

4th. The dancing-master came, whom standing by,
seeing him instructing my wife, when he had done
with her, he would needs have me try the steps of a
coranto; and what with his desire and my wife's
importunity, I did begin, and then was obliged to
give him entry money 10s., and am become his
scholar. The truth is I think it is a thing very useful
for any gentleman.

8th. Took my wife and Ashwell to the Theatre
Royal, being the second day of its being opened. The
house is made with extraordinary good contrivance,
and yet hath some faults, as the narrowness of the
passages in and out of the pit, and the distance from
the stage to the boxes, which I am confident cannot
hear; but for all other things is well; only, above all,
the music being below, and most of it sounding under
the very stage, there is no hearing of the basses at all,
nor very well of the trebles, which sure must be
mended. The play was *The Humorous Lieutenant*, a
play that hath little good in it, nor much in the very
part which, by the King's command, Lacy now acts,
instead of Clun. In the dance, the tall devil's actions
was very pretty. The play being done, we home by
water, having been a little shamed that my wife and
woman were in such a pickle, all the ladies being
finer and better dressed in the pit than they used, I
think, to be. To my office, to set down this day's passage; and, though my oath against going to plays do
not oblige me against this house, because it was not
then in being, yet, believing that at the time my
meaning was against all public houses, I am resolved
to deny myself the liberty of two plays at Court, which
are in arrear to me for the months of March and
April. At supper comes Pembleton, and afterwards

we all up to dancing till late. They say that I am like to make a dancer.

11th. On foot to Greenwich, where going, I was set upon by a great dog, who got hold of my garters, and might have done me hurt; but, Lord! to see in what a maze I was, that, having a sword about me, I never thought of it, or had the heart to make use of it, but might, for want of that courage, have been worried! I went homeward, after a little discourse with Mr. Pierce, the surgeon, who tells me that my Lady Castlemaine hath now got lodgings near the King's chamber at Court; and that the other day Dr. Clerke and he did dissect two bodies, a man and a woman, before the King, with which the King was highly pleased. I called upon Mr. Crumlum, and did give him the 10s. remaining not laid out, of the £5 I promised him for the school, with which he will buy strings, and golden letters upon the books I did give them.

12th. A little angry with my wife for minding nothing now but the dancing-master, having him come twice a day, which is folly.

June 1663

June 2nd. With the vintner's man, who came by my direction to taste again my tierce of claret, to go down to the cellar with him to consult about the drawing of it; and there, to my great vexation, I find that the cellar door hath long been kept unlocked, and above half the wine drunk.

13th. To the Royal Theatre; here we saw *The Faithful Shepherdess*, a most simple thing, and yet much thronged after, and often shown, but it is only for the scenes' sake, which is very fine indeed, and worth seeing; but I quite out of opinion of any of their actings but Lacy's, compared with the other house.

In our way saw my Lady Castlemaine, who, I fear, is not so handsome as I have taken her for, and now she begins to decay something. This is my wife's opinion also, for which I am sorry. Thence by coach, with a mad coachman, that drove like mad, and down byways, through Bucklersbury home—everybody through the street cursing him, being ready to run over them. Yesterday, upon conference with the King in the Banqueting House, the Parliament did agree with much ado, it being carried but by forty-two voices, that they would supply him with a sum of money; but what, and how, is not yet known, but expected to be done with great disputes the next week. But if done at all, it is well.

15th. I was forced to go to Thames Street; thence home; but, finding my wife gone, I took coach and after her to her inn, where I am troubled to see her forced to sit in the back of the coach, though pleased to see her company none but women and one parson, and so kissing her often, and Ashwell once, I bid them adieu. To the Trinity House; where, among others, I found my Lords Sandwich and Craven, and my cousin Roger Pepys, and Sir William Wheeler. Great variety of talk. Mr. Prin, among many, had a pretty tale of one that brought in a bill in Parliament for the impowering him to dispose his land to such children as he should have that should bear the name of his wife. It was in Queen Elizabeth's time. One replied that there are many species of creatures where the male gives the denomination to both sexes, as swan and woodcock, but not above one where the female do, and that is goose. Both at and after dinner we had great discourses of the nature and power of spirits, and whether they can animate dead bodies; in all which, as of the general appearance of spirits, my Lord Sandwich is very sceptical. He says the greatest warrants that ever he had to believe any, is the present appearing of the Devil in Wiltshire, much of late talked of, who beats a drum up and down. There are books of it, and, they say, very true; but my Lord observes, though he do answer any tune that you will play to him upon another drum, yet one tune he tried to play and could not; which makes him suspect the whole; and I think it is a good argument. They talked of handsome women, and Sir J. Minnes saying that there was no beauty like what he sees in the country-markets, and specially at Bury, in which I will agree with him. My Lord replied thus: " Sir John, what do you think of your neighbour's wife? " looking upon me. " Do you not think that he hath a great beauty to his wife? " " Upon my word he hath." Which I was not a little proud of.

21st. (Lord's day.) To church, and slept all the sermon; the Scot (Creighton), to whose voice I am not to be reconciled, preaching.

July 1663

July 4th. This day, in the Duke's chamber there being a Roman story in the hangings, and upon the standard written these four letters—S. P. Q. R., Sir G. Carteret came to me to know what the meaning of those four letters were; which ignorance is not to be borne in a Privy Councillor, methinks, what a school-boy should be whipped for not knowing.

10th. I met Pierce, the surgeon, who tells me that for certain the King is grown colder to my Lady Castlemaine than ordinary, and that he believes he begins to love the Queen, and do make much of her, more than he used to do. Mr. Coventry tells me that my Lord Bristol hath this day impeached my Lord Chancellor in the House of Lords of High Treason. The chief of the articles are these:—1st, That he should be the occasion of the peace made with Holland lately upon such disadvantageous terms, and that he was bribed to it. 2nd, That Dunkirk was also sold by his advice chiefly, so much to the damage of England. 3rd, That he had £6000 given him for the drawing-up or promoting of the Irish declaration lately, concerning the division of the lands there. 4th, He did carry on the design of the Portugal match, so much to the prejudice of the Crown of England, notwithstanding that he knew the Queen is not capable of bearing children. 5th, That the Duke's marrying of his daughter was a practice of his, thereby to raise his family; and that it was done by indirect courses. 6th, As to the breaking off of the match with Parma, in which he was employed at the very time when the match with Portugal was made up here, which he took as a great slur to him, and so it was; and that indeed is the chief occasion of all this feud. 7th, That he hath endeavoured to bring in Popery, and wrote to the Pope for a cap for a subject of the King of England's (my Lord Aubigny). And some say that he lays it to the Chancellor that a good Protestant Secretary, Sir Edward Nicholas, was laid aside, and a Papist, Sir H. Bennet, put in his room: which is very strange, when the last of these two is his own creature, and such an enemy accounted to the Chancellor, that they never did nor do agree; and all the world did judge the Chancellor to be falling from the time that Sir H. Bennet was brought in. Besides, my Lord Bristol being a Catholic himself, all this is very strange. These are the main of the Articles. Upon which my Lord Chancellor desired the noble Lord that brought in these Articles would sign to them with his hand; which my Lord Bristol did presently. Then the House did order that the Judges should, against Monday next, bring in their opinion, Whether these articles are treason, or no? and next, they would know, Whether they were brought

in regularly or no, without the leave of Lords'
House ?

13th. I walked to the Temple; and there, from
my cousin Roger, hear that the Judges have this day
brought in their answer to the Lords, That the articles
against my Lord Chancellor are not Treason; and
to-morrow they are to bring in their arguments to the
House for the same. This day also the King did send
by my Lord Chamberlain to the Lords, to tell them
from him, that the most of the articles against my
Lord Chancellor he himself knows to be false. I met
the Queen-mother walking in the Pell-Mell, led by
my Lord St. Albans. And finding many coaches at
the Gate, I found upon enquiry that the Duchess is
brought to bed of a boy; and hearing that the King
and Queen are rode abroad with the Ladies of Honour
to the Park, and seeing a great crowd of gallants
staying here to see their return, I also stayed walking
up and down. By and by the King and Queen, who
looked in this dress, a white laced waistcoat and a
crimson short petticoat, and her hair dressed *à la
négligence*, mighty pretty; and the King rode hand in
hand with her. Here was also my Lady Castlemaine,
who rode amongst the rest of the ladies; but the King
took, methought, no notice of her; nor, when she
'light, did anybody press, as she seemed to expect, and
stayed for it, to take her down, but was taken down by
her own gentleman. She looked mighty out of humour,
and had a yellow plume in her hat, which all took
notice of, and yet is very handsome, but very melancholy; nor did anybody speak to her, or she so much
as smile or speak to anybody. I followed them up into
Whitehall, and into the Queen's presence, where all
the ladies walked, talking and fiddling with their hats
and feathers, and changing and trying one another's
by one another's heads, and laughing. But it was the
finest sight to me, considering their great beauties and

dress, that ever I did see in all my life. But, above all, Mrs. Stewart in this dress, with her hat cocked and a red plume, with her sweet eye, little Roman nose, and excellent *taille*, is now the greatest beauty I ever saw, I think, in my life; and, if ever woman can, do exceed my Lady Castlemaine, at least in this dress: nor do I wonder if the King changes, which I verily believe is the reason of his coldness to my Lady Castlemaine.

22nd. To my Lord Crewe's. My Lord not being come home, I met and stayed below with Captain Ferrers, who was come to wait upon my Lady Jemimah to St. James's, she being one of the four ladies that hold up the mantle at the christening this afternoon of the Duke's child, a boy. In discourse of the ladies at Court, Captain Ferrers tells me that my Lady Castlemaine is now as great again as ever she was; and that her going away was only a fit of her own upon some slighting words of the King, so that she called for her coach at a quarter of an hour's warning, and went to Richmond; and the King the next morning, under pretence of going a-hunting, went to see her and make friends, and never was a-hunting at all. After which she came back to Court, and commands the King as much as ever, and hath and doth what she will. No longer ago than last night, there was a private entertainment made for the King and Queen at the Duke of Buckingham's, and she was not invited: but being at my Lady Suffolk's, her aunt's, where my Lady Jemimah and Lord Sandwich dined, yesterday, she was heard to say, " Well, much good may it do them, and for all that, I will be as merry as they "; and so she went home, and caused a great supper to be prepared. And after the King had been with the Queen at Wallingford House, he came to my Lady Castlemaine's, and was there all night, and my Lord Sandwich with him. He tells me he believes that, as soon as the King can get a husband for Mrs. Stewart, however, my Lady Castlemaine's nose will be out of joint; for that she comes to be in great esteem, and is more handsome than she.

25th. Having intended this day to go to Banstead Downs to see a famous race, I sent Will. to get himself ready to go with me; but I hear it is put off, because the Lords do sit in Parliament to-day. Towards the evening we bade them adieu, and took horse; being resolved that, instead of the race which fails us, we would go to Epsom. When we came there, we could hear of no lodging, the town so full; but, which was better, I went towards Ashted, and there we got a lodging in a little hole we could not stand upright in. While supper was getting, I walked up and down behind my cousin Pepys's house that was, which I find comes little short of what I took it to be, when I was a little boy.

26th. (Lord's day.) Up and to the Wells, where a great store of citizens, which was the greatest part of the company, though there were some others of better quality. Thence I walked to Mr. Minnes's house, and thence to Durdans, and walked within the Courtyard and to the Bowling-green, where I have seen so much mirth in my time; but now no family in it, my Lord Barkeley, whose it is, being with his family at London. Then rode through Epsom, the whole town over, seeing the various companies that were there walking; which was very pleasant to see how they are there, without knowing what to do, but only in the morning to drink waters. But, Lord! to see how many I met there of citizens, that I could not have thought to have seen there; that they had ever had it in their heads or purses to go down thither.

27th. We rode hard home, and set up our horses at Fox Hall, and I by water (observing the King's barge attending his going to the House this day) home, it being about one o'clock. By water to Westminster, and there came most luckily to the Lords' House, as the House of Commons were going into the Lords' House, and there I crowded in along with the Speaker, and got to stand close behind him, where he made his speech to the King, who sat with his crown on and robes, and so all the Lords in their robes, a fine sight; wherein he told his Majesty what they have done this Parliament, and now offered for his royal consent. The greatest matters were a bill for the Lord's day, which it seems the Lords have lost, and so cannot be passed, at which the Commons are displeased; the bills against Conventicles and Papists, but it seems the Lords have not passed them; and giving his Majesty four entire subsidies; which last, with about twenty smaller Acts, were passed with this form: The Clerk of the House reads the title of the bill, and then looks at the end, and there finds (writ by the King, I suppose), " Le Roy le veult," and that he reads. And to others he reads, " Soit fait comme vous desirez." And to the Subsidies, as well that for the Commons, I mean the Laity, as for the Clergy, the King writes, " Le Roy remerciant les Seigneurs et Prelats, accepte leur benevolence." The Speaker's speech was far from any oratory, but was as plain, though good matter, as anything could be, and void of elocution. After the bills passed, the King sitting on his throne, with his speech writ in a paper which he held in his lap, and scarce looked off of it all the time, he made his speech to them, giving them thanks for their subsidies, of which, had he not need, he would not have asked or received them; and that need, not from any extravagances of his, he was sure, in anything, but the disorders of the times compelling him to be at greater charge than he hoped for the future, by their care in their country, he should be: and that for his family expenses and others, he would labour, however, to retrench in many things convenient, and would have all others to do so too. He desired that nothing of old faults should be remembered, or severity for the same used to any in the country, it being his desire to have all forgot, as well as forgiven. But, however, to use all care in suppressing any tumults, etc.; assuring them that the restless spirits of his and their adversaries have great expectations of something to be done this summer. And promised that though the Acts about Conventicles and Papists were not ripe for passing this Session, yet he would take care himself that neither of them should in this interval be encouraged to the endangering of the peace; and that at their next meeting he would himself prepare two bills for them concerning them. So he concluded that for the better proceeding of justice he did think fit to make this a Session, and do prorogue them to the 16th of March next. His speech was very plain, nothing at all of spirit in it, nor spoke with any; but rather, on the contrary, imperfectly, repeating many times his words, though he read all: which I am sorry to see, it having not been hard for him to have got all the speech without book. So they all went away, the King out of the House at the upper end, he being by and by to go to Tunbridge to the Queen; and I in the Painted Chamber spoke with my Lord Sandwich while he was putting off his robes, who tells me he will now hasten down into the country. By water to Whitehall, and walked over the Park to St. James's, but missed Mr. Coventry; and so out again, and there the Duke was coming along the Pell-Mell. It being a little darkish, I stayed not to take notice of him, but went directly back again. And in our walk over the Park, one of the Duke's footmen came running behind us, and came looking just in our faces to see who we were, and went back again. What his meaning is I know not, but was fearful that I might not go far enough with my hat off.

    31st. Dr. Pierce tells me, as a friend, the great injury

that he thinks I do myself by being so severe in the Yards, and contracting the ill-will of the whole Navy for those offices, singly upon myself. Now I discharge a good conscience therein, and I tell him that no man can, nor do he say any say it, charge me with doing wrong; but rather do as many good offices as any man. They think, he says, that I have a mind to get a good name with the King and Duke, who he tells me do not consider any such thing; but I shall have as good thanks to let all alone, and do as the rest. But I believe the contrary; and yet I told him I never go to the Duke alone, as others do, to talk of my own services. However, I will make use of his counsel, and take some course to prevent having the single ill-will of the office.

September 1663

September 10th. All the morning making a great contract with Sir W. Warren for £3000 worth of masts; but, good God! to see what a man might do, were I a knave. Mr. Moore tells me of the good peace that is made at Tangier with the Moors, but to continue but from six months to six months.

11th. This morning, about two or three o'clock, knocked up in our back-yard and rising to the window, being moonshine, I found it was the constable and his watch, who had found our back-yard door open, and so came in to see what the matter was. So I desired them to shut the door, and bid them good-night.

14th. By coach to Bishop's Gate Street, it being a very promising fair day. There at the Dolphin we met my uncle Thomas, and his son-in-law, which seems a very sober man, and Mr. Moore: so Mr. Moore and my wife set out before, and my uncle and I stayed for his son Thomas, who, by a sudden resolution, is preparing to go with us, which makes me fear something of mischief which they design to do us. He staying a great while, the old man and I before, and about eight miles off his son comes after us, and about six miles farther we overtake Mr. Moore and my wife, which makes me mightily consider what a great deal of ground is lost in a little time, when it is to be got up again by another, who is to go his own ground and the others too; and so, after a little bait (I paying all the reckonings the whole journey) at Ware, to Buntingford, where my wife, by drinking some cold beer, being hot herself, presently after 'lighting begins to be sick, and became so pale, and I alone with her in a great chamber there, that I thought she would have died, and so in great horror, and having a great trial of my true love and passion for her, called the maids and mistress of the house, and so with some strong water she came to be pretty well again; and so to bed, and I having put her to bed with great content, I called in my company, and supped in the chamber by her, and, being very merry in talk, supped and then parted. This day my cousin Thomas dropped his hanger, and it was lost.

19th. Up pretty betimes; and I to Brampton, where I find my father ill in bed still, and Madam Norbery, whom and her fair daughter and sister I was ashamed to kiss, but did—my lip being sore with riding in the wind, and bit with the gnats; and, they being gone, I told my father my success. My wife and I took horse, and rode with marvellous, and the first and only hour of, pleasure that ever I had in this estate since I had to do with it, to Brampton woods; and through the wood rode, and gathered nuts in my way, and then at Graffam, to an old woman's house, to drink, where my wife used to go; and being in all circumstances highly pleased, and in my wife's riding and good company at this time, I rode, and she showed me the river behind my father's house, which is very pleasant; and so saw her home, and I straight to Huntingdon; and there a barber came and trimmed me; and thence walked to Hinchingbroke, where my Lord and ladies all are just alighted.

October 1663

October 14th. After dinner my wife and I, by Mr. Rawlinson's conduct, to the Jewish Synagogue; where the men and boys in their veils, and the women behind a lattice out of sight; and some things stand up, which I believe is their Law, in a press, to which all coming in do bow; and in the putting on their veils do say something, to which others that hear him do cry, Amen, and the party do kiss his veil. Their service all in a singing way, and in Hebrew. And anon their Laws that they take out of the press are carried by several men, four or five several burdens in all, and they do relieve one another: and whether it is that every one desires to have the carrying of it, thus they carried it round about the room while such a service is singing. And in the end they had a prayer for the King, which they pronounced his name in Portuguese; but the prayer, like the rest, in Hebrew. But, Lord! to see the disorder, laughing, sporting, and no attention, but confusion in all their service, more like brutes than people knowing the true God, would make a man forswear ever seeing them more: and indeed I never did see so much, or could have imagined there had been any religion in the whole world so absurdly performed as this.

17th. Some discourse of the Queen's being very sick, if not dead, the Duke and Duchess of York being sent for betimes this morning to come to Whitehall to her.

19th. Waked with a very high wind, and said to my wife, " I pray God I hear not of the death of any great person, this wind is so high! " fearing that the

Queen might be dead. So up; and going by coach with Sir W. Batten and Sir J. Minnes to St. James's, they tell me that Sir W. Compton, who it is true had been a little sickly for a week or fortnight, but was very well upon Friday at night last at the Tangier Committee with us, was dead—died yesterday: at which I was most exceedingly surprised, he being, and so all the world saying that he was, one of the worthiest men and best officers of State now in England; and so in my conscience he was: of the best temper, valour, ability of mind, integrity, birth, fine person, and diligence of any one man he hath left behind him in the three kingdoms; and yet not forty years old, or if so, that is all. I find the sober men of the Court troubled for him; and yet not so as to hinder or lessen their mirth, talking, laughing, and eating, drinking, and doing everything else, just as if there was no such thing. Coming to St. James's, I hear that the Queen did sleep five hours pretty well tonight, and that she waked and gargled her mouth, and to sleep again; but that her pulse beats fast, beating twenty to the King's or my Lady Suffolk's eleven; but not so strong as it was. It seems she was so ill as to be shaved, and pigeons put to her feet, and to have the extreme unction given her by the priests, who were so long about it that the doctors were angry. The King, they all say, is most fondly disconsolate for her, and weeps by her, which makes her weep; which one this day told me he reckons a good sign, for that it carries away some rheum from the head. This morning Captain Allen tells me how the famous Ned Mullins, by a slight fall, broke his leg at the ankle, which festered; and he had his leg cut off on Saturday, but so ill done, notwithstanding all the great surgeons about the town at the doing of it, that they fear he will not live with it. Being invited to dinner to my Lord Barkeley's, and so, not

knowing how to spend our time till noon, Sir W.
Batten and I took coach and to the Coffee-house in
Cornhill; where much talk about the Turks' proceedings, and that the plague is got to Amsterdam,
brought by a ship from Algiers; and it is also carried
to Hambrough. The Duke says the King purposes
to forbid any of their ships coming into the river.
The Duke also told us of several Christian commanders
(French) gone over to the Turks to serve them; and,
upon enquiry, I find that the King of France do by
this aspire to the Empire, and so to get the Crown of
Spain also upon the death of the King, which is very
probable, it seems. Back to St. James's, and there
dined with my Lord Barkeley and his lady, where
Sir G. Carteret, Sir W. Batten, and myself, with two
gentlemen more: my lady, and one of the ladies of
honour to the Duchess, no handsome woman, but a
most excellent hand. A fine French dinner.

29th. Up, it being Lord Mayor's day, Sir Anthony
Bateman. This morning was brought home my new
velvet cloak, that is, lined with velvet, a good cloth
the outside—the first that ever I had in my life; and
I pray God it may not be too soon now that I begin
to wear it. I thought it better to go without it
because of the crowd, and so I did not wear it. At
noon I went to Guildhall; and, meeting with Mr.
Proby, Sir R. Ford's son, and Lieutenant-Colonel
Baron, a City commander, we went up and down to
see the tables; where under every salt there was a
bill of fare, and at the end of the table the persons
proper for the table. Many were the tables, but
none in the Hall but the Mayor's and the Lords of
the Privy Council that had napkins or knives, which
was very strange. We went into the Buttery, and
there stayed and talked, and then into the Hall again,
and there wine was offered, and they drank, I only
drinking some hypocras, which do not break my vow,

it being, to the best of my present judgment, only a mixed compound drink, and not any wine. If I am mistaken, God forgive me! but I do hope and think I am not. By and by met with Creed: and we, with the others, went within the several Courts, and there saw the tables prepared for the Ladies, and Judges, and Bishops: all great signs of a great dinner to come. By and by, about one o'clock, before the Lord Mayor came, came into the Hall, from the room where they were first led into, the Chancellor (Archbishop before him), with the Lords of the Council, and other Bishops, and they to dinner. Anon comes the Lord Mayor, who went up to the lords, and then to the other tables to bid welcome; and so all to dinner. I sat near Proby, Baron, and Creed at the Merchant Strangers' table; where ten good dishes to a mess, with plenty of wine of all sorts, of which I drank none; but it was very unpleasing that we had no napkins or change of trenchers, and drank out of earthen pitchers and wooden dishes. It happened that after the lords had half dined, came the French Ambassador up to the lords' table, where he was to have sat: he would not sit down nor dine with the Lord Mayor, who was not yet come, nor have a table to himself, which was offered; but in a discontent went away again. After I had dined, I and Creed rose and went up and down the house, and up to the ladies' room, and there stayed gazing upon them. But though there were many and fine, both young and old, yet I could not discern one handsome face there; which was very strange. I expected music, but there was none but only trumpets and drums, which displeased me. The dinner, it seems, is made by the Mayor and two Sheriffs for the time being, the Mayor paying one half, and they the other. And the whole, Proby says, is reckoned to come to about £700 or £800 at most. Being wearied with looking upon a company of ugly women, Creed and I went away, and took coach, and through Cheapside, and there saw the pageants, which were very silly. The Queen mends apace, they say; but yet talks idle still.

November 1663

November 2nd. Up, and by coach to Whitehall, and there in the long Matted Gallery I find Sir G. Carteret, Sir J. Minnes, and Sir W. Batten; and by and by comes the King to walk there with three or four with him; and, soon as he saw us, says he, "Here is the Navy Office," and there walked twenty turns the length of the gallery, talking, methought, but ordinary talk. By and by came the Duke, and he walked, and at last they went into the Duke's lodgings. The King stayed so long, that we could not discourse with the Duke, and so we parted. I heard the Duke say that he was going to wear a periwig; and they say the King also will. I never till this day observed that the King is mighty grey.

3rd. Home, and by and by comes Chapman, the periwig-maker, and upon my liking it, without more ado I went up, and there he cut off my hair, which went a little to my heart at present to part with it; but, it being over, and my periwig on, I paid him £3 for it; and away went he with my own hair, to make up another of; and I, by and by, went abroad, after I had caused all my maids to look upon it; and they conclude it do become me; though Jane was mightily troubled for my parting of my own hair, and so was Bess.

8th. (Lord's day.) To church, where I found that my coming in a periwig did not prove so strange as I was afraid it would, for I thought that all the church would presently have cast their eyes all upon me, but I found no such thing.

15th. (Lord's day.) In the afternoon drew up a letter to my Lord, stating to him what the world talks concerning him, and leaving it to him and myself to be thought of by him as he pleases; but I have done but my duty in it. I wait Mr. Moore's coming, for his advice about sending it. This day being our Queen's birthday, the guns of the Tower went all off; and in the evening the Lord Mayor sent from church to church to order the constables to cause bonfires to be made in every street, which methinks is a poor thing to be forced to be commanded. After a good supper with my wife, and hearing of the maids read in the Bible, to prayers and to bed.

18th. This morning I sent Will with my great letter of reproof to Lord Sandwich, who did give it into his own hand. I pray God give a blessing to it; but I confess I am afraid what the consequence may be to me of good or bad, which is according to the ingenuity that he do receive it with. However, I am satisfied that it will do him good, and that he needs it.

My Lord,

I do verily hope that neither the manner nor matter of this advice will be condemned by your Lordship, when for my defence in the first I shall allege my double attempt, since your return from Hinchinbroke, of doing it personally, in both of which your Lordship's occasions, no doubtfulness of mine, prevented me; and that being now fearful of a sudden summons to Portsmouth, for the discharge of some ships there, I judge it very unbecoming the duty which every bit of bread I eat tells me I owe to your Lordship to expose the safety of your honour to the uncertainty of my return. For the matter, my Lord, it is such as, could I in any measure think safe to conceal from, or likely to be discovered to you by any other hand, I should not have dared so far to own what from my heart I believe is false, as to make myself but the relater of others' discourse; but, sir, your Lordship's honour being such as I ought to value it to be, and finding both in city and court that discourses pass to your prejudice, too generally for mine or any man's controllings but your Lordship's, I shall, my Lord, without the least greatening or lessening the matter, do my duty in laying it shortly before you.

People of all conditions, my Lord, raise matter of wonder from your Lordship's so little appearance at Court: some concluding thence their disfavour thereby, to which purpose I have had questions asked me; and endeavouring to put off such insinuations by asserting the contrary, they have replied that your Lordship's living so beneath your quality, out of the way, and declining of Court attendance, hath been more than once discoursed about the King. Others, my Lord, when the chief Ministers of State, and those most active of the Council have been reckoned up, wherein your Lordship never used to want an eminent place, have said, touching your Lordship, that now your turn was served, and the King had given you a good estate, you left him to stand or fall as he would, and, particularly in that of the Navy, have enlarged upon your letting fall all service there.

Another sort, and those the most, insist upon the bad report of the house wherein your Lordship, now observed in perfect health again, continues to sojourn, and by name have charged one of the daughters for a common courtesan, alleging both places and persons where and with whom she hath been too well known, and how much her wantonness occasions, though unjustly, scandal to your Lordship, and that as well to gratifying of some enemies as to the wounding of more friends I am not able to tell.

Lastly, my Lord, I find a general coldness in all

persons towards your Lordship, such as, from my first dependence on you, I never yet knew, wherein I shall not offer to interpose any thoughts or advice of mine, well knowing your Lordship needs not any. But with a most faithful assurance, that no person nor papers under Heaven is privy to what I here write, besides myself and this, which I shall be careful to have put into your own hands, I rest confident of your Lordship's just construction of my dutiful intentions herein, and in all humility take my leave. May it please your Lordship,

Your Lordship's most obedient Servant,

S. P.

The foregoing letter was sealed up and enclosed in this that follows—

My Lord,

If this find your Lordship either not alone, or not at leisure, I beg the suspending your opening the enclosed till you shall have both, the matter very well bearing such a delay, and in all humility remain, etc.,

November 17, 1663.   S. P.

My servant hath my directions to put this into your Lordship's own hand, but not to stay for any answer.

19th. With Sir G. Carteret, to my Lord Treasurer, to discourse with him about Mr. Gauden's having of money, and to offer to him whether it would not be necessary, Mr. Gauden's credit being so low as it is, to take security of him if he demands any great sum, such as £20,000, which now ought to be paid him upon his next year's declaration; which is a sad thing that, being reduced to this by us, we should be the first to doubt his credit; but so it is. However, it will be managed with great tenderness to him. My Lord Treasurer we found in his bed-chamber, being laid up of the gout. I find him a very ready man, and certainly a brave servant to the King: he spoke so quick and sensibly of the King's charge. Nothing displeased me in him but his long nails, which he lets grow upon a pretty thick white short hand, that it troubled me to see them. In our way Sir G. Carteret told me there is no such thing likely yet as a Dutch war, neither they nor we being in condition for it, though it will come certainly to that in some time, our interests lying the same way, that is to say, in trade. But not yet. To speak with Mr. Moore, and met him by the way, who tells me, to my great content, that he believes my letter to my Lord Sandwich hath wrought well upon him, and that he will look after himself and his business upon it, for he begins already to do so. But I dare not conclude anything till I see him, which shall be to-morrow morning, that I may be out of my pain to know how he takes it of me.

20th. To my Lord Sandwich's lodgings, but he was gone out before, and so I am defeated of my expectation of being eased one way or other in the business of my Lord. But I up to Mr. Howe, whom I saw this day the first time in a periwig, which becomes him very well. He tells me that my Lord is of a sudden much changed, and he do believe that he do take my letter well. However, we both bless God that it hath so good an effect upon him. Thence I home again.

22nd. (Lord's day.) I walked as far as the Temple, and there took coach, and to my Lord's lodgings, whom I found ready to go to Chapel; but I coming, he began, with a very serious countenance, to tell me that he had received my late letter, wherein first he took notice of my care of him and his honour, and did give me thanks for that part of it where I say that from my heart I believe the contrary of what I do there relate to be the discourse of others; but, since

I intended it not a reproach, but matter of information, and for him to make a judgement of it for his practice, it was necessary for me to tell him the persons of whom I have gathered the several particulars which I there insist on. I would have made excuses in it; but, seeing him so earnest in it, I found myself forced to it, and so did tell him Mr. Pierce, the surgeon, in that of his Lordship's living being discoursed of at Court; a maid-servant that I kept, that lived at Chelsea school; and also Mr. Pickering, about the report touching the young woman; and also Mr. Hunt, in Axe Yard, near whom she lodged. I told him the whole city do discourse concerning his neglect of business; and so I many times asserting my dutiful intention in all this, and he owning his accepting of it as such. That that troubled me most in particular is that he did there assert the civility of the people of the house, and the young gentlewoman, for whose reproach he was sorry. His saying that he was resolved how to live, and that though he was taking a house, meaning to live in another manner, yet it was not to please any people, or to stop report, but to please himself, though this I do believe he might say that he might not seem to me to be so much wrought upon by what I have writ; and lastly, and most of all, when I spoke of the tenderness that I have used in declaring this to him, there being nobody privy to it, he told me that I must give him leave to except one. I told him that possibly somebody might know of some thoughts of mine—I having borrowed some intelligence in this matter from them, but nobody could say they knew of the thing itself what I writ. This, I confess, however, do trouble me, for that he seemed to speak it as a quick retort, and it must sure be Will. Howe, who did not see anything of what I writ, though I told him indeed that I would write; but in this, methinks, there is no great hurt.

I find him, though he cannot but own his opinion of my good intention, and so he did again and again profess it, that he is troubled in his mind at it; and I confess I think I may have done myself an injury for his good, which, were it to do again, and that I believed he would take it no better, I think I should sit quietly without taking any notice of it; for I doubt there is no medium between his taking it very well or very ill. I could not forbear weeping before him at the latter end; which, since, I am ashamed of, though I cannot see what he can take it to proceed from but my tenderness and good will to him. After this discourse was ended, he began to talk very cheerfully of other things, and I walked with him to Whitehall, and we discoursed of the pictures in the gallery, which it may be he might do out of policy, that the boy might not see any strangeness in him; but I rather think that his mind was somewhat eased, and hope that he will be to me as he was before.

23rd. To St. Paul's Churchyard, and there bespoke Rushworth's *Collections*, and Scobell's *Acts of the Long Parliament*, etc., which I will make the King pay for as to the office, and so I do not break my vow at all. With Alderman Backwell, talking of the new money, which he says will never be counterfeited, he believes; but it is so deadly inconvenient for telling, it is so thick, and the edges are made to turn up.

26th. The plague, it seems, grows more and more at Amsterdam; and we are going upon making of all ships coming from thence and Hambrough, or any other infected places, to perform their Quarantine, for thirty days, as Sir Richard Browne expressed it in the order of the Council, contrary to the import of the word, though, in the general acceptation, it signifies now the thing, not the time spent in doing it, in Holehaven; a thing never done by us before.

28th. I met with Mr. Pierce, the surgeon, who

tells me for good news that my Lord Sandwich is resolved to go no more to Chelsea, and told me he believed that I had been giving my Lord some counsel, which I neither denied nor affirmed. To Paul's Churchyard, and there looked upon the second part of *Hudibras*, which I buy not, but borrow to read, to see if it be as good as the first, which the world cried so mightily up, though it hath not a good liking in me, though I had tried by twice or three times reading to bring myself to think it witty. To-day, for certain, I am told how in Holland publicly they have pictured our King with reproach: one way is with his pockets turned the wrong side outward, hanging out empty; another with two courtiers picking of his pockets; and a third, leading of two ladies, while others abuse him; which amounts to great contempt.

December 1663

December 10th. To St. Paul's Churchyard, to my bookseller's, and, having gained this day in the office by my stationer's bill to the King about 40s. or £3, calling for twenty books to lay this money out upon, and found myself at a great loss where to choose, and do see how my nature would gladly return to the laying out of money in this trade. Could not tell whether to lay out my money for books of pleasure, as plays, which my nature was most earnest in; but at last, after seeing Chaucer, Dugdale's *History of Paul's*, Stow's *London*, Gesner, *History of Trent*, besides Shakespeare, Jonson, and Beaumont's plays, I at last chose Dr. Fuller's *Worthies*, the *Cabbala or Collections of Letters of State*, and a little book, *Delices de Hollande*, with another little book or two, all of good use or serious pleasure; and *Hudibras*, both parts, the book now in greatest fashion for drollery, though I cannot, I confess, see enough where the wit lies. My mind being thus settled, I went by link home, and so to my office, and to read in Rushworth; and so home to supper and to bed. Calling at Wotton's, my shoemaker's, to-day, he tells me that Sir H. Wright is dying; and that Harris is come to the Duke's house again; and of a rare play to be acted this week of Sir William Davenant's, the story of Henry the Eighth, with all his wives.

21st. To my Lord Sandwich's, and there I had a pretty kind salute from my Lord. To Mrs. Turner's, and there saw the achievement pretty well set up, and it is well done. To Shoe Lane, to see a cock-fighting at a new pit there, a sport I was never at in my life; but, Lord! to see the strange variety of people, from Parliament man (by name Wildes, that was Deputy Governor of the Tower, when Robinson was Lord Mayor), to the poorest 'prentices, bakers, brewers, butchers, draymen, and what not; and all these fellows one with another cursing and betting. I soon had enough of it. It is strange to see how people of this poor rank, that look as if they had not bread to put in their mouths, shall bet three or four pounds at one bet, and lose it, and yet bet as much the next battle; so that one of them will lose £10 or £20 at a meeting.

January 1664

January 6th. (Twelfth day.) This morning I began a practice, which I find, by the case I do it with, that I shall continue, it saving me money and time; that is, to trim myself with a razor; which pleases me mightily.

21st. Up, and after sending my wife to my aunt Wight's, to get a place to see Turner hanged, I to the 'Change; and seeing people flock in the City, I enquired, and found that Turner was not yet hanged.

So I went among them to Leadenhall Street, at the end of Lyme Street, near where the robbery was done; and to St. Mary Axe, where he lived. And there I got for a shilling to stand upon the wheel of a cart, in great pain, above an hour before the execution was done; he delaying the time by long discourses and prayers, one after another, in hopes of a reprieve; but none came, and at last he was flung off the ladder in his cloak. A comely-looked man he was, and kept his countenance to the end; I was sorry to see him. It was believed there were at least 12,000 or 14,000 people in the street. To the Coffeehouse, and heard the full of Turner's discourse on the cart, which was chiefly to clear himself of all things laid to his charge but this fault, for which he now suffers, which he confesses. He deplored the condition of his family, but his chief design was to lengthen time, believing still a reprieve would come, though the sheriff advised him to expect no such thing, for the King was resolved to grant none. To my aunt Wight's, where Dr. Burnett did tell me how poorly the sheriffs did endeavour to get one jewel returned by Turner, after he was convicted, as a due to them, and not to give it to Mr. Tryan, the true owner, but ruled against them, to their great dishonour.

30th. The day kept solemnly for the King's murder. In the evening signed and sealed my last will and testament, which is to my mind, and I hope to the liking of God Almighty. This evening I tore some old papers; among others, a romance which, under the title of *Love a Cheat*, I began ten years ago at Cambridge; and, reading it over to-night, I liked it very well, and wondered a little at myself, at my vein at that time when I wrote it, doubting that I cannot do so well now if I would try.

A SHADY TRANSACTION

February 1664

February 1st. I hear how two men last night, jostling for the wall about the new Exchange, did kill one another, each thrusting the other through; one of them of the King's Chapel, one Cave, and the other a retainer of my Lord General Middleton's. I to Whitehall; where, in the Duke's chamber, the King came and stayed an hour or two laughing at Sir W. Petty, who was there, about his boat; and at Gresham College in general; at which poor Petty was, I perceive, at some loss; but did argue discreetly, and bear the unreasonable follies of the King's objections and other bystanders with great discretion; and offered to take odds against the King's best boats; but the King would not lay, but cried him down with words only. Gresham College he mightily laughed at, for spending time only in weighing of air, and doing nothing else since they sat.

2nd. To the 'Change, and thence on to the Sun Tavern with Sir W. Warren. He did give me a pair of gloves for my wife wrapt up in a paper, which I would not open, feeling it hard; but did tell him that my wife should thank him, and so went on in discourse. When I came home, Lord! in what pain I was to get my wife out of the room without bidding her go, that I might see what these gloves were; and, by and by, she being gone, it proves a pair of white gloves for her, and forty pieces in good gold, which did so cheer my heart, that I could eat no victuals almost for dinner. I was at a great loss what to do, whether to tell my wife of it or no, for fear of making her think me to be in a better condition, or in a better way of getting money, than yet I am.

3rd. In Covent Garden to-night, going to fetch home my wife, I stopped at the great Coffee-house there, where I never was before: where Dryden, the poet (I knew at Cambridge), and all the wits of the town.

March 1664

March 15th. My poor brother Tom died. I left my wife to see him laid out, and I by coach home, carrying my brother's papers, all I could find, with me.

18th. Up betimes, and walked to my brother's, where a great while putting things in order against anon; and so to Wotton, my shoemaker, and there got a pair of shoes blacked on the soles against anon for me: so to my brother's. To church, and, with the grave-maker, chose a place for my brother to lie in, just under my mother's pew. But to see how a man's tombs are at the mercy of such a fellow, that for sixpence he would, as his own words were, " I will jostle them together, but I will make room for him "; speaking of the fulness of the middle aisle, where he was to lie; and that he would, for my father's sake, do my brother, that is dead, all the civility he can; which was to disturb other corpses that are not quite rotten, to make room for him; and methought his manner of speaking it was very remarkable; as of a thing that now was in his power to do a man a courtesy or not. I dressed myself, and so did my servant Bess; and so to my brother's again: whither, though invited, as the custom is, at one or two o'clock, they came not till four or five. But, at last, one after another, they came, many more than I bid: and my reckoning that I bid was one hundred and twenty; but I believe there was nearer one hundred and fifty. Their service was six biscuits a-piece, and what they pleased of burnt claret. My cousin Joyce Norton kept the wine and cakes above; and did give out to them that served, who had white gloves given them. But, above all, I am beholden to Mrs. Holden, who was most kind, and did take mighty pains not only in getting the house and everything else ready, but this day in going up and down to see the house filled and served, in order to mine and their great content, I think: the men sitting by themselves in some rooms, and the women by themselves in others, very close, but yet room enough. Anon to church, walking out into the street to the conduit, and so across the street: and had a very good company along with the corpse. And, being come to the grave as above, Dr. Pierson, the minister of the parish, did read the service for burial: and so I saw my poor brother laid into the grave: and so all broke up; and I and my wife, and Madam Turner and her family, to her brother's, and by and by fell to a barrel of oysters, cake, and cheese, of Mr. Honiwood's, with him, in his chamber and below, being too merry for so late a sad work. But, Lord! to see how the world makes nothing of the memory of a man, an hour after he is dead! And, indeed, I must blame myself; for, though at the sight of him dead and dying I had real grief for a while, while he was in my sight, yet presently after, and ever since, I have had very little grief indeed for him.

April 1664

April 23rd. (Coronation day.) I met with Mr. Coventry, who himself is now full of talk of a Dutch war; for it seems the Lords have concurred in the Commons' vote about it; and so the next week it will be presented to the King, insomuch that he do desire we would look about to see what stores we lack, and buy what we can. Home to dinner, where I and my wife much troubled about my money that is in my Lord Sandwich's hand, for fear of his going

to sea and being killed; but I will get out of it what
I can.

25th. The Duke, which gives me great good hopes,
do talk of setting up a good discipline in the fleet.
In the Duke's chamber there is a bird, given him by
Mr. Pierce, the surgeon, come from the East Indies,
black the greatest part, with the finest collar of white
about the neck; but talks many things, and neighs
like the horse and other things, the best almost that
ever I heard bird in my life. To my Lord Sandwich's, where by agreement I met my wife, and there
dined with the young ladies; my Lady, being not
well, kept her chamber. Much simple discourse at
table among the young ladies. After dinner walked
in the garden, talking with Mr. Moore about my
Lord's business. He told me my Lord runs in debt
every day more and more, and takes little care how
to come out of it. He counted to me how my Lord
pays use now for above £9000, which is a sad thing,
especially considering the probability of his going to
sea, in great danger of his life, and his children,
many of them, to provide for. Thence, the young
ladies going out to visit, I took my wife by coach out
through the city, discoursing how to spend the afternoon; and conquered, with much ado, a desire of
going to the play; but took her out at White Chapel,
and to Bednal Green; so to Hackney, where I have
not been many a year, since a little child I boarded
there. Thence to Kingsland, by my nurse's house,
Goody Lawrence, where my brother Tom and I was
kept when young. Then to Newington Green, and
saw the outside of Mrs. Herbert's house, where she
lived, and my aunt Ellen with her; but Lord! how
in every point I find myself to overvalue things when
a child. Thence to Islington, and so to St. John's
to the Red Bull, and there saw the latter part of a
rude prize fought; and thence back to Islington,

and at the King's Head, where Pitts lived, we 'lighted, and ate and drank for remembrance of the old house' sake; and so through Kingsland again, and so to Bishopsgate, and so home with great pleasure. The country mighty pleasant—only a little troubled at the young ladies leaving my wife so to-day, and from some passages fearing my Lady might be offended. But I hope for the best.

May 1664

May 4th. To my cousin Scott's. There condoled with him the loss of my cousin his wife, and talked about his matters, as attorney to my father, in his administering to my brother Tom. The plague increases at Amsterdam.

5th. My eyes beginning every day to grow less and less able to bear with long reading or writing, though it be by daylight; which I never observed till now.

13th. Up before three o'clock, and a little after upon the water, it being very light as at noon, and a bright sunrising; but by and by a rainbow appeared, the first that ever in a morning I saw.

16th. With Mr. Pierce, the surgeon, to see an experiment of killing a dog, by letting opium into his hind leg. He and Dr. Clerke did fail mightily in hitting the vein, and in effect did not do the business after many trials; but, with the little they got in, the dog did presently fall asleep, and so lay till we cut him up, and a little dog also, which they put it down his throat; he also staggered first, and then fell asleep, and so continued. Whether he recovered or no, after I was gone, I know not.

June 1664

June 4th. Mr. Coventry discoursing this noon
about Sir W. Batten (what a sad fellow he is!) told me
how the King told him the other day how Sir W.
Batten, being in the ship with him and Prince Rupert
when they expected to fight with Warwick, did walk
up and down sweating, with a napkin under his throat
to dry up his sweat; and that Prince Rupert, being
a most jealous man, and particularly of Batten, do
walk up and down swearing bloodily to the King
that Batten had a mind to betray them to-day, and
that the napkin was a signal; " but, by God," says
he, " if things go ill, the first thing I will do is to
shoot him." He discoursed largely and bravely to
me concerning the different sort of valours, the active
and passive valour. For the latter, he brought as
an instance General Blake, who, in the defending of
Taunton and Lyme for the Parliament, did, through
his stubborn sort of valour, defend it the most
opiniastrément that ever any man did anything; and
yet never was the man that ever made an attack by
land or sea, but rather avoided it on all, even fair,
occasions. On the other side, Prince Rupert, the
boldest attacker in the world for personal courage;
and yet, in the defending of Bristol, no man ever did
anything worse, he wanting the patience and seasoned
head to consult and advise for defence, and to bear
with the evils of a siege. The like he says of my
Lord Teviot, who was the boldest adventurer of his
person in the world; and from a mean man in few
years was come to this greatness of command and
repute only by the death of all his officers, he many
times having the luck of being the only survivor of
them all, by venturing upon services for the King of
France that nobody else would; and yet no man

upon a defence, he being all fury and of no judgement in a fight. He tells me, above all, of the Duke of York, that he is more himself and more of judgement is at hand in him in the middle of a desperate service than at other times, as appeared in the business of Dunkirk, wherein no man ever did braver things, or was in hotter service in the close of that day, being surrounded with enemies; and then, contrary to the advice of all about him, his counsel carried himself and the rest through them safe, by advising that he might make his passage with but a dozen with him; "For," says he, "the enemy cannot move after me so fast with a great body, and with a small one we shall be enough to deal with them"; and, though he is a man naturally martial to the highest degree, yet a man that never in his life talks one word of himself or service of his own, but only that he saw such or such a thing, and lays it down for a maxim that a Hector can have no courage. He told me also, as a great instance of some men, that the Prince of Condé's excellence is that, there not being a more furious man in the world, danger in fight never disturbs him more than just to make him civil, and to command in words of great obligation to his officers and men; but without any the least disturbance in his judgement or spirit.

24th. To Whitehall; and Mr. Pierce showed me the Queen's bed-chamber, and her closet where she had nothing but some pretty pious pictures and books of devotion, and her holy water at her head as she sleeps, with a clock by her bedside, wherein a lamp burns that tells her the time of the night at any time. Thence with him to the Park, and there met the Queen coming from Chapel, with her Maids of Honour, all in silver-lace gowns again; which is new to me, and that which I did not think would have been brought up again. Thence he carried me to the King's closet; where such variety of pictures, and other things of value and rarity, that I was properly confounded, and enjoyed no pleasure in the sight of them; which is the only time in my life that ever I was so at a loss for pleasure, in the greatest plenty of objects to give it me.

July 1664

July 11th. Betimes up this morning, and, getting ready, we by coach to Holborn, where, at nine o'clock, they set out, and I and my man Will on horseback by my wife to Barnet; a very pleasant day; and there dined with her company, which was very good —a pretty gentlewoman with her, that goes but to Huntingdon, and a neighbour to us in town. Here we stayed two hours, and then parted for altogether, and my poor wife I shall soon want, I am sure. Thence I and Will to see the Wells, half a mile off, and there I drank three glasses, and walked, and came back and drank two more; and so we rode home, round by Kingsland, Hackney, and Mile End, till we were quite weary; and, not being very well, I betimes to bed. About eleven o'clock, knowing what money I have in the house, and hearing a noise, I began to sweat worse and worse, till I melted almost to water. I rang, and could not in half an hour make either of the wenches hear me; and this made me fear the more, lest they might be gagged; and then I began to think that there was some design in a stone being flung at the window over our stairs this evening, by which the thieves meant to try what looking there would be after them, and know our company. These thoughts and fears I had, and do hence apprehend the fears of all rich men that are covetous, and have much money by them. At last Jane rose, and then I understand it was only the dog wants a lodging, and so made a noise.

14th. I rose a little after four o'clock, and abroad. Walked to my Lord's and nobody up, but the porter rose out of bed to me : so I back again to Fleet Street, and there bought a little book of law; and thence hearing a psalm sung I went into St. Dunstan's, and there heard prayers read, which, it seems, is done there every morning at six o'clock; a thing I never did do at a chapel, but the College chapel, in all my life. Thence to my Lord's again, and my Lord being up, was sent for up, and he and I alone. He did begin with a most solemn profession of the same confidence in and love for me that he ever had, and then told me what a misfortune was fallen upon me and him : on me, by a displeasure which my Lord Chancellor did show to him last night against me, in the highest and most passionate manner that ever any man did speak, even to the not hearing of anything to be said to him; but he told me that he did say all that could be said for a man as to my faithfulness and duty to his Lordship, and did me the greatest right imaginable. And what should the business be, but that I should be forward to have the trees in Clarendon Park marked and cut down, which he, it seems, hath bought of my Lord Albemarle; when, God knows! I am the most innocent man in the world in it, and did nothing of myself, nor knew of his concernment therein, but barely obeyed my Lord Treasurer's warrant for the doing thereof. And said that I did most ungentlemanlike with him, and had justified the rogues in cutting down a tree of his; and that I had sent the veriest Fanatic [Deane] that is in England to mark them, on purpose to nose him. All which, I did assure my Lord, was most properly false, and nothing like it true; and told my Lord the whole passage. My Lord do seem most nearly affected; he is partly, I believe, for me, and partly for himself. So he advised me to wait presently upon my Lord, and clear myself in the most perfect manner I could, with all submission and assurance that I am his creature both in this and all other things; and that I do own that all I have is derived through my Lord Sandwich from his Lordship. So, full of horror, I went, and found him busy in trials of law in his great room; and, it being Sitting-day, durst not stay, but went to my Lord and told him so: whereupon he directed me to take him after dinner; and so away I home, leaving my Lord mightily concerned for me. So I to my Lord Chancellor's; and there, coming out after dinner, I accosted him, telling him that I was the unhappy Pepys that had fallen into his high displeasure, and come to desire him to give me leave to make myself better understood to his Lordship, assuring him of my duty and service. He answered me very pleasingly that he was confident upon the score of my Lord Sandwich's character of me, but that he had reason to think what he did, and desired me to call upon him some evening: I named to-night, and he accepted of it. To my Lord Chancellor's, and there heard several trials, wherein I perceive my Lord is a most able and ready man. After all done, he himself called, " Come, Mr. Pepys, you and I will take a turn in the garden." So he was led downstairs, having the gout, and there walked with me, I think, above an hour, talking most friendly, yet cunningly. I told him clearly how things were; how ignorant I was of his Lordship's concernment in it; how I did not do nor say one word singly, but what was done was the act of the whole Board. He told me by name that he was more angry with Sir G. Carteret than with me, and also with the whole body of the Board. But, thinking who it was of the Board that did know him least, he did place his fear upon me; but he finds that he is indebted to none of his friends there. I think I did thoroughly appease him, till he thanked me for my desire and pains to satisfy him; and, upon my desiring to be directed who I should of his servants advise with about this business, he told me nobody, but would be glad to hear from me himself. He told me he would not direct me in anything, that it might not be said that the Lord Chancellor did labour to abuse the King; or, as I offered, direct the suspending the Report of the Purveyors: but I see what he means, and will make it my work to do him service in it. But, Lord! to see how he is incensed against poor Deane, as a fanatic rogue, and I know not what: and what he did was done in spite to his Lordship among all his friends and tenants. He did plainly say that he would not direct me in anything, for he would not put himself into the power of any man to say that he did so and so; but plainly told me, as if he would be glad I did something. Lord! to see how we poor wretches dare not do the King good service for fear of the greatness of these men. He named Sir G. Carteret, and Sir J. Minnes, and the rest; and that he was as angry with them all as with me. But it was pleasant to think that, while he was talking to me, comes into the garden Sir G. Carteret; and my Lord avoided speaking with him, and made him and many others stay expecting him, while I walked up and down above an hour, I think; and would have me walk with my hat on. And yet, after all, there has been so little ground for his jealousy of me, that I am sometimes afraid that he do this only in policy to bring me to his side by scaring me; or else, which is worse, to try how faithful I would be to the King: but I rather think the former of the two. I parted with great assurance how I acknowledged all I had to come from his Lordship; which he did not seem to refuse, but with great kindness and respect parted.

15th. With Creed to St. James's; and, missing Mr. Coventry, to Whitehall; where, staying for him in one of the galleries, there comes out of the chair-room Mrs. Stewart, in a most lovely form, with her hair all about her ears, having her picture taking there. There was the King and twenty more, I think, standing by all the while, and a lovely creature she in the dress seemed to be.

20th. With Mr. Deane, discoursing upon the business of my Lord Chancellor's timber in Claren-don Park, and how to make a report therein without offending him; which at last I drew up, and hope it will please him. But I would to God neither I nor he ever had had anything to have done with it! To Whitehall, to the Committee for Fishing; but nothing done, it being a great day to-day there upon drawing at the Lottery of Sir Arthur Slingsby. I got in, and stood by the two Queens and the Duchess of York, and just behind my Lady Castlemaine, whom I do heartily admire; and good sport to see how most that did give their ten pounds did go away with a pair of gloves only for their lot, and one gentlewoman, one Mrs. Fish, with the only blank. And one I stayed to see draw a suit of hangings valued at £430, and they say are well worth the money, or near it. One other suit there is better than that; but very many lots of three and fourscore pounds. I observed the King and Queen did get but as poor lots as any else. But the wisest man I met with was Mr. Cholmley, who insured as many as would, from the drawing of the one blank for 12d.; in which case there was the whole number of persons to one, which, I think, was three or four hundred. And so he insured about 200 for 200 shillings, so he could not have lost if one of them had drawn it, for there was enough to pay the

£10; but it happened another drew it, and so he got all the money he took.

31st. (Lord's day.) Up, and to church, where I have not been these many weeks.

August 1664

August 13th. Comes Mr. Reeve, with a microscope and scotoscope. For the first I did give him £5 10s., a great price, but a most curious bauble it is, and he says, as good, nay, the best he knows in England. The other he gives me, and is of value; and a curious curiosity it is to discover objects in a dark room with. Mr. Creed dining with me, I got him to give my wife and me a play this afternoon, lending him money to do it, which is a fallacy that I have found now once, to avoid my vow with, but never to be more practised, I swear. To the new play, at the Duke's house, of *Henry the Fifth*; a most noble play, writ by my Lord Orrery, wherein Betterton, Harris, and Ianthe's parts are most incomparably wrote and done, and the whole play the most full of height and raptures of wit and sense that ever I heard; having but one incongruity, that King Harry promises to plead for Tudor to their mistress, Princess Katherine of France, more than, when it comes to it, he seems to do; and Tudor refused by her with some kind of indignity, not with a difficulty and honour that it ought to have been done in to him.

27th. To Cutler's house, and there had a very good dinner; and had two or three pretty young ladies of their relations there. Home, and there find my boy Tom Edwards come, sent me by Captain Cooke, having been bred in the King's Chapel these four years. I propose to make a clerk of him; and, if he deserves well, to do well by him. Find him a very schoolboy, that talks innocently and impertinently. All the news this day is that the Dutch are, with twenty-two sail of ships of war, cruising up and down about Ostend; at which we are alarmed. My Lord Sandwich is come back into the Downs, with only eight sail, which is, or may be, a prey to the Dutch, if they knew our weakness and inability to set out any more speedily.

September 1664

September 3rd. I have had a bad night's rest to-night, not sleeping well, as my wife observed; and I thought myself to be mightily bit with fleas, and in the morning she chid her maids for not looking the fleas a-days. But, when I rose, I found that it is only the change of the weather from hot to cold, which, as I was two winters ago, do stop my pores, and so my blood tingles and itches all day, all over my body.

6th. Called upon Doll, our pretty 'Change woman, for a pair of gloves trimmed with yellow ribbon, to [match] the petticoat my wife bought yesterday, which cost me 20s.; but she is so pretty, that, God forgive me! I could not think it too much, which is a strange slavery that I stand in to beauty, that I value nothing near it.

November 1664

November 9th. To Whitehall, and there the King being in his Cabinet Council, I desiring to speak with Sir G. Carteret, I was called in, and demanded by the King himself many questions, to which I did give him full answers. There were at this Council my Lord Chancellor, Archbishop of Canterbury, Lord Treasurer, the two Secretaries, and Sir G. Carteret. Not a little contented at this chance of being made known to these persons, and called often by my name by the King.

13th. (Lord's day.) This morning to church, where mighty sport to hear our clerk sing out of tune, though his master sits by him that begins and keeps the time aloud for the parish. With my wife within doors, and getting a speech out of *Hamlet*, "To be or not to be," without book. In the evening to sing psalms, and so to prayers and to bed.

15th. To a Committee of Tangier, where, and everywhere else, thank God, I find myself growing in repute; and so home, and late, very late, at business, nobody minding it but myself, and so home to bed, weary and full of thoughts.

22nd. To my Lord Treasurer's, where with Sir Philip Warwick studying all we could to make the last year swell as high as we could. And it is much to see how he do study for the King, to do it to get all the money from the Parliament he can: and I shall be serviceable to him therein, to help him to heads upon which to enlarge the report of the expense. He did observe to me how obedient this Parliament was for awhile, and the last Session how they begin to differ, and to carp at the King's officers; and what they will do now, he says, is to make agreement for the money, for there is no guess to be made of it. He told me he was prepared to convince the Parliament that the Subsidies are a most ridiculous tax, the four last not rising to £40,000, and unequal. He talks of a tax of Assessment of £70,000 for five years; the people to be secured that it shall continue no longer than there is really a war; and the charges thereof to be paid. He told me that one year of the late Dutch war cost £1,623,000. Thence to my Lord Chancellor's, and there stayed long with Sir W. Batten and Sir J. Minnes, to speak with my Lord about our Prize-Office business; but, being sick and full of visitants, we could not speak with him, and so away home, where Sir Richard Ford did meet us with letters from Holland this day, that it is likely the Dutch fleet will not come out this year; they have not victuals to keep them out, and it is likely they will be frozen before they can get back.

25th. At my office all the morning, to prepare an account of the charge we have been put to extraordinary by the Dutch already; and I have brought it to appear £852,700: but God knows this is only a scare to the Parliament, to make them give the more money. Thence to the Parliament House, and there did give it to Sir Philip Warwick; the House being hot upon giving the King a supply of money. Mr. Jennings tells me the mean manner that Sir Samuel Morland lives near him, in a house that he hath bought and laid out money upon, in all to the value of £1200; but is believed to be a beggar.

December 1664

December 15th. To the Coffee-house, where great talk of the comet seen in several places; and among our men at sea, and by my Lord Sandwich, to whom I intend to write about it to-night. This night I began to burn wax candles in my closet at the office, to try the charge, and to see whether the smoke offends like that of tallow candles.

24th. Having sat up all night till past two o'clock this morning, our porter, being appointed, comes and tells us that the bellman tells him that the star is seen upon Tower Hill; so I, that had been all night setting in order all my old papers in my chamber, did leave off all, and my boy and I to Tower Hill, it being a most fine, bright, moonshine night, and a great frost, but no comet to be seen. At noon to the 'Change, to the Coffee-house; and there heard Sir Richard Ford tell the whole story of our defeat at Guinea, wherein our men are guilty of the most horrid cowardice and perfidiousness, as he says and tells it, that ever Englishmen were. Captain Raynolds, that was the only commander of any of the King's ships there, was shot at by De Ruyter, with a bloody flag flying. He, instead of opposing, which, indeed, had been to no purpose, but only to maintain honour, did poorly go on board himself, to ask what De Ruyter would have, and so yield to whatever Ruyter would desire. The King and Duke are highly vexed at it, it seems, and the business deserves it. I saw the comet, which now, whether worn away or no I know not, appears not with a tail, but only is larger and duller than any other star, and is come to rise betimes, and to make a great arch, and is gone quite to a new place in the heavens than it was before; but I hope in a clearer night something more will be seen.

26th. To Sir W. Batten's, where Mr. Coventry and all our families here, and Sir R. Ford and his, and a great feast, and good discourse and merry, and so home to bed, where my wife and people innocently at cards, very merry. I to bed, leaving them to their sport and blindman's-buff.

31st. To my accounts of the whole year till past twelve at night, it being bitter cold, but yet I was well satisfied with my work; and, above all, to find myself, by the great blessing of God, worth £1349, by which, as I have spent very largely, so I have laid up above £500 this year above what I was worth this day twelvemonth. The Lord make me for ever thankful to his holy name for it! Soon as ever the clock struck one, I kissed my wife in the kitchen by the fireside, wishing her a merry new year.

So ends the old year, I bless God, with great joy to me, not only from my having made so good a year of profit, as having spent £420 and laid up £540 and upwards; but I bless God I never have been in so good plight as to my health in so very cold weather as this is, nor indeed in any hot weather, these ten years, as I am at this day, and have been these four or five months. But I am at a great loss to know whether it be my hare's foot, or taking every morning of a pill of turpentine, or my having left off the wearing of a gown. My family is my wife, in good health, and happy with her; her woman Mercer, a pretty, modest, quiet maid; her chamber-maid Bess, her cook-maid Jane, the little girl Susan, and my boy, which I have had about half a year, Tom Edwards, which I took from the King's Chapel; and a pretty and loving quiet a family I have as any man in England. My credit in the world and my office grows daily, and I am in good esteem with everybody, I think. My troubles of my uncle's estate pretty well over; but it comes to be of little profit to us, my father being much supported by my purse. But great vexations remain upon my father and me from my brother Tom's death and ill condition, both to our disgrace and discontent, though no great reason for either. Public matters are all in a hurry about a Dutch war. Our preparations great; our provocations against them great; and, after all our presumption, we are now afraid as much of them as we lately contemned them. Everything else in the State quiet, blessed be God! My Lord Sandwich at sea with the fleet at Portsmouth; sending some about to cruise for taking of ships, which we have done to a great number. This Christmas I judged it fit to look over all my papers and books, and to tear all that I found either boyish or not to be worth keeping, or fit to be seen, if it should please God to take me away suddenly.

January 1665

January 20th. To my bookseller's, and there took home Hooke's book of Microscopy, a most excellent piece, and of which I am very proud. Homeward, in my way buying a hare, and taking it home, which arose upon my discourse to-day with Mr. Batten, in Westminster Hall, who showed me my mistake that my hare's foot hath not the joint to it; and assures me he never had his colic since he carried it about him; and it is a strange thing how fancy works, for I no sooner handled his foot, but I became very well, and so continue.

February 1665

February 4th. I to the Sun behind the 'Change, to dinner to my Lord Bellasis. He told us a very handsome passage of the King's sending him his message about holding out the town of Newark, of which he was then governor for the King. This message he sent in a slug-bullet, being writ in cypher, and wrapped up in lead and swallowed. So the messenger came to my Lord, and told him he had a message from the King, but it was yet in his belly; so they did give him some physic, and out it came. This was a month before the King's flying to the Scots; and therein he told him that, at such a day, the 3rd or 6th of May, he should hear of his being come to the Scots, being assured by the King of France that in coming to them he should be used with all the liberty, honour, and safety that could be desired. And at the just day he did come to the Scots. He told us another odd passage: how the King having newly put out Prince Rupert of his generalship, upon some miscarriage at Bristol, and Sir Richard Willis of his governorship of Newark, at the entreaty of the gentry of the county, and put in my Lord Bellasis, the great officers of the King's army mutinied, and came in that manner with swords drawn into the market-place of the town where the King was; which the King hearing, says, " I must horse." And there himself personally, when everybody expected they should have been opposed, the King came, and cried to the head of the mutineers, which was Prince Rupert, " Nephew, I command you to be gone." So the Prince, in all his fury and discontent, withdrew, and his company scattered.

9th. Sir William Petty tells me that Mr. Barlow is dead; for which, God knows my heart, I could be as sorry as is possible for one to be for a stranger, by whose death he gets £100 per annum.

15th. Busy all the morning. At noon with Creed to the Trinity-house, where a very good dinner among the old soakers, and an extraordinary discourse of the manner of the loss of the *Royal Oak* coming home from Bantam, upon the rocks of Scilly. Thence with Creed to Gresham College, where I had been by Mr. Povy the last week proposed to be admitted a member; and was this day admitted, by signing a book and being taken by the hand of the President, my Lord Brouncker, and some words of admittance said to me. But it is a most acceptable thing to hear their discourse, and see their experiments; which were this day on fire, and how it goes out in a place where the air is not free, and sooner out where the air is exhausted, which they showed by an engine on purpose.

19th. (Lord's day.) Hearing by accident of my maid's letting in a roguing Scotch woman that haunts the office, to help them to wash and scour in our house, and that very lately, I fell mightily out, and made my wife, to the disturbance of the house and neighbours, to beat our little girl, and then we shut her down into the cellar, and there she lay all night.

20th. Rode into the beginning of my Lord Chancellor's new house, near St. James's; which common people have already called Dunkirk-house, from their opinion of his having a good bribe for the selling of that town.

25th. At noon to the 'Change; where, just before I came, the Swede that had told the King and the Duke so boldly a great lie of the Dutch flinging our men back to back into the sea at Guinea, so particularly, and readily, and confidently, was whipped round the 'Change; he confessing it a lie, and that he did it in hopes to get something. It is said the Judges, upon demand, did give it their opinion that the law would judge him to be whipped, to lose his ears, or to have his nose slit; but I do not hear that anything more is to be done to him.

March 1665

March 1st. Being the day that by a promise, a great while ago made to my wife, I was to give her £20 to lay out in clothes against Easter, I did give it her, and then she abroad to buy her things. To Gresham College, where Mr. Hooke read a second very curious lecture about the late comet; among other things, proving very probably that this is the verysame comet that appeared before in the year 1618, and that in such a time probably it will appear again, which is a very new opinion; but all will be in print. Then to the meeting, where Sir G. Carteret's two sons, his own, and Sir N. Slaning, were admitted of the society: and this day I did pay my admission money, 40s., to the society. Here was very fine discourses and experiments, but I do lack philosophy enough to understand them, and so cannot remember them. Among others, a very particular account of the making of the several sorts of bread in France, which is accounted the best place for bread in the world.

4th. This day was proclaimed at the 'Change the war with Holland.

26th. (Lord's day and Easter-day.) With my wife to church. Home to dinner, my wife and I, Mercer staying to the sacrament, alone. This is the day seven years which, by the blessing of God, I have survived of my being cut of the stone, and am now in very perfect good health, and have long been; and though the last winter hath been as hard a winter as any have been these many years, yet I never was better in my life, nor have not, these ten years, gone colder in the summer than I have done all this winter, wearing only a doublet and a waistcoat cut open on the back; abroad, a cloak, and within doors a coat I slipped on. Now I am at a loss to know whether it be my hare's foot which is my preservative, for I never had a fit of the colic since I wore it, or whether it be my taking of a pill of turpentine every morning.

27th. Up betimes to Mr. Povy's, and there did sign and seal my agreement with him about my place of being Treasurer for Tangier. Thence to the Duke of Albemarle, the first time that we officers of the Navy have waited upon him since the Duke of York's going, who hath deputed him to be Admiral in his absence; and I find him a quiet heavy man, that will help business when he can, and hinder nothing. I did afterwards alone give him thanks for his favour to me about my Tangier business, which he received kindly, and did speak much of his esteem of me. Thence, and did the same to Sir H. Bennet, who did the like to me very fully. To my Lord Peterborough's; where Povy, Creed, Williamson, Auditor Beale, and myself, and mighty merry to see how plainly my Lord and Povy do abuse one another about their accounts, each thinking the other a fool, and I thinking they were not either of them, in that point, much in the wrong, though in everything, and even in this manner of reproaching one another, very witty and pleasant.

April 1665

April 24th. To the Cockpit, and there walked an hour with my Lord Duke of Albemarle alone in his garden, where he expressed in great words his opinion of me; that I was the right hand of the Navy here, nobody but I taking any care of anything therein; so that he should not know what could be done without me. At which I was (from him) not a little proud.

May 1665

May 13th. To the 'Change, after office, and received my watch from the watchmaker, and a very fine one it is, given me by Briggs, the scrivener. But, Lord, to see how much of my old folly and childishness hangs upon me still, that I cannot forbear carrying my watch in my hand in the coach all this afternoon, and seeing what o'clock it is one hundred times, and am apt to think with myself, how could I be so long without one; though I remember since I had one, and found it a trouble, and resolved to carry one no more about me while I lived.

June 1665

June 7th. This morning my wife and mother rose about two o'clock; and with Mercer, Mary, the boy, and W. Hewer, as they had designed, took boat, and down to refresh themselves on the water to Gravesend. To the Dolphin tavern, where Sir J. Minnes, Lord Brouncker, Sir Thomas Harvy, and myself dined, upon Sir G. Carteret's charge, and very merry we were, Sir Thomas Harvy being a very droll. To the New Exchange, and there drunk whey, with much entreaty getting it for our money, and they would not be entreated to let us have one glass more. So took water to Fox Hall, to the Spring garden, and there walked an hour or two with great pleasure, saving our minds ill at ease concerning the fleet and my Lord Sandwich, that we have no news of them, and ill reports run up and down of his being killed, but without ground. Here stayed, pleasantly walking, and spending but 6d. till nine at night. The hottest day that ever I felt in my life. This day, much against my will, I did in Drury Lane see two or three houses marked with a red cross upon the doors, and ' Lord have mercy upon us! ' writ there; which was a sad sight to me, being the first of the kind that, to my remembrance, I ever saw. It put me into an ill conception of myself and my smell, so that I was forced to buy some roll-tobacco to smell to and chaw, which took away the apprehension. By water home, where weary with walking, and with the mighty heat of the weather, and for my wife's not coming home, I staying walking in the garden till twelve at night, when it begun to lighten exceedingly, through the greatness of the heat. Then, despairing of her coming home, I to bed.

10th. In the evening home to supper; and there, to my great trouble, hear that the plague is come into the City, though it hath, these three or four weeks since its beginning, been wholly out of the City; but where should it begin but in my good friend and neighbour's, Dr. Burnett, in Fenchurch Street; which, in both points, troubles me mightily.

15th. Up, and put on my new stuff suit with close knees, which becomes me most nobly, as my wife says. At noon put on my first laced band, all lace; and to Kate Joyce's to dinner, where my mother, wife, and abundance of their friends, and good usage. At Woolwich discoursed with Mr. Sheldon about my bringing my wife down for a month or two to his house, which he approves of, and, I think, will be very convenient. This day, the *Newsbook* (upon Mr. Moore's showing L'Estrange Captain Ferrers's letter) did do my Lord Sandwich great right as to the late victory. The Duke of York not yet come to town. The town grows very sickly, and people to be afraid of it; there dying this last week of the plague 112, from 43 the week before; whereof but one in Fenchurch Street, and one in Broad Street, by the Treasurer's office.

17th. At the office find Sir W. Pen come home, who looks very well; and I am gladder to see him than otherwise I should be because of my hearing so well of him for his serviceableness in this late great action. It struck me very deep this afternoon going with a hackney coach from Lord Treasurer's down Holborn, the coachman I found to drive easily and easily, at last stood still, and came down hardly able to stand, and told me that he was suddenly struck very sick, and almost blind, he could not see; so I 'lighted, and went into another coach, with a sad heart for the poor man and for myself also, lest he should have been struck with the plague. Sir John Lawson, I hear, is worse than yesterday: the King went to see him to-day most kindly. It seems his wound is not very bad; but he hath a fever, a thrush, and a hiccup, all three together, which are, it seems, very bad symptoms.

21st. I find our tallies will not be money in less than sixteen months, which is a sad thing for the King to pay all that interest for every penny he spends; and, which is strange, the goldsmiths with whom I spoke do declare that they will not be moved to part with money upon the increase of their consideration of ten per cent which they have. I find all the town almost going out of town, the coaches and waggons being all full of people going into the country.

30th. To Whitehall, to the Duke of Albemarle, who I find at Secretary Bennet's, there being now no other great statesman, I think, but my Lord Chancellor, in town. At night back by water, and in the dark and against the tide shot the bridge, groping with their pole for the way, which troubled me before I got through. So home, about one or two o'clock in the morning, my family at a great loss what was become of me. Thus this book of two years ends. Myself and family in good health, consisting of myself and wife, Mercer, her woman, Mary, Alice, and Susan, our maids, and Tom, my boy. In a sickly time of the plague growing on. Having upon my hands the troublesome care of the Treasury of Tangier, with great sums drawn upon me, and nothing to pay them with; also the business of the office great. Considering of removing my wife to Woolwich; she lately busy in learning to paint, with great pleasure and success. All other things well; especially a new interest I am making, by a match in hand between the eldest son of Sir G. Carteret and my Lady Jemimah Montagu. The Duke of York gone down to the fleet; but all suppose not with the intent to stay there, as it is not fit, all men conceive, he should.

July 1665

July 7th. At this time I have two tierces of claret, two quarter-casks of canary, and a smaller vessel of sack; a vessel of tent, another of malaga, and another of white wine; all in my wine-cellar together; which, I believe, none of my friends of my name now alive ever had of his own at one time.

12th. After doing what business I could in the morning, it being a solemn fast-day for the plague growing upon us, I took boat, and down to Deptford, where I stood with great pleasure an hour or two by my Lady Sandwich's bedside, talking to her.

13th. By water, at night late, to Sir G. Carteret's, but, there being no oars to carry me, I was fain to call a sculler that had a gentleman already in it, and he proved a man of love to music, and he and I sang together the way down with great pleasure. Above 700 died of the plague this week.

15th. Mr. Carteret and I to the ferry-place at Greenwich, and there stayed an hour crossing the water to and again to get our coach and horses over; and by and by set out, and so toward Dagenhams. But, Lord! what silly discourse we had as to love-matters, he being the most awkward man ever I met with in my life as to that business. Thither we came, and by that time it began to be dark, and were kindly received by Lady Wright and my Lord Crewe. And to discourse they went, my Lord discoursing with him, asking of him questions of travel, which he answered well enough in a few words; but nothing to the lady from him at all. To supper, and after supper to talk again, he yet taking no notice of the lady. My Lord would have had me have consented to leaving the young people together to-night, to begin their amours, his staying being but to be little. But I advised against it, lest the lady might be too much surprised. So they led him up to his chamber, where I stayed a little, to know how he liked the lady, which he told me he did mightily; but, Lord! in the dullest insipid manner that ever lover did. So I bid him good-night, and down to prayers, with my Lord Crewe's family; and, after prayers, my Lord, and Lady Wright, and I, to consult what to do; and it was agreed at last to have them go to church together, as the family used to do, though his lameness was a great objection against it. But at last my Lady Jem. sent me word by my Lady Wright that it would be better to do just as they used to do before his coming; and therefore she desired to go to church, which was yielded to them.

16th. (Lord's day.) I up, having lain with Mr.

Moore in the chaplain's chamber. And, having trimmed myself, down to Mr. Carteret; and we walked in the gallery an hour or two, it being a most noble and pretty house that ever, for the bigness, I saw. Here I taught him what to do: to take the lady always by the hand to lead her, and telling him that I would find opportunity to leave them together, he should make these and these compliments, and also take a time to do the like to Lord Crewe and Lady Wright. After I had instructed him, which he thanked me for, owning that he needed my teaching him, my Lord Crewe came down and family, the young lady among the rest; and so by coaches to church four miles off; where a pretty good sermon, and a declaration of penitence of a man that had undergone the Church's censure for his wicked life. Thence back again by coach, Mr. Carteret having not had the confidence to take his lady once by the hand, coming or going, which I told him of when we came home, and he will hereafter do it. So to dinner. My Lord excellent discourse. Then to walk in the gallery, and to sit down. By and by my Lady Wright and I go out, and then My Lord Crewe (he not by design), and lastly my Lady Crewe came out, and left the young people together. And a little pretty daughter of my Lady Wright's most innocently came out afterwards, and shut the door to, as if she had done it, poor child, by inspiration; which made us without have good sport to laugh at. They together an hour, and by and by church-time, whither he led her into the coach and into the church, where several handsome ladies. But it was most extraordinary hot that ever I knew it. So home again, and to walk in the gardens, where we left the young couple a second time; and my Lady Wright and I to walk together, who tells me that some new clothes must of necessity be made for Lady Jemimah, which and other things I took care of. Anon to supper, and excellent discourse and dispute between my Lord Crewe and the chaplain, who is a good scholar, but a nonconformist. Here this evening I spoke with Mrs. Carter, my old acquaintance, that hath lived with my Lady these twelve or thirteen years, the sum of all whose discourse (and others for her) is that I would get her a good husband; which I have promised, but know not when I shall perform. After Mr. Carteret was carried to his chamber, we to prayers, and then to bed.

26th. To Greenwich, to the Park, where I heard the King and Duke are come by water this morn from Hampton Court. They asked me several questions. The King mightily pleased with his new buildings there. I followed them to Castle's ship, in building, and there met Sir W. Batten, and thence to Sir G. Carteret's, where all the morning with them; they not having any but the Duke of Monmouth, and Sir W. Killigrew, and one gentleman, and a page more. Great variety of talk, and was often led to speak to the King and Duke. By and by they to dinner, and all to dinner and sat down to the King, saving myself, which, though I could not in modesty expect, yet, God forgive my pride! I was sorry I was there, that Sir W. Batten should say that he could sit down where I could not. The King having dined, he came down, and I went in the barge with him, I sitting at the door. Down to Woolwich, and there I just saw and kissed my wife, and saw some of her painting, which is very curious; and away again to the King, and back again with him in the barge, hearing him and the Duke talk, and seeing and observing their manner of discourse. And, God forgive me! though I admire them with all the duty possible, yet the more a man considers and observes them, the less he finds of difference between them

149

and other men, though, blessed be God! they are both princes of great nobleness and spirits. The Duke of Monmouth is the most skittish leaping gallant that ever I saw, always in action, vaulting, or leaping, or clambering. Sad news of the death of so many in the parish of the plague; forty last night; the bell always going. To the Exchange, where I went up and sat talking with my beauty, Mrs. Batelier, a great while, who is indeed one of the finest women I ever saw in my life. This day poor Robin Shaw at Backewell's died, and Backewell himself now in Flanders. The King himself asked about Shaw, and, being told he was dead, said he was very sorry for it. The sickness is got into our parish this week, and is got, indeed, everywhere; so that I begin to think of setting things in order, which I pray God enable me to put, both as to soul and body.

27th. With Mr. Gauden to Hampton Court, where I saw the King and Queen set out towards Salisbury, and after them the Duke and Duchess, whose hands I did kiss. And it was the first time I did ever, or did see anybody else, kiss her hand, and it was a most fine white and fat hand. But it was pretty to see the young pretty ladies dressed like men, in velvet coats, caps with ribbons, and with laced bands, just like men. Only the Duchess herself it did not become. They gone, we, with great content, took coach again; and, hungry, came to Clapham about one o'clock, and Creed there, too, before us; where a good dinner, the house having dined, and so to walk up and down in the gardens, mighty pleasant. By and by comes, by promise to me, Sir G. Carteret, and viewed the house above and below, and sat and drank there, and I had a little opportunity to kiss and spend some time with the ladies above, his daughter, a buxom lass, and his sister Fissant, a serious lady, and a little daughter of hers, that begins to sing prettily. Thence, with mighty pleasure, with Sir G. Carteret by coach, with great discourse of kindness with him to my Lord Sandwich, and to me also; and I every day see more good by the alliance. To Half-way House, and so home, in my way being shown my cousin Patience's house, which seems, at distance, a pretty house. At home met the weekly Bill, where above 1000 increased in the Bill; and of them, in all about 1700 of the plague, which hath made the officers this day resolve of sitting at Deptford, which puts me to some consideration what to do.

August 1665

August 3rd. By and by met my Lord Crewe; Mr. Marr telling me, by the way, how a maid servant of Mr. John Wright's, who lives thereabouts, falling sick of the plague, she was removed to an out-house, and a nurse appointed to look to her; who, being once absent, the maid got out of the house at the window and ran away. The nurse coming and knocking, and, having no answer, believed she was dead, and went and told Mr. Wright so; who and his lady were in a great strait what to do to get her buried. At last, resolved to go to Burntwood, hard by, being in the parish, and there get people to do it. But they would not: so he went home full of trouble, and in the way met the wench walking over the common, which frighted him worse than before; and was forced to send people to take her, which he did; and they got one of the pest-coaches, and put her into it, to carry her to a pest-house. And, passing in a narrow lane, Sir Anthony Browne, with his brother and some friends in the coach, met this coach with the curtains drawn close. The brother, being a young man, and believing there might be some lady in it that would not be seen, and the way being narrow, he thrust his head out of his own into her coach, and to look, and there saw somebody look very ill, and in a sick dress, and stunk mightily; which the coachman also cried out upon. And presently they came up to some people that stood looking after it, and told our gallants that it was a maid of Mr. Wright's carried away sick of the plague; which put the young gentleman into a fright had almost cost him his life, but is now well again.

8th. To my office a little, and then to the Duke of Albemarle's about some business. The streets empty all the way now, even in London, which is a sad sight. And to Westminster Hall, where talking, hearing very sad stories from Mrs. Mumford; among others, of Michell's son's family. And poor Will, that used to sell us ale at the Hall-door, his wife and three children died, all, I think, in a day. So home, through the City again, wishing I may have taken no ill in going; but I will go, I think, no more thither. The news of De Ruyter's coming home is certain; and told to the great disadvantage of our fleet, and the praise of De Ruyter; but it cannot be helped.

10th. My she-cousin Porter, the turner's wife, to tell me that her husband was carried to the Tower, for buying of some of the King's powder, and would have my help, but I could give her none, not daring to appear in the business. By and by to the office, where we sat all the morning; in great trouble to see the Bill this week rise so high, to above 4000 in all, and of them above 3000 of the plague. Home, to draw over anew my will, which I had bound myself by oath to dispatch by to-morrow night; the town growing so unhealthy, that a man cannot depend upon living two days.

12th. Sent for by Sir G. Carteret, to meet him and my Lord Hinchingbroke at Deptford, but my Lord did not come thither, he having crossed the river at Gravesend to Dagenhams, whither I dare not follow him, they being afraid of me; but Sir G. Carteret says he is a most sweet youth in every circumstance. Sir G. Carteret being in haste of going to the Duke of Albemarle and the Archbishop, he was pettish. The people die so, that now it seems they are fain to carry the dead to be buried by daylight, the nights not sufficing to do it in. And my Lord Mayor commands people to be within at nine at night all, as they say, that the sick may have liberty to go abroad for air. There is one also dead out of one of our ships at Deptford, which troubles us mightily—the *Providence* fire-ship, which was just fitted to go to sea; but they tell me to-day no more sick on board. And this day W. Bodham tells me that one is dead at Woolwich, not far from the Ropeyard. I am told, too, that a wife of one of the grooms at Court is dead at Salisbury; so that the King and Queen are speedily to be all gone to Milton. So God preserve us!

13th. (Lord's day.) It being very wet all day, clearing all matters, and giving instructions in writing to my executors, thereby perfecting the whole business of my will, to my very great joy; so that I shall be in much better state of soul, I hope, if it should please the Lord to call me away this sickly time. I find myself worth, besides Brampton estates, the sum of £2164, for which the Lord be praised!

15th. It was dark before I could get home, and so land at Churchyard stairs, where, to my great trouble, I met a dead corpse of the plague, in the narrow alley, just bringing down a little pair of stairs. But I thank God I was not much disturbed at it. However, I shall beware of being late abroad again.

16th. To the Exchange, where I have not been a great while. But, Lord! how sad a sight it is to see the streets empty of people, and very few upon the

'Change! Jealous of every door that one sees shut up, lest it should be the plague; and about us two shops in three, if not more, generally shut up. This day I had the ill news from Dagenhams, that my poor Lord of Hinchingbroke his indisposition is turned to the smallpox. Poor gentleman! that he should be come from France so soon to fall sick, and of that disease too, when he should be gone to see a fine lady, his mistress! I am most heartily sorry for it.

20th. (Lord's day.) Took horse for Staines, and thence to Brainford, to Mr. Povy's. Mr. Povy not being at home, I lost my labour—only ate and drank there with his lady, and told my bad news, and hear the plague is round about them there. So away to Brainford; and there, at the inn that goes down to the waterside, I 'light and paid off my post-horses, and so slipped on my shoes, and laid my things by, the tide not serving, and to church, where a dull sermon, and many Londoners. After church to my inn, and ate and drank, and so about seven o'clock by water, and got between nine and ten to Queenhive, very dark; and I could not get my waterman to go elsewhere, for fear of the plague. Thence with a lantern, in great fear of meeting of dead corpses, carrying to be buried; but, blessed be God! met none, but did see now and then a link, which is the mark of them, at a distance.

28th. To Mr. Colvill, the goldsmith's, having not for some days been in the streets; but now how few people I see, and those looking like people that had taken leave of the world. To the Exchange, and there was not fifty people upon it, and but few more like to be, as they told me. I think to take adieu to-day of the London streets. In much the best posture I ever was in in my life, both as to the quantity and the certainty I have of the money I am worth; having most of it in my hand. But then this is a trouble to me what to do with it, being myself this day going to be wholly at Woolwich; but for the present I am resolved to venture it in an iron chest, at least for a while. Just now comes news that the fleet is gone, or going this day, out again, for which God be praised! and my Lord Sandwich hath done himself great right in it, in getting so soon out again. I met my wife walking to the waterside with her painter, Mr. Browne, and her maids. There I met Commissioner Pett and my Lord Brouncker; and the lady at his house had been there to-day, to see her.

31st. Up; and after putting several things in order to my removal, to Woolwich; the plague having a great increase this week, beyond all expectation, of almost 2000, making the general Bill 7000, odd 100; and the plague above 6000. Thus this month ends with great sadness upon the public, through the greatness of the plague everywhere through the kingdom almost. Every day sadder and sadder news of its increase. In the City died this week 7496, and of them 6102 of the plague. But it is feared that the true number of the dead this week is near 10,000; partly from the poor that cannot be taken notice of, through the greatness of the number, and partly from the Quakers and others that will not have any bell ring for them. Our fleet gone out to find the Dutch, we having about 100 sail in our fleet, and in them the *Sovereign* one; so that it is a better fleet than the former with which the Duke was. All our fear is that the Dutch should be got in before them; which would be a very great sorrow to the public, and to me particularly, for my Lord Sandwich's sake. A great deal of money being spent, and the kingdom not in a condition to spare, nor a parliament, without much difficulty to meet, to give more. And to that; to have it said, what hath been done by our late fleets? As to myself, I am very well, only in fear of the plague, and as much of an ague, by being forced to go early and late to Woolwich, and my family to lie there continually. My late gettings have been very great, to my great content, and am likely to have yet a few more profitable jobs in a little while; for which Tangier and Sir W. Warren I am wholly obliged to.

September 1665

September 3rd. (Lord's day.) Up; and put on my coloured silk suit, very fine, and my new periwig, bought a good while since, but durst not wear, because the plague was in Westminster when I bought it; and it is a wonder what will be the fashion after the plague is done, as to periwigs, for nobody will dare to buy any hair, for fear of the infection, that it had been cut off the heads of people dead of the plague. I took my Lady Pen home, and her daughter Peg; and after dinner I made my wife show them her pictures, which did mad Peg Pen, who learns of the same man. My Lord Brouncker, Sir J. Minnes, and I up to the Vestry at the desire of the Justices of the Peace, in order to the doing something for the keeping of the plague from growing; but, Lord! to consider the madness of people of the town, who will, because they are forbid, come in crowds along with the dead corpses to see them buried; but we agreed on some orders for the prevention thereof. Among other stories, one was very passionate, methought, of a complaint brought against a man in the town for taking a child from London from an infected house. Alderman Hooker told us it was the child of a very able citizen in Gracious Street, a saddler, who had buried all the rest of his children of the plague; and himself and wife, now being shut up in despair of escaping, did desire only to save the life of this little child, and so prevailed to have it received stark-naked into the arms of a friend, who brought it, having put it into new fresh clothes, to Greenwich; where, upon hearing the story, we did agree it should be permitted to be received and kept in the town.

10th. (Lord's day.) Walked home; being forced thereto by one of my watermen falling sick yesterday, and it was God's great mercy I did not go by water with them yesterday, for he fell sick on Saturday night, and it is to be feared of the plague. So I sent him away to London with his fellow; but another boat came to me this morning. My wife, before I came out, telling me the ill news that she hears, that her father is very ill, and then I told her I feared of the plague, for that the house is shut up. And so she much troubled, and did desire me to send them something, and I said I would, and will do so. But, before I came out, there happened news to come to me by an express from Mr. Coventry, telling me the most happy news of my Lord Sandwich's meeting with part of the Dutch; his taking two of their East India ships, and six or seven others, and very good prizes; and that he is in search of the rest of the fleet, which he hopes to find upon the Wellbank, with the loss only of the *Hector*, poor Captain Cuttle. To Greenwich, and there sending away Mr. Andrews, I to Captain Cocke's, where I find my Lord Brouncker and his mistress, and Sir J. Minnes, where we supped; there was also Sir W. Doyly and Mr. Evelyn; but the receipt of this news did put us all into such an ecstasy of joy, that it inspired into Sir J. Minnes and Mr. Evelyn such a spirit of mirth, that in all my life I never met with so merry a two hours as our company this night was. Among other humours, Mr. Evelyn's repeating of some verses made up of nothing but the various acceptations of *may* and *can*, and doing it so aptly upon occasion of something of that nature, and so fast, did make us all die almost with laughing, and did so stop the mouth of Sir J. Minnes in the middle of all his mirth, and in a thing agreeing with his own manner of genius, that I never saw any man so outdone in all my life; and Sir J. Minnes's mirth, too, to see himself outdone, was the crown of all our mirth. In this humour we sat till about ten at night, and so my Lord and his mistress home, and we to bed.

October 1665

October 7th. Did business, though not much, at the office, because of the horrible crowd and lamentable moan of the poor seamen that lie starving in the streets for lack of money, which do trouble and perplex me to the heart; and more at noon, when we were to go through them, for then above a whole hundred of them followed us; some cursing, some swearing, and some praying to us. A letter came this afternoon from the Duke of Albemarle, signifying the Dutch to be in sight, with 80 sail, yesterday morning, off Solebay, coming right into the bay. God knows what they will and may do to us, we having no force abroad able to oppose them, but to be sacrificed to them. At night came two waggons from Rochester, with more goods from Captain Cocke; and in housing them came two of the Custom-house, and did seize them; but I showed them my *Transire*. However, after some angry words, we locked them up, and sealed up the key, and did give it to the constable to keep till Monday, and so parted. But, Lord! to think how the poor constable came to me in the dark, going home; "Sir," says he, "I have the key, and, if you would have me do any service for you, send for me betimes to-morrow morning, and I will do what you would have me." Whether the fellow do this out of kindness or knavery, I cannot tell; but it is pretty to observe. Talking with him in the highway, came close by the bearers with a dead corpse of the plague; but, Lord! to see what custom is, that I am come almost to think nothing of it.

11th. Comes up my landlady, Mrs. Clerke, to make an agreement for the time to come; and I, for the having room enough, and to keep out strangers, and to have a place to retreat to for my wife, if the sickness should come to Woolwich, am to pay dear; so, for three rooms and a dining-room, and for linen, and bread and beer and butter, at nights and mornings, I am to give her £5 : 10s. per month. To Erith, and there we met Mr. Seymour, one of the Commissioners for Prizes, and a Parliament-man, and he was mighty high, and had now seized our goods on their behalf; and he mighty imperiously would have all forfeited. But I could not but think it odd that a Parliament-man, in a serious discourse before such persons as we and my Lord Brouncker, and Sir John Minnes, should quote *Hudibras*, as being the book I doubt he hath read most. To Woolwich, where we had appointed to keep the night merrily; and so, by Captain Cocke's coach, had brought a very pretty child, a daughter of one Mrs. Tooker's, next door to my lodging, and so she and a daughter and kinsman of Mrs. Pett's made up a fine company at my lodgings at Woolwich, where my wife, and Mercer, and Mrs. Barbara danced, and mighty merry we were, but especially at Mercer's dancing a jig, which she does the best I ever did see, having the most natural way of it, and keeps time the most perfectly I ever did see. This night is kept in lieu of yesterday, for my wedding-day of ten years; for which God be praised! being now in an extreme good condition of health and estate and honour, and a way of getting more money, though at this hour under some discomposure, rather than damage, about some prize-goods that I have bought off the fleet, in partnership with Captain Cocke, and for the discourse about the world concerning my Lord Sandwich, that he hath done a thing so bad; and indeed it must needs have been a very rash act; and the rather because of a Parliament now newly met to give money, and will have some account of what hath already been spent, besides the precedent for a General to take what prizes he pleases, and the giving a pretence to take away much more than he intended, and all will lie upon him; and not giving to all the Commanders, as well as the Flags, he displeases all them, and offends even some of the Flags, thinking others to be better served than themselves; and, lastly, puts himself out of a power of begging anything again a great while of the King. Having danced with my people as long as I saw fit to sit up, I to bed, and left them to do what they would.

15th. (Lord's day.) Up, and, while I stayed for the barber, tried to compose a duo of counterpoint; and I think it will do very well, it being by Mr. Berkenshaw's rule.

16th. Upon the Exchange, which is very empty, God knows! and but mean people there. The news for certain that the Dutch are come with their fleet before Margate, and some men were endeavouring to come on shore when the post came away, perhaps to steal some sheep. I walked to the Tower; but, Lord! how empty the streets are, and melancholy, so many poor sick people in the streets full of sores; and so many sad stories overheard as I walk, everybody talking of this dead, and that man sick, and so many in this place, and so many in that. And they tell me that in Westminster there is never a physician and but one apothecary left, all being dead; but that there are great hopes of a great decrease this week; God send it! At the Tower found my Lord

Duke and Duchess at dinner; so I sat down; and much good cheer, the Lieutenant and his lady and several officers with the Duke. But, Lord! to hear the silly talk was there would make one mad; the Duke having none almost but fools about him. Much talk about the Dutch, in reproach of them in whose hands the fleet is; but, Lord help him! there is something will hinder him and all the world in going to sea, which is want of victuals; for we have not wherewith to answer our service; and how much better it would have been if the Duke's advice had been taken for the fleet to have gone presently out; but God help the King while no better counsels are given, and what is given no better taken. I have received letters from my Lord Sandwich to-day, speaking very high about the prize-goods, that he would have us to fear nobody, but be very confident in what we have done, and not to confess any fault or doubt of what he hath done; for the King hath allowed it, and do now confirm it, and do send orders, as he says, for nothing to be disturbed that his Lordship hath ordered therein as to the division of the goods to the fleet; which do comfort us. To the Still Yard, which place, however, is now shut up of the plague; but I was there, and we now make no bones of it. Much talk there is of the Chancellor's speech and the King's at the Parliament's meeting, which are very well liked; and that we shall certainly, by their speeches, fall out with France, at this time, together with the Dutch, which will find us work.

November 1665

November 1st. Lay very long in bed, discoursing with Mr. Hill of most things of a man's life, and how little merit do prevail in the world, but only favour; and that, for myself, chance without merit brought me in; and that diligence only keeps me so, and will, living as I do among so many lazy people that the diligent man becomes necessary, that they cannot do anything without him.

5th. (Lord's day.) To the Cockpit, where I heard the Duke of Albemarle's chaplain make a simple sermon; among other things, reproaching the imperfection of human learning, he cried, " All our physicians cannot tell what an ague is, and all our arithmetic is not able to number the days of a man "; which, God knows, is not the fault of arithmetic, but that our understandings reach not the thing. I hear that the plague increases much at Lambeth, St. Martin's, and Westminster, and fear it will all over the city. By water to Deptford, and there made a visit to Mr. Evelyn, who, among other things, showed me most excellent painting in little, in distemper, in Indian ink, water-colours; graving; and, above all, the whole secret of mezzotinto, and the manner of it, which is very pretty, and good things done with it. He read to me very much also of his discourse, he hath been many years and now is about, about Gardenage, which will be a most noble and pleasant piece. He read me part of a play or two of his making, very good, but not as he conceits them, I think, to be. He showed me his *Hortus Hiemalis*; leaves laid up in a book of several plants kept dry, which preserve colour, however, and look very finely, better than an herbal. In fine, a most excellent person he is, and must be allowed a little for a little conceitedness; but he may well be so, being a man so much above others. He read me, though with too much gusto, some little poems of his own, that were not transcendent, yet one or two very pretty epigrams; among others, of a lady looking in at a grate, and being pecked at by an eagle that was there.

15th. To the King's Head tavern, where all the

Trinity House dined to-day, to choose a new Master in the room of Hurlestone, that is dead, and Captain Crispe is chosen. After dinner who comes in but my Lady Batten, and a troop of a dozen women almost, and expected, as I found afterwards, to be made mighty much of, but nobody minded them; but the best jest was, that when they saw themselves not regarded, they would go away, and it was horrible foul weather; and my Lady Batten walking through the dirty lane with new spick and span white shoes, she dropped one of her galoshes in the dirt, where it stuck, and she forced to go home without one, at which she was horribly vexed, and I led her; and, after vexing her a little more in mirth, I parted, and to Glanville's, where I knew Sir John Robinson, Sir G. Smith, and Captain Cocke were gone, and then, with the company of Mrs. Pennington, whose father, I hear, was one of the Court of Justice, and died prisoner, of the stone, in the Tower, I made them, against their resolutions, to stay from hour to hour, till it was almost midnight, and a furious, dark, and rainy, and windy, stormy night, and, which was best, I, with drinking small beer, made them all drunk drinking wine, at which Sir John Robinson made great sport. But, they being gone, the lady and I very civilly sat an hour by the fireside, showing the folly of this Robinson, that makes it his work to praise himself, and all he says and do, like a heavy-headed coxcomb. The plague, blessed be God! is decreased 400; making the whole this week but 1300 and odd; for which the Lord be praised!

23rd. Up betimes, and so, being trimmed, I to get papers ready against Sir H. Cholmely come to me by appointment, he being newly come over from Tangier. He did by and by come, and we settled all matters about his money, and he is a most satisfied man in me, and do declare his resolution to give me

£200 per annum. It continuing to be a great frost, which gives us hopes for a perfect cure of the plague, he and I to walk in the Park, and there discoursed with grief of the calamity of the times. I brought him home, and had a good dinner for him. Captain Cuttance tells me how W. Howe is laid by the heels, and confined to the *Royal Katharine*, and his things all seized; and how, also, for a quarrel, which indeed my Lord the other night told me, Captain Ferrers having cut all over the back of another of my Lord's servants, is parted from my Lord. We in extraordinary lack of money and everything else to go to sea next year. My Lord Sandwich is gone from the fleet yesterday towards Oxford.

24th. To London, and there, in my way, at my old oyster-shop in Gracious Street, bought two barrels of my fine woman of the shop, who is alive after all the plague, which now is the first observation or inquiry we make at London concerning everybody we know. To the 'Change, where very busy with several people, and mightily glad to see the 'Change so full, and hopes of another abatement still the next week. I went home with Sir G. Smith to dinner, sending for one of my barrels of oysters, which were good, though come from Colchester, where the plague hath been so much. Here a very brave dinner, though no invitation; and, Lord! to see how I am treated, that come from so mean a beginning, is matter of wonder to me. But it is God's mercy to me, and His blessing upon my taking pains, and being punctual in my dealings. Visited Mr. Evelyn, where most excellent discourse with him; among other things he showed me a ledger of a Treasurer of the Navy, his great grandfather, just 100 years old; which I seemed mighty fond of, and he did present me with it, which I take as a great rarity; and he hopes to find me more, older than it. He also showed us several letters of the old Lord of Leicester's, in Queen Elizabeth's time, under the very handwriting of Queen Elizabeth, and Queen Mary, Queen of Scots; and others, very venerable names. But, Lord! how poorly, methinks, they wrote in those days, and in what plain uncut paper.

30th. At noon comes Sir Thomas Allen, and I made him dine with me, and very friendly he is, and a good man, I think, but one that professes he loves to get and to save. Great joy we have this week in the weekly Bill, it being come to 544 in all, and but 333 of the plague; so that we are encouraged to get to London soon as we can. And my father writes as great news of joy to them, that he saw York's waggon go again this week to London, and was full of passengers; and tells me that my aunt Bell hath been dead of the plague these seven weeks.

December 1665

December 6th. Up betimes, it being fast-day; and by water to the Duke of Albemarle, who came to town from Oxford last night. He is mighty brisk, and very kind to me, and asks my advice principally in everything. He surprises me with the news that my Lord Sandwich goes Ambassador to Spain speedily; though I know not whence this arises, yet I am heartily glad of it. I spent the afternoon upon a song of Solyman's words to Roxalana that I have set, and so with my wife walked and Mercer to Mrs. Pierce's, where Captain Rolt and Mrs. Knipp, Mr. Coleman and his wife, and Laneare, Mrs. Worship and her singing daughter met; and by and by unexpectedly comes Mr. Pierce from Oxford. Here the best company for music I ever was in, in my life, and wish I could live and die in it, both for music and the face of Mrs. Pierce, and my wife, and Knipp, who is pretty enough; but the most excellent mad-humoured thing, and sings the noblest that ever I heard in my life, and Rolt, with her, some things together most excellently. I spent the night in an ecstasy almost; and, having invited them to my house a day or two hence, we broke up, Pierce having told me how the King hath done my Lord Sandwich all the right imaginable, by showing him his countenance before all the world on every occasion, to remove thoughts of discontent; and that he is to go Ambassador, and the Duke of York is made General of all forces by land and sea, and the Duke of Albemarle Lieutenant-General.

30th. All the afternoon to my accounts; and there find myself, to my great joy, a great deal worth above £4000, for which the Lord be praised! and is principally occasioned by my getting £500 of Cocke for my profit in his bargains of prize-goods, and from Mr. Gauden's making me a present of £500 more, when I paid him £8000 for Tangier.

31st. (Lord's day.) Thus ends this year, to my great joy, in this manner. I have raised my estate from £1300 in this year to £4400. I have got myself greater interest, I think, by my diligence, and my employments increased by that of Treasurer for Tangier and Surveyor of the Victuals. It is true we have gone through great melancholy because of the great plague, and I put to great charges by it, by keeping my family long at Woolwich, and myself and another part of my family, my clerks, at my charge, at Greenwich, and a maid at London; but I hope the King will give us some satisfaction for that. But now the plague is abated almost to nothing, and I intending to get to London as fast as I can. The Dutch war goes on very ill, by reason of lack of money; having none to hope for, all being put into disorder by a new Act that is made as an experiment to bring credit to the Exchequer, for goods and money to be advanced upon the credit of that Act. The great evil of this year, and the only one indeed, is the fall of my Lord Sandwich, whose mistake about the prizes hath undone him, I believe, as to interest at Court; though sent (for a little palliating it) Ambassador into Spain, which he is now fitting himself for. But the Duke of Albemarle goes with the Prince to sea this next year, and my Lord is very meanly spoken of; and, indeed, his miscarriage about the prize-goods is not to be excused, to suffer a company of rogues to go away with ten times as much as himself, and the blame of all to be deservedly laid upon him. My whole family hath been well all this while, and all my friends I know of, saving my aunt Bell, who is dead, and some children of my cousin Sarah's, of the plague. But many of such as I know very well, dead; yet, to our great joy, the town fills apace, and shops begin to be open again. Pray God continue the plague's decrease! for that keeps the Court away from the place of business, and so all goes to rack as to public matters, they at this distance not thinking of it.

January 1666

January 6th. To a great dinner and much company. Mr. Cuttle and his lady and I went, hoping to get Mrs. Knipp to us, having wrote a letter to her in the morning, calling myself " Dapper Dicky," in answer to her's of " Barbary Allen," but could not, and am told by the boy that carried my letter that he found her crying; and I fear she lives a sad life with that ill-natured fellow her husband: so we had a great, but I a melancholy, dinner. After dinner to cards, and then comes notice that my wife is come unexpectedly to me to town: so I to her. It is only to see what I do, and why I come not home; and she is in the right that I would have a little more of

Mrs. Knipp's company before I go away. My wife
to fetch away my things from Woolwich, and I back
to cards, and after cards to choose King and Queen,
and a good cake there was, but no marks found; but
I privately found the clove, the mark of the knave,
and privately put it into Captain Cocke's piece,
which made some mirth, because of his lately being
known by his buying of clove and mace of the East
India prizes. At night home to my lodging, where I
find my wife returned with my things. It being
Twelfth-Night, they had got the fiddler, and mighty
merry they were; and I above came not to them,
leaving them dancing, and choosing King and Queen.

28th. (Lord's day.) Took coach, and to Hampton
Court, where we find the King, and Duke, and Lords,
all in council; so we walked up and down: there being
none of the ladies come, and so much the more business
I hope will be done. The Council being up, out
comes the King, and I kissed his hand, and he grasped
me very kindly by the hand. The Duke also, I
kissed his, and he mighty kind, and Sir W. Coventry.
I found my Lord Sandwich there, poor man! I see
with a melancholy face, and suffers his beard to grow
on his upper lip more than usual. I took him a
little aside, to know when I should wait on him, and
where: he told me that it would be best to meet at his
lodgings, without being seen to walk together; which
I liked very well; and, Lord! to see in what difficulty
I stand, that I dare not walk with Sir W. Coventry,
for fear my Lord or Sir G. Carteret should see me;
nor with either of them, for fear Sir W. Coventry
should. I went down into one of the Courts, and there
met the King and Duke; and the Duke called me to
him. And the King came to me of himself, and told
me, " Mr. Pepys," says he, " I do give you thanks for
your good service all this year, and I assure you I am
very sensible of it." And the Duke of York did tell

me with pleasure that he had read over my discourse about pursers, and would have it ordered in my way, and so fell from one discourse to another. I walked with them quite out of the Court into the fields, and then back, and to my Lord Sandwich's chamber, where I find him very melancholy, and not well satisfied, I perceive, with my carriage to Sir G. Carteret, but I did not satisfy him that I have a very hard game to play; and he told me that he was sorry to see it, and the inconveniences which likely may fall upon me with him; but, for all that, I am not much afraid, if I can but keep out of harm's way. He hath got over the business of the prizes, so far as to have a privy seal passed for all that was in his distribution to the officers, which I am heartily glad of; and, for the rest, he must be answerable for what he is proved to have. But for his pardon for anything else, he thinks it not seasonable to ask it, and not useful to him; because that will not stop a Parliament's mouth, and for the King, he is sure of him. Took boat, and by water to Kingston, and so to our lodgings.

February 1666

February 10th. To the office. This day comes first Sir Thomas Harvy after the plague, having been out of town all this while. He was coldly received by us, and he went away before we rose also, to make himself appear yet a man less necessary. To supper, and to bed, being nowadays, for these four or five months, mightily troubled with my snoring in my sleep, and know not how to remedy it.

March 1666

March 8th. To Hales's, where my wife is sitting; and, indeed, her face and neck, which are now finished, do so please me that I am not myself almost, in consideration of the fine picture that I shall be master of.

17th. To Hales's, and paid him £14 for the picture, and £1 : 5s. for the frame. This day I began to sit, and he will make me, I think, a very fine picture. He promises it shall be as good as my wife's, and I to sit to have it full of shadows, and do almost break my neck looking over my shoulder to make the posture for him to work by. Home, having a great cold: so bed, drinking butter-ale.

April 1666

April 11th. To Hales's, where there was nothing found to be done more to my picture, but the music, which now pleases me mightily, it being painted true. To Gresham College, where a great deal of do and formality in choosing of the Council and officers. I had three votes to be of the Council, who am but a stranger, nor expected any, my Lord Brouncker being confirmed President.

29th. (Lord's day.) To church, where Mr. Mills, a lazy sermon upon the Devil's having no right to anything in this world. To Mr. Evelyn's, where I walked in his garden till he came from church, with great pleasure reading Ridly's Discourse, all my way going and coming, upon the Civil and Ecclesiastical Law. He being come home, he and I walked together in the garden with mighty pleasure, he being a very ingenious man; and the more I know him, the more I love him. Weary to bed, after having my hair of my head cut shorter, even close to my skull, for coolness, it being mighty hot weather.

May 1666

May 8th. Comes Mr. Downing, the anchor-smith, who had given me 50 pieces in gold the last month to speak for him to Sir W. Coventry, for his being smith at Deptford; but, after I had got it granted to him, he finds himself not fit to go on with it, so lets it fall. I therefore in honour and conscience took him home and forced him to take the money again, and glad to have given him so much cause to speak well of me.

June 1666

June 13th. With Balty to Hales's by coach. Here I find my father's picture begun, and so much to my content, that it joys my very heart to think that I should have his picture so well done; who, besides that he is my father, and a man that loves me, and hath ever done so, is also, at this day, one of the most careful and innocent men in the world. Invited to Sir Christopher Mings's funeral, but find them gone to church. However, I go into the church, which is a fair large church, and a great chapel, and there heard the service, and stayed till they buried him, and then out; and there met with Sir W. Coventry, who was there out of great generosity, and no person of quality there but he, and went with him into his coach; and, being in it with him, there happened this extraordinary case, one of the most romantic that I ever heard of in my life, and could not have believed, but that I did see it; which was this. About a dozen able, lusty, proper men came to the coach-side with tears in their eyes, and one of them that spoke for the rest began, and said to Sir W. Coventry, " We are here a dozen of us that have long known, and loved, and served our dead commander, Sir Christopher Mings, and have now done the last office of laying him in the ground.

We would be glad we had any other to offer after him, and in revenge of him. All we have is our lives; if you will please to get His Royal Highness to give us a fireship among us all, here is a dozen of us, out of all which, choose you one to be commander; and the rest of us, whoever he is, will serve him; and, if possible, do that which shall show our memory of our dead commander, and our revenge." Sir W. Coventry was herewith much moved, as well as I, who could hardly abstain from weeping, and took their names, and so parted; telling me that he would move His Royal Highness as in a thing very extraordinary, which was done. The truth is Sir Christopher Mings was a very stout man, and a man of great parts and most excellent tongue among ordinary men; and, as Sir W. Coventry says, could have been the most useful man at such a pinch of time as this. He was come into great renown here at home, and more abroad in the West Indies. He had brought his family into a way of being great; but, dying at this time, his memory and name (his father being always, and at this day, a shoemaker, and his mother a hoyman's daughter), of which he was used frequently to boast, will be quite forgot in a few months, as if he had never been, nor any of his name be the better by it; he having not had time to will any estate, but is dead poor rather than rich. So we left the church and crowd. Walked to Mrs. Bagwell's, and went into her house; but I was not a little fearful of what she told me but now, which is, that her servant was dead of the plague, and that she had new-whitened the house all below stairs, but that above stairs they are not so fit for me to go up to, they being not so. So I parted thence with a very good will, but very civilly, and away to the water-side, and sent for a pint of sack, and drank what I would, and gave the waterman the rest.

29th. To the office; where I met with a letter from
Dover, which tells me, and it came by express, that
news is brought over by a gentleman from Callice,
that the Dutch fleet, 130 sail, are come upon the
French coast; and that the country is bringing in
pick-axes, and shovels, and wheel-barrows into
Callice; that there are 6000 men armed on head,
back, and breast, Frenchmen, ready to go on board the
Dutch fleet, and will be followed by 12,000 more.
That they pretend they are to come to Dover; and
that thereupon the Governor of Dover Castle is getting
the victuallers' provisions out of the town into the
Castle to secure it. But I do think this a ridiculous
conceit; but a little time will show.

30th. Late to bed; and, while I was undressing
myself, our new ugly maid, Luce, had like to have
broken her neck in the dark, going down our upper
stairs; but, which I was glad of, the poor girl did only
bruise her head, but at first did lie on the ground
groaning and drawing her breath, like one a-dying.

July 1666

July 1st. (Sunday.) Comes Sir W. Pen to town,
which I little expected, having invited my Lady and
her daughter Peg to dine with me to-day; which at
noon they did, and Sir W. Pen with them; and pretty
merry we were. And though I do not love him, yet
I find it necessary to keep in with him; his good
service at Sheerness, in getting out the fleet, being
much taken notice of, and reported to the King and
Duke, even from the Prince and Duke of Albemarle
themselves, and made the most of to me and them by
Sir W. Coventry; therefore, I think it discretion,
great and necessary discretion, to keep in with him.
To the Tower several times about the business of the
pressed men, and late at it till twelve at night, shipping

of them. But, Lord! how some poor women did cry; and in my life I never did see such natural expression of passion as I did here in some women's bewailing themselves, and running to every parcel of men that were brought, one after another, to look for their husbands, and wept over every vessel that went off, thinking they might be there, and looking after the ship as far as ever they could by moonlight, that it grieved me to the heart to hear them. Besides, to see poor patient labouring men and house-keepers, leaving poor wives and families, taken up on a sudden by strangers, was very hard, and that without press-money, but forced against all law to be gone. It is a great tyranny.

6th. To the Tower, about shipping of some more pressed men, and, that done, away to Broad Street, to Sir G. Carteret, who is at a pay of tickets all alone; and I believe not less than one thousand people in the streets. But it is a pretty thing to observe that, both there and everywhere else, a man shall see many women now-a-days of mean sort in the streets, but no men; men being so afraid of the press. I dined with Sir G. Carteret, and, after dinner, had much discourse about our public business; and he do seem to fear every day more and more what I do; which is, a general confusion in the State; plainly answering me to the question, who is it that the weight of the war depends upon? that it is only Sir W. Coventry. He tells me, too, the Duke of Albemarle is dissatisfied, and that the Duchess do curse Coventry as the man that betrayed her husband to the sea; though I believe that it is not so. Thence to Lombard Street, and received £2000, and carried it home: whereof £1000 in gold. This I do for security sake, and convenience of carriage; though it costs me above £70 the change of it, at 18½d. per piece. Being at home, I there met with a letter from Bab. Allen, to invite me to be godfather to her boy, with Mrs. Williams, which I consented to, but know not the time when it is to be.

10th. To the office; the yard being very full of women (I believe above three hundred) coming to get money for their husbands and friends that are prisoners in Holland; and they lay clamouring and swearing, and cursing us, that my wife and I were afraid to send a venison-pasty that we have for supper to-night to the cook's to be baked, for fear of their offering violence to it; but it went, and no hurt done. To the Tower to speak with Sir John Robinson about the bad condition of the pressed men for want of clothes. Home, and there find my wife and the two Mrs. Bateliers walking in the garden; and then they and we and Mrs. Mercer, the mother, and her daughter Anne, and our Mercer, to supper to a good venison-pasty and other good things, and had a good supper, and very merry, Mistress Bateliers being both very good-humoured. We sang and talked, and then led them home, and there they made us drink; and, among other things, did show us, in cages, some birds brought from Bordeaux, that are all fat, and examining one of them, they are so, almost all fat. Their name is ortolans, which are brought over to the King for him to eat, and indeed are excellent things.

28th. To the Pope's Head, where my Lord Brouncker and his mistress dined and Commissioner Pett, Dr. Charleton, and myself entertained with a venison-pasty by Sir W. Warren. Here very pretty discourse of Dr. Charleton's, concerning Nature's fashioning every creature's teeth according to the food she intends them; and that men's, it is plain, was not for flesh, but for fruit, and that he can at any time tell the food of a beast unknown by the teeth; and that all children love fruit, and none brought to flesh, but against their wills at first. Thence with my Lord to his coach-house, and there put in six horses into his coach, and he and I alone to Highgate. Being come thither, we went to my Lord Lauderdale's house to speak with him, and find him and his lady, and some Scotch people, at supper: pretty odd company, though my Lord Brouncker tells me my Lord Lauderdale is a man of mighty good reason and judgement. But at supper there played one of their servants upon the violin some Scotch tunes only; several, and the best of their country, as they seemed to esteem them, by their praising and admiring them; but, Lord! the strangest air that ever I heard in my life, and all of one cast. But strange to hear my Lord Lauderdale say himself that he had rather hear a cat mew than the best music in the world; and the better the music, the more sick it makes him; and that of all instruments, he hates the flute most, and next to that the bagpipe.

August 1666

August 7th. Comes Mr. Reeve, with a twelve-foot glass. Up to the top of the house, and there we endeavoured to see the moon, and Saturn, and Jupiter; but the heavens proved cloudy, and so we lost our labour, having taken pains to get things together, in order to the managing of our long glass. I receive fresh intelligence that Deptford and Greenwich are now afresh exceedingly afflicted with the sickness more than ever.

8th. Discoursed with Mr. Hooke about the nature of sounds, and he did make me understand the nature of musical sounds made by strings, mighty prettily; and told me that having come to a certain number of vibrations proper to make any tone, he is able to tell how many strokes a fly makes with her wings (those flies that hum in their flying) by the note that it answers to in music during their flying. That, I suppose, is a little too much refined; but his discourse in general of sound was mighty fine. To St. James's, where we attended with the rest of my fellows on the Duke, whom I found with two or three patches upon his nose and about his right eye, which came from his being struck with the bough of a tree the other day in his hunting; and it is a wonder it did not strike out his eye. After we had done our business with him, which is now but little, the want of money being such as leaves us but little to do but to answer complaints of the want thereof, the representing of our want of money being now become useless. To Bow, to my Lady Pooly's, where my wife was with Mr. Batelier and his sisters; and there I found a noble supper. About ten o'clock we rose from table, and sang a song; and so home in two coaches, Mr. Batelier and his sister Mary, and my wife and I in one, and Mercer alone in the other; and, after being examined at Allgate whether we were husbands and wives, home. I find Reeves there, it being a mighty fine bright night, and so upon my leads, though very sleepy, till one in the morning, looking on the moon and Jupiter, with his twelve-foot glass, and another of six foot that he hath brought with him to-night, and the sights mighty pleasant, and one of the glasses I will buy. So to bed mighty sleepy, but with much pleasure, Reeves lying at my house; and mighty proud I am, and ought to be thankful to God Almighty that I am able to have a spare bed for my friends.

September 1666

September 2nd. (Lord's day.) Some of our maids sitting up late last night to get things ready against our feast to-day, Jane called us up about three in the morning, to tell us of a great fire they saw in the City. So I rose, and slipped on my night-gown, and went to her window; and thought it to be on the backside of Mark Lane at the farthest; but, being unused to such fires as followed, I thought it far enough off; and so went to bed again, and to sleep. About seven rose again to dress myself, and there looked out at the window, and saw the fire not so much as it was, and farther off. So to my closet to set things to rights, after yesterday's cleaning. By and by Jane comes and tells me that she hears that above 300 houses have been burned down to-night by the fire we saw, and that it is now burning down all Fish Street, by London Bridge. So I made myself ready presently, and walked to the Tower; and there got up upon one of the high places, Sir J. Robinson's little son going up with me; and there I did see the houses at that end of the bridge all on fire, and an infinite great fire on this and the other side the end of the bridge; which, among other people, did trouble me for poor little Michell and our Sarah on the bridge. So down, with my heart full of trouble, to the Lieutenant of the Tower, who tells me that it began this morning in the King's baker's house in Pudding Lane, and that it hath burned down St. Magnus's Church and most part of Fish Street already. So I down to the waterside, and there got a boat, and through bridge, and there saw a lamentable fire. Poor Michell's house, as far as the Old Swan, already burned that way, and the fire running farther, that in a very little time it got as far as the Steelyard, while I was there. Everybody endeavouring to remove their goods, and flinging into the river, or bringing them into lighters that lay off; poor people staying in their houses as long as till the very fire touched them, and then running into boats, or clambering from one pair of stairs, by the waterside,

to another. And, among other things, the poor
pigeons, I perceive, were loath to leave their houses,
but hovered about the windows and balconies, till
they burned their wings, and fell down. Having
stayed, and in an hour's time seen the fire rage every
way; and nobody, to my sight, endeavouring to
quench it, but to remove their goods, and leave all to
the fire; and, having seen it get as far as the Steelyard,
and the wind mighty high and driving it into the City;
and everything, after so long a drought, proving com-
bustible, even the very stones of churches, and,
among other things, the poor steeple by which pretty
Mrs. —— lives, and whereof my old schoolfellow
Elborough is parson, taken fire in the very top, and
there burned till it fell down; I to Whitehall, with a
gentleman with me, who desired to go off from the
Tower, to see the fire, in my boat; and there up to
the King's closet in the Chapel, where people came
about me, and I did give them an account dismayed
them all, and word was carried in to the King. So I
was called for, and did tell the King and Duke of
York what I saw; and that unless his Majesty did
command houses to be pulled down nothing could
stop the fire. They seemed much troubled, and the
King commanded me to go to my Lord Mayor from
him, and command him to spare no houses, but to
pull down before the fire every way. The Duke of
York bid me tell him that if he would have any more
soldiers he shall; and so did my Lord Arlington afterwards, as a great secret. Here meeting with Captain
Cocke, I in his coach, which he lent me, and Creed
with me to Paul's; and there walked along Watling
Street, as well as I could, every creature coming away
loaden with goods to save, and here and there sick
people carried away in beds. Extraordinary good
goods carried in carts and on backs. At last met my
Lord Mayor in Canning Street, like a man spent,

with a handkerchief about his neck. To the King's message he cried, like a fainting woman, "Lord! what can I do? I am spent: people will not obey me. I have been pulling down houses; but the fire overtakes us faster than we can do it." That he needed no more soldiers; and that, for himself, he must go and refresh himself, having been up all night. So he left me, and I him, and walked home, seeing people all almost distracted, and no manner of means used to quench the fire. The houses, too, so very thick thereabouts, and full of matter for burning, as pitch and tar, in Thames Street; and warehouses of oil, and wines, and brandy, and other things. Here I saw Mr. Isaac Houblon, the handsome man, prettily dressed and dirty, at his door at Dowgate, receiving some of his brother's things, whose houses were on fire; and, as he says, have been removed twice already; and he doubts, as it soon proved, that they must be in a little time removed from his house also, which was a sad consideration. And to see the churches all filling with goods by people who themselves should have been quietly there at this time. By this time it was about twelve o'clock; and so home, and there find my guests, who were Mr. Wood and his wife Barbary Sheldon, and also Mr. Moone; she mighty fine, and her husband, for aught I see, a likely man. But Mr. Moone's design and mine, which was to look over my closet, and please him with the sight thereof, which he hath long desired, was wholly disappointed; for we were in great trouble and disturbance at this fire, not knowing what to think of it. However, we had an extraordinary good dinner, and as merry as at this time we could be. While at dinner, Mrs. Batelier came to enquire after Mr. Woolfe and Stanes, who, it seems, are related to them, whose houses in Fish Street are all burned, and they in a sad condition. She would not stay in the fright. Soon as dined, I and Moone away, and walked through the City, the streets full of nothing but people and horses and carts loaden with goods, ready to run over one another, and removing goods from one burned house to another. They now removing out of Canning Street, which received goods in the morning, into Lombard Street, and farther; and, among others, I now saw my little goldsmith, Stokes, receiving some friend's goods, whose house itself was burned the day after. We parted at Paul's; he home, and I to Paul's Wharf, where I had appointed a boat to attend me, and took in Mr. Carcasse and his brother, whom I met in the street, and carried them below and above bridge to and again to see the fire, which was now got farther, both below and above, and no likelihood of stopping it. Met with the King and Duke of York in their barge, and with them to Queenhithe, and there called Sir Richard Browne to them. Their order was only to pull down houses apace, and so below bridge at the waterside; but little was or could be done, the fire coming upon them so fast. Good hopes there was of stopping it at the Three Cranes above, and at Buttulph's Wharf below bridge, if care be used; but the wind carries it into the City, so as we know not by the waterside what it do there. River full of lighters and boats taking in goods, and good goods swimming in the water; and only I observed that hardly one lighter or boat in three that had the goods of a house in, but there was a pair of virginals in it. Having seen as much as I could now, I away to Whitehall by appointment, and there walked to St. James's Park; and there met my wife, and Creed, and Wood and his wife, and walked to my boat; and there upon the water again, and to the fire up and down, it still increasing, and the wind great. So near the fire as we could for smoke; and all over the Thames, with one's face in the wind, you were almost burned with a shower of fire-drops. This is very true; so as houses were burned by these drops and flakes of fire, three or four, nay, five or six houses, one from another. When we could endure no more upon the water, we to a little alehouse on the Bankside, over against the Three Cranes, and there stayed till it was dark almost, and saw the fire grow; and, as it grew darker, appeared more and more, and in corners and upon steeples, and between churches and houses, as far as we could see up the hill of the City, in a most horrid, malicious, bloody flame, not like the fine flame of an ordinary fire. Barbary and her husband away before us. We stayed till, it being darkish, we saw the fire as only one entire arch of fire from this to the other side the bridge, and in a bow up the hill for an arch of above a mile long: it made me weep to see it. The churches, houses, and all on fire, and flaming at once; and a horrid noise the flames made, and the cracking of houses at their ruin. So home with a sad heart, and there find everybody discoursing and lamenting the fire; and poor Tom Hater came with some few of his goods saved out of his house, which was burned upon Fish Street Hill. I invited him to lie at my house, and did receive his goods, but was deceived in his lying there, the news coming every moment of the growth of the fire; so as we were forced to begin to pack up our own goods, and prepare for their removal; and did by moonshine, it being brave dry, and moonshine, and warm weather, carry much of my goods into the garden; and Mr. Hater and I did remove my money and iron chests into my cellar, as thinking that the safest place. And got my bags of gold into my office, ready to carry away, and my chief papers of accounts also there, and my tallies into a box by themselves. So great was our fear, as Sir W. Batten hath carts come out of the country to fetch away his goods this night. We did put Mr. Hater, poor man! to bed a little; but he got very little rest, so much noise being in my house, taking down of goods.

3rd. About four o'clock in the morning, my Lady Batten sent me a cart to carry away all my money, and plate, and best things, to Sir W. Rider's, at Bednall Green. Which I did, riding myself in my nightgown, in the cart; and, Lord! to see how the streets and the highways are crowded with people running and riding, and getting of carts at any rate to fetch away things. I find Sir W. Rider tired with being called up all night, and receiving things from several friends. His house full of goods, and much of Sir W. Batten's and Sir W. Pen's. I am eased at my heart to have my treasure so well secured. Then home, and with much ado to find a way, nor any sleep all this night to me nor my poor wife. But then and all this day she and I and all my people labouring to get away the rest of our things, and did get Mr. Tooker to get me a lighter to take them in, and we did carry them, myself some, over Tower Hill, which was by this time full of people's goods, bringing their goods thither; and down to the lighter, which lay at the next quay, above the Tower Dock. And here was my neighbour's wife, Mrs. ———, with her pretty child, and some few of her things, which I did willingly give way to be saved with mine; but there was no passing with anything through the postern, the crowd was so great. The Duke of York came this day by the office, and spoke to us, and did ride with his guard up and down the City to keep all quiet, he being now General, and having the care of all. This day, Mercer being not at home, but against her mistress's order gone to her mother's, and my wife going thither to speak with W. Hewer, met her there, and was angry; and her mother saying that she was not a 'prentice girl, to ask leave every time she goes abroad, my wife with good reason was angry, and, when she came home, did bid her be gone again. And so she went away, which troubled me, but yet less than it would, because of the condition we are in, in fear of coming in a little time to being less able to keep one in her quality. At night lay down a little upon a quilt of W. Hewer's in the office, all my own things being packed up or gone; and after me my poor wife did the like, we having fed upon the remains of yesterday's dinner, having no fire nor dishes, nor any opportunity of dressing anything.

4th. Up by break of day, to get away the remainder of my things; which I did by a lighter at the Iron gate; and my hands so few, that it was the afternoon before we could get them all away. Sir W. Pen and I to the Tower Street, and there met the fire burning three or four doors beyond Mr. Howell's, whose goods, poor man, his trays, and dishes, shovels, etc., were flung all along Tower Street in the kennels, and people working therewith from one end to the other; the fire coming on in that narrow street, on both sides, with infinite fury. Sir W. Batten, not knowing how to remove his wine, did dig a pit in the garden, and laid it in there; and I took the opportunity of laying all the papers of my office that I could not otherwise dispose of. And in the evening Sir W. Pen and I did dig another, and put our wine in it; and I my parmesan cheese, as well as my wine and some other things. The Duke of York was at the Office this day, at Sir W. Pen's; but I happened not to be within. This afternoon, sitting melancholy with Sir W. Pen in our garden, and thinking of the certain burning of this office, without extraordinary means, I did propose for the sending up of all our workmen from the Woolwich and Deptford yards (none whereof yet appeared), and to write to Sir W. Coventry to have the Duke of York's permission to pull down

houses, rather than lose this office, which would much
hinder the King's business. So Sir W. Pen went
down this night, in order to the sending them up to-
morrow morning; and I wrote to Sir W. Coventry
about the business, but received no answer. This
night Mrs. Turner (who, poor woman, was removing
her goods all this day, good goods, into the garden, and
knows not how to dispose of them) and her husband
supped with my wife and me at night, in the office,
upon a shoulder of mutton from the cook's without
any napkin or anything, in a sad manner, but were
merry. Only now and then walking into the garden,
and saw how horribly the sky looks, all on a fire in the
night, was enough to put us out of our wits; and,
indeed, it was extremely dreadful, for it looks just as
if it was at us, and the whole heaven on fire. I after
supper walked in the dark down to Tower Street, and
there saw it all on fire, at the Trinity House on that
side, and the Dolphin Tavern on this side, which was
very near us; and the fire with extraordinary
vehemence. Now begins the practice of blowing up
of houses in Tower Street, those next the Tower,
which at first did frighten people more than anything;
but it stopped the fire where it was done, it bringing
down the houses to the ground in the same places they
stood, and then it was easy to quench what little fire
was in it, though it kindled nothing almost. W.
Hewer this day went to see how his mother did, and
comes late home, telling us how he hath been forced
to remove her to Islington, her house in Pye Corner
being burned; so that the fire is got so far that way,
and all the Old Bailey, and was running down to
Fleet Street; and Paul's is burned, and all Cheapside. I wrote to my father this night, but, the post-
house being burned, the letter could not go.

5th. I lay down in the office again upon W. Hewer's
quilt, being mighty weary, and sore in my feet with

going till I was hardly able to stand. About two in the morning my wife calls me up, and tells me of new cries of fire, it being come to Barking Church, which is the bottom of our lane. I up; and finding it so, resolved presently to take her away, and did, and took my gold, which was about £2350, W. Hewer and Jane down by Proundy's boat to Woolwich; but, Lord! what a sad sight it was by moonlight to see the whole City almost on fire, that you might see it as plain at Woolwich, as if you were by it. There, when I came, I find the gates shut, but no guard kept at all; which troubled me, because of discourses now begun, that there is a plot in it, and that the French had done it. I got the gates open, and to Mr. Sheldon's, where I locked up my gold, and charged my wife and W. Hewer never to leave the room without one of them in it, night or day. So back again, by the way seeing my goods well in the lighters at Deptford, and watched well by people. Home, and whereas I expected to have seen our house on fire, it being now about seven o'clock, it was not. But to the fire, and there find greater hopes than I expected; for my confidence of finding our office on fire was such, that I durst not ask anybody how it was with us, till I came and saw it was not burned. But, going to the fire, I find, by the blowing up of houses, and the great help given by the workmen out of the King's yards, sent up by Sir W. Pen, there is a good stop given to it, as well at Mark Lane end as ours; it having only burned the dial of Barking Church, and part of the porch, and was there quenched. I up to the top of Barking steeple, and there saw the saddest sight of desolation that I ever saw; everywhere great fires, oil-cellars, and brimstone, and other things burning. I became afraid to stay there long, and therefore down again as fast as I could, the fire being spread as far as I could see; and to Sir W. Pen's, and there ate a piece of cold meat, having eaten nothing since Sunday, but the remains of Sunday's dinner. Here I met with Mr. Young and Whistler; and, having removed all my things, and received good hopes that the fire at our end is stopped, they and I walked into the town, and find Fenchurch Street, Gracious Street, and Lombard Street all in dust. The Exchange a sad sight, nothing standing there of all the statues or pillars, but Sir Thomas Gresham's picture in the corner. Into Moorfields (our feet ready to burn, walking through the town among the hot coals), and find that full of people, and poor wretches carrying their goods there, and everybody keeping his goods together by themselves; and a great blessing it is to them that it is fair weather for them to keep abroad night and day; drank there, and paid twopence for a plain penny loaf. Thence homeward, having passed through Cheapside and Newgate market, all burned, and seen Anthony Joyce's house on fire; and took up, which I keep by me, a piece of glass of the Mercers' chapel in the street, where much more was, so melted and buckled with the heat of the fire like parchment. I also did see a poor cat taken out of a hole in a chimney, joining to the wall of the Exchange, with the hair all burned off the body, and yet alive. So home at night, and find there good hopes of saving our office; but great endeavours of watching all night, and having men ready; and so we lodged them in the office, and had drink and bread and cheese for them. And I lay down and slept a good night about midnight; though, when I rose, I heard that there had been a great alarm of French and Dutch being risen, which proved nothing. But it is a strange thing to see how long this time did look since Sunday, having been always full of variety of actions, and little sleep, that it looked like a week or more, and I had forgot almost the day of the week.

6th. Up about five o'clock, and met Mr. Gauden

at the gate of the office (I intending to go out, as I used, every now and then to-day, to see how the fire is) to call our men to Bishopsgate, where no fire had yet been near, and there is now one broke out; which did give great grounds to people, and to me too, to think that there is some kind of plot in this, on which many by this time have been taken, and it hath been dangerous for any stranger to walk in the streets, but I went with the men, and we did put it out in a little time; so that that was well again. It was pretty to see how hard the women did the work in the cannels, sweeping of water; but then they would scold for drink, and be as drunk as devils. I saw good butts of sugar broken open in the street, and people give and take handfuls out, and put into beer, and drink it. And now all being pretty well, I took boat, and over to Southwark, and took boat on the other side the bridge, and so to Westminster, thinking to shift myself, being all in dirt from top to bottom; but could not there find any place to buy a shirt or pair of gloves. Westminster Hall being full of people's goods, those in Westminster having removed all their goods, and the Exchequer money put into vessels to carry to Nonsuch; but to the Swan, and there was trimmed: and then to Whitehall, but saw nobody; and so home. A sad sight to see how the river looks; no houses nor church near it, to the Temple, where it stopped. At home did go with Sir W. Batten, and our neighbour, Knightly (who, with one more, was the only man of any fashion left in all the neighbourhood thereabouts, they all removing their goods and leaving their houses to the mercy of the fire), to Sir R. Ford's, and there dined in an earthen platter—a fried breast of mutton; a great many of us, but very merry, and indeed as good a meal, though as ugly a one, as ever I had in my life. Thence down to Deptford, and there with great satisfaction landed all my goods at Sir G. Carteret's safe, and nothing missed I could see, or hurt. This being done to my great content, I home, and to Sir W. Batten's, and there, with Sir R. Ford, Mr. Knightly, and one Withers, a professed lying rogue, supped well, and mighty merry, and our fears over. From them to the office, and there slept with the office full of labourers, who talked, and slept, and walked all night long there. But strange it was to see Clothworkers' Hall on fire these three days and nights in one body of flame, it being the cellar full of oil.

7th. Up by five o'clock; and, blessed be God! find all well; and by water to Paul's Wharf. Walked thence, and saw all the town burned, and a miserable sight of Paul's church, with all the roofs fallen, and the body of the choir fallen into St. Faith's; Paul's school also, Ludgate and Fleet Street; my father's house, and the church, and a good part of the Temple the like. So to Creed's lodging, near the New Exchange, and there find him laid down upon a bed; the house all unfurnished, there being fears of the fire's coming to them. There borrowed a shirt of him, and washed. To Sir W. Coventry at St. James's, who lay without curtains, having removed all his goods; as the King at Whitehall, and everybody had done, and was doing. He hopes we shall have no public distractions upon this fire, which is what everybody fears, because of the talk of the French having a hand in it. And it is a proper time for discontents; but all men's minds are full of care to protect themselves and save their goods: the militia is in arms everywhere. Our fleets, he tells me, have been in sight one of another, and most unhappily by foul weather were parted, to our great loss, as in reason they do conclude; the Dutch being come out only to make a show, and please their people; but in very bad condition as to stores, victuals, and men. They are at Boulogne, and our fleet come to St. Ellen's. We have got nothing, but have lost one ship, but he knows not what. Thence to the Swan, and there drank; and so home, and find all well. My Lord Brouncker, at Sir W. Batten's, tells us the General is sent for up, to come to advise with the King about business at this juncture, and to keep all quiet; which is great honour to him, but I am sure is but a piece of dissimulation. So home, and did give orders for my house to be made clean; and then down to Woolwich, and there find all well. Dined, and Mrs. Markham came to see my wife. This day our Merchants first met at Gresham College, which, by proclamation, is to be their Exchange. Strange to hear what is bid for houses all up and down here; a friend of Sir W. Rider's having £150 for what he used to let for £40 per annum. Much dispute where the Custom House shall be; thereby the growth of the City again to be foreseen. My Lord Treasurer, they say, and others, would have it at the other end of the town. I home late to Sir W. Pen's, who did give me a bed, but without curtains or hangings, all being down. So here I went the first time into a naked bed, only my drawers on; and did sleep pretty well; but still both sleeping and waking had a fear of fire in my heart, that I took little rest. People do all the world over cry out of the simplicity of my Lord Mayor in general; and more particularly in this business of the fire, laying it all upon him. A proclamation is come out for markets to be kept at Leadenhall and Mile End Green, and several other places about the town; and Tower Hill, and all churches to be set open to receive poor people.

8th. I stopped with Sir G. Carteret to desire him to go with us, and to enquire after money. But the first he cannot do, and the other as little, or says, " when we can get any, or what shall we do for it ? " He, it seems, is employed in the correspondence between the City and the King every day, in settling of things. I find him full of trouble to think how things will go. I left him, and to St. James's, where we met first at Sir W. Coventry's chamber, and there did what business we could, without any books. Our discourse, as everything else, was confused. The fleet is at Portsmouth, there staying a wind to carry them to the Downs, or towards Boulogne, where they say the Dutch fleet is gone, and stays. We concluded upon private meetings for a while, not having any money to satisfy any people that may come to us. I bought two eels upon the Thames, cost me six shillings. Thence with Sir W. Batten to the Cockpit, whither the Duke of Albemarle is come. It seems the King holds him so necessary at this time, that he hath sent for him, and will keep him here. Indeed, his interest in the City, being acquainted, and his care in keeping things quiet, is reckoned that wherein he will be very serviceable. We to him: he is courted in appearance by everybody. He very kind to us; and I perceive he lays by all business of the fleet at present, and minds the City, and is now hastening to Gresham College, to discourse with the Aldermen. Sir W. Batten and I home, where met my brother John, come to town to see how things are done with us, and then presently he with me to Gresham College; where infinity of people, partly through novelty to see the new place, and partly to find out and hear what is become one man of another. I met with many people undone, and more that have extraordinary great losses. People speaking their thoughts variously about the beginning of the fire, and the rebuilding of the City. Then to Sir W. Batten's, and took my brother with me, and there dined with a great company of neighbours, and much good discourse; among others, of the low spirits of some rich men in the City, in sparing any encouragement to the poor people that wrought for the saving their houses. Among others, Alderman Starling, a very rich man, without children, the fire at next door to him in our lane, after our men had saved his house, did give 2s. 6d. among thirty of them, and did quarrel with some that would remove the rubbish out of the way of the fire, saying that they came to steal. Sir W. Coventry told me of another this morning in Holborn, which he showed the King: that when it was offered to stop the fire near his house for such a reward that came to but 2s. 6d. a man among the neighbours he would give but 18d. Thence to Bednall Green by coach, my brother with me, and saw all well there, and fetched away my journal-book, to enter for five days past. I was much frighted and kept awake in my bed by some noise I heard a great while below stairs; and the boy's not coming up to me when I knocked. It was by their discovery of some people stealing of some neighbour's wine that lay in vessels in the streets. So to sleep; and all well all night.

9th. (Sunday.) Up; and was trimmed, and sent my brother to Woolwich to my wife, to dine with her. I to church, where our parson made a melancholy but good sermon; and many and most in the church cried, specially the women. The church mighty full; but few of fashion, and most strangers. I walked to Bednall Green, and there dined well (but a bad venison pasty) at Sir W. Rider's. Good people they are, and good discourse; and his daughter, Middleton, a fine woman, discreet. Thence home, and to church again, and there preached Dean Harding; but, me-thinks a bad poor sermon, though proper for the time; nor eloquent, in saying at this time that the City is reduced from a large folio to a decimo-tertio. So to my office, there to write down my journal, and take leave of my brother, whom I sent back this afternoon, though raining, which it hath not done a good while before. But I had no room or convenience for him here till my house is fitted; but I was very kind to him, and to take very well of him his journey. I did give him 40s. for his pocket, and so, he being gone, and it presently raining, I was troubled for him, though it is good for the fire. Anon to Sir W. Pen's to bed, and make my boy Tom to read me asleep.

15th. Captain Cocke says he hath computed that the rents of the houses lost by this fire in the City comes to £600,000 per annum; that this will make the Parliament more quiet than otherwise they would have been, and give the King a more ready supply; that the supply must be by excise, as it is in Holland; that the Parliament will see it necessary to carry on the war; that the late storm hindered our beating the Dutch fleet, who were gone out only to satisfy the people, having no business to do but to avoid us; that the French, as late in the year as it is, are coming; that the Dutch are really in bad condition, but that this unhappiness of ours do give them heart; that there was a late difference between my Lord Arlington and Sir W. Coventry about neglect in the latter to send away an express of the other's in time; that it came before the King, and the Duke of York concerned himself in it; but this fire hath stopped it. The Dutch fleet is not gone home, but rather to the North, and so dangerous to our Gottenburgh fleet. That the Parliament is likely to fall foul upon some persons; and, among others, on the Vice-chamberlain; though, we both believe, with little ground. That certainly never so great a loss as this was borne so well by citizens in the world; he believing that not one merchant upon the 'Change will break upon it. That he do not apprehend there will be any disturbance in State upon it; for that all men are busy in looking after their own business to save themselves. He gone, I to finish my letters, and home to bed; and find, to my infinite joy, many rooms clean; and myself and wife lie in our own chamber again. But much terrified in the nights nowadays with dreams of fire and falling down of houses.

23rd. (Lord's day.) Mr. Wayth and I by water to Whitehall, and there at Sir G. Carteret's lodgings Sir W. Coventry met, and we did debate the whole business of our accounts to the Parliament; where it appears to us that the charge of the war from September 1, 1664 to this Michaelmas will have been but £3,200,000, and we have paid, in that time, somewhat about £2,200,000; so that we owe above £900,000: but our method of accounting, though it cannot, I believe, be far wide from the mark, yet will not abide a strict examination if the Parliament should be troublesome. Here happened a pretty question of Sir W. Coventry, whether this account of ours will not put my Lord Treasurer to a difficulty to tell what is become of all the money the Parliament have given in this time for the war, which hath amounted to about £4,000,000, which nobody there could answer; but I perceive they did doubt what his answer could be. My wife and I for pleasure to Foxhall, and there ate and drank, and so back home.

26th. By coach home, calling at Bennet's, our late mercer, who is come into Covent Garden to a fine house, looking down upon the Exchange; and I perceive many Londoners every day come; and Mr. Pierce hath let his wife's closet, and the little blind bedchamber, and a garret to a silk-man for £50 fine, and £30 per annum, and £40 per annum more for dieting the master and two prentices. By Mr. Dugdale I hear the great loss of books in St. Paul's Churchyard, and at their Hall also, which they value at about £150,000; some booksellers being wholly undone, and among others, they say, my poor Kirton. And Mr. Crumlum, all his books and household stuff burned; they trusting to St. Faith's, and the roof of the church falling broke the arch down into the lower church, and so all the goods burned. A very great loss. His father hath lost above £1000 in books; one book newly printed, a Discourse, it seems, of Courts. Here I had the hap to see my Lady Denham; and at night went into the dining-room, and saw several fine ladies; among others, Castlemaine, but chiefly Denham again: and the Duke of York, taking her aside and talking to her in the sight of all the world, all alone; which was strange, and what I also did not like. Mr. Evelyn observes that none of the nobility come out of the country at all to help the King, or comfort him, or prevent commotions at this fire, but do as if the King were nobody; nor ne'er a priest comes to give the King and Court good counsel, or to comfort the poor people that suffer; but all is dead, nothing of good in any of their minds: he bemoans it, and says he fears more ruin hangs over our heads. My wife tells me she hath bought a gown of 15s. a yard; the same, before her face, my Lady Castlemaine this day bought also, which I seemed vexed for, though I do not grudge it her, but to incline her to have Mercer again. Our business was tendered to the House to-day, and a Committee of the whole House chosen to examine our accounts, and a great many Hotspurs enquiring into it. Sir W. Pen proposes his and my looking out into Scotland about timber, and to use Pett there; for timber will be a good commodity this time of building the City. Our fleet abroad, and the Dutch too, for all we know; the weather very bad; and under the command of an unlucky man, I fear. God bless him, and the fleet under him!

October 1666

October 7th. (Lord's day.) To Whitehall, where met by Sir W. Batten and Lord Brouncker, to attend the King and Duke of York at the Cabinet; but nobody had determined what to speak of, but only in general to ask for money. So I was forced immediately to prepare in my mind a method of discoursing. And anon we were called in to the Green Room, where the King, Duke of York, Prince Rupert, Lord Chancellor, Lord Treasurer, Duke of Albemarle, Sirs G. Carteret, W. Coventry, Morrice. Nobody beginning, I did, and made a current, and, I thought, a good speech, laying open the ill state of the Navy: by the greatness of the debt; greatness of the work to do against next year; the time and materials it would take; and our incapacity, through a total want of money. I had no sooner done, but Prince Rupert rose up and told the King, in a heat, that whatever the gentleman had said, he had brought home his fleet in as good a condition as ever any fleet was brought home; that twenty boats would be as many as the fleet would want; and all the anchors and cables left in the storm might be taken up again. This arose from my saying, among other things we had to do, that the fleet was come in—the greatest fleet that ever his Majesty had yet together, and that in as bad condition as the enemy or weather could put it; and to use Sir W. Pen's words, who is upon the place taking a survey, he dreads the reports he is to receive from the Surveyors of its defects. I therefore did only answer, that I was sorry for his Highness's offence, but that what I said was but the report we received from those entrusted in the fleet to inform us. He muttered and repeated what he had said; and so, after a long silence on all hands, nobody, not so much as the Duke of Albemarle, seconding the Prince, nor taking notice of what he said, we withdrew. I was not a little troubled at this passage, and the more when speaking with Jack Fenn about it, he told me that the Prince will be asking who this Pepys is, and find him to be a creature of my Lord Sandwich's, and therefore this was done only to disparage him. Anon they broke up, and Sir W. Coventry came out; so I asked his advice. He told me he had said something to salve it, which was, that his Highness had, he believed, rightly informed the King that the fleet is come in good condition to have stayed out yet longer, and have fought the enemy, but yet that Mr. Pepys his meaning might be that, though in so good condition, if they should come in and lie all the winter, we shall be very loath to send them to sea for another year's service without great repairs. He said it would be no hurt if I went to him, and showed him the report himself brought up from the fleet, where every ship, by the Commander's report, do need more or less, and not to mention more of Sir W. Pen for doing him a mischief. So I said I would, but do not think that all this will redound to my hurt, because the truth of what I said will soon appear. Thence, having been informed that, after all this pains, the King hath found out how to supply us with £5000 or £6000, when £100,000 were at this time but absolutely necessary, and we mention £50,000. This is every day a greater and greater omen of ruin. God fit us for it! I made my brother, in his cassock, to say his grace this day, but I like his voice so ill, that I begin to be sorry he hath taken this order.

November 1666

November 10th. The Parliament did fall foul of our accounts again yesterday; and we must arm to have them examined, which I am sorry for; it will bring great trouble to me, and shame upon the office. With my Lord Brouncker and Sir Thomas Harvy to Cocke's house, and there Mrs. Williams and other company, and an excellent dinner. Mr. Temple's wife, after dinner, fell to play on the harpsichon, till she so tired everybody, that I left the house without taking leave, and no creature left standing by her to hear her. Read an hour, to make an end of Potter's *Discourse of 666*, which I like all along, but his close is most excellent; and, whether it be right or wrong, is mighty ingenious. This is the fatal day that everybody hath discoursed for a long time to be the day that the Papists, or I know not who, have designed to commit a massacre upon; but, however, I trust in God we shall rise to-morrow morning as well as ever. I hear that my Lady Denham is exceeding sick, even to death, and that she says, and everybody else discourses, that she is poisoned; and Creed tells me that it is said that there hath been a design to poison the King. What the meaning of all these sad signs is, the Lord only knows; but every day things look worse and worse. God fit us for the worst!

14th. Dr. Croone told me that, at the meeting at Gresham College to-night, which, it seems, they now have every Wednesday again, there was a pretty experiment of the blood of one dog let out, till he died, into the body of another on one side, while all his own ran out on the other side. The first died upon the place, and the other very well, and likely to do well. This did give occasion to many pretty wishes, as of the blood of a Quaker to be let into an Archbishop, and such like; but, as Dr. Croone says, may, if it takes, be of mighty use to man's health, for the amending of bad blood by borrowing from a better body.

December 1666

December 17th. Spent the evening in fitting my books, to have the number set upon each, in order to my having an alphabet of my whole, which will be of great ease to me.

19th. Talked of the King's family with Mr. Hingston, the organist. He says many of the music are ready to starve, they being five years behindhand for their wages; nay, Evans, the famous man upon the harp, having not his equal in the world, did the other day die for mere want, and was fain to be buried at the alms of the parish, and carried to his grave in the dark at night without one link, but that Mr. Hingston met it by chance, and did give 12d. to buy two or three links. Thence home, and upon Tower Hill saw about 300 or 400 seamen get together; and one, standing upon a pile of bricks, made his sign, with his handkercher, upon his stick, and called all the rest to him, and several shouts they gave. This made me afraid; so I got home as fast as I could. But by and by Sir W. Batten and Sir R. Ford do tell me, that the seamen have been at some prisons to release some seamen, and the Duke of Albemarle is in arms, and all the Guards at the other end of the town; and the Duke of Albemarle is gone with some forces to Wapping, to quell the seamen; which is a thing of infinite disgrace to us. I sat long talking with them; and among other things, Sir R. Ford made me understand how the House of Commons is a beast not to be understood, it being impossible to know beforehand the success almost of any small plain thing, there being so many to think and speak to any business, and they of so uncertain minds and interests and passions. He did tell me, and so did Sir W. Batten, how Sir Allen Broderick and Sir Allen Apsly did come drunk the other day into the House, and did both speak for half an hour together, and could not be either laughed, or pulled, or bid to sit down and hold their peace, to the great contempt of the King's servants and cause; which I am grieved at with all my heart.

25th. (Christmas day.) Lay pretty long in bed, and then rose, leaving my wife desirous to sleep, having sat up till four this morning seeing her maids make mince-pies. I to church, where our parson Mills made a good sermon. Then home, and dined well on some good ribs of beef roasted and mince-pies; only my wife, brother, and Barker, and plenty of good wine of my own, and my heart full of true joy; and thanks to God Almighty for the goodness of my condition at this day. After dinner I began to teach my wife and Barker my song, "It is decreed," which pleases me mightily. Walked alone on foot to the Temple, thinking to have seen a play all alone; but there, missing of any bills, concluded there was none, and so back home; and there with my brother reducing the names of all my books to an alphabet, and then to supper and to bed.

January 1667

January 20th. I to church, and there, beyond expectation, find our seat, and all the church, crammed by twice as many people as used to be; and to my great joy find Mr. Frampton in the pulpit; and I think the best sermon, for goodness and oratory, without affectation or study, that ever I heard in my life. The truth is, he preaches the most like an apostle that ever I heard man; and it was much the best time that I ever spent in my life at church. His text, Ecclesiastes xi., verse 8th,— "But if a man live many years, and rejoice in them all, yet let him remember the days of darkness, for they shall be many. All that cometh is vanity."

23rd. To take up my wife and Mercer, and to Temple Bar to the Ordinary, and had a dish of meat for them, they having not dined, and thence to the King's house, and there saw *The Humorous Lieutenant*: a silly play, I think; only the Spirit in it that grows very tall, and then sinks again to nothing, having two heads breeding upon one, and then Knipp's singing, did please us. Here, in a box above, we spied Mrs. Pierce; and, going out, they called us, and so we stayed for them; and Knipp took us all in, and brought to us Nelly, a most pretty woman, who acted the great part of Celia to-day very fine, and did it pretty well: I kissed her, and so did my wife; and a mighty pretty soul she is.

February 1667

February 2nd. This night comes home my new silver snuff-dish, which I do give myself for my closet. I am very well pleased this night with reading a poem I brought home with me last night from Westminster Hall, of Dryden's upon the present war; a very good poem.

5th. All the talk is that my Lord Sandwich hath perfected the peace with Spain; which is very good, if true. To the King's house, to see *The Chances*. A good play I find it, and the actors most good in it; and pretty to hear Knipp sing in the play very properly, "All night I weep"; and sang it admirably.

The whole play pleases me well; and most of all, the sight of many fine ladies—among others, my Lady Castlemaine and Mrs. Middleton: the latter of the two hath also a very excellent face and body, I think. Thence by coach to the New Exchange, and there laid out money, and I did give Betty Michell two pair of gloves and a dressing-box; and so home in the dark, over the ruins, with a link. To the office. There came to me Mr. Young and Whistler, flag-makers, and with mighty earnestness did present me with, and press me to take a box, wherein I could not guess there was less than £100 in gold; but I do wholly refuse, and did not at last take it. The truth is, not thinking them safe men to receive such a gratuity from, nor knowing any considerable courtesy that ever I did do them, but desirous to keep myself free from their reports, and to have it in my power to say I had refused their offer.

7th. Talking with my brother upon matters relating to his journey to Brampton to-morrow, I looking another way heard him fall down, and turned my head, and he was fallen down all along upon the ground dead, which did put me into a great fright; and, to see my brotherly love! I did presently lift him up from the ground, he being as pale as death; and, being upon his legs, he did presently come to himself, and said he had something come into his stomach very hot. He knew not what it was, nor ever had such a fit before. To the office, late doing business, and then home, and find my brother pretty well. I did this night give him 20s. for books, and as much for his pocket, and 15s. to carry him down. Poor fellow! he is so melancholy, and withal, my wife says, harmless, that I begin to love him, and would be loath he should not do well.

10th. (Lord's day.) To church, where Mr. Mills made an unnecessary sermon upon Original Sin, neither understood by himself nor the people. Home, where came Mr. Carter, my old acquaintance of Magdalene College, who hath not been here of many years. He hath spent his time in the country with the Bishop of Carlisle much. He is grown a very comely person, and of good discourse, and one that I like very much. We had much talk of all our old acquaintance of the College, concerning their various fortunes; wherein, to my joy, I met not with any that have sped better than myself.

12th. With my Lord Brouncker by coach to his house, there to hear some Italian music; and here we met Tom Killigrew, Sir Robert Murray, and the Italian Signor Baptista, who hath composed a play in Italian for the Opera, which T. Killigrew do intend to have up; and here he did sing one of the acts. He himself is the poet as well as the musician; which is very much; and did sing the whole from the words without any music pricked, and played all along upon a harpsicon most admirably, and the composition most excellent. The words I did not understand, and so know not how they are fitted, but believe very well, and all in the recitativo very fine. But I perceive there is a proper accent in every country's discourse, and that do reach in their setting of notes to words, which, therefore, cannot be natural to anybody else but them; so that I am not so much smitten with it as, it may be, I should be, if I were acquainted with their accent. But the whole composition is certainly most excellent; and the poetry, T. Killigrew and Sir R. Murray, who understood the words, did say most excellent. I confess I was mightily pleased with the music. He pretends not to voice, though it be good, but not excellent. This done, T. Killigrew and I to talk; and he tells me how the audience at his house is not above half so much as it used to be before the late fire. That

Knipp is like to make the best actor that ever came upon the stage, she understanding so well: that they are going to give her £30 a year more. That the stage is now by his pains a thousand times better and more glorious than ever heretofore. Now, wax-candles, and many of them; then, not above 3 lbs. of tallow: now, all things civil, no rudeness any-where; then, as in a bear-garden: then, two or three fiddlers; now, nine or ten of the best: then, nothing but rushes upon the ground, and everything else mean; now, all otherwise: then, the Queen seldom and the King never would come; now, not the King only for state, but all civil people do think they may come as well as any. He tells me that he hath gone several times, eight or ten times he tells me, hence to Rome, to hear good music; so much he loves it, though he never did sing or play a note. That he hath ever endeavoured in the late King's time and in this to introduce good music, but he never could do it, there never having been any music here better than ballads. Nay, says " Hermit poor " and " Chevy Chase " was all the music we had; and yet no ordinary fiddlers get so much money as ours do here, which speaks our rudeness still. That he hath gathered our Italians from several Courts in Christendom, to come to make a concert for the King, which he do give £200 a year apiece to: but badly paid, and do come in the room of keeping four ridiculous gondolas, he having got the King to put them away, and lay out money this way; and indeed I do commend him for it, for I think it is a very noble undertaking. He do intend to have some times of the year these operas to be performed at the two present theatres, since he is defeated in what he intended in Moorfields on purpose for it; and he tells me plainly that the City audience was as good as the Court, but now they are most gone. Baptista

tells me that Giacomo Charissimi is still alive at
Rome, who was master to Vinnecotio, who is one of
the Italians that the King hath here, and the chief
composer of them. My great wonder is, how this
man do to keep in memory so perfectly the music
of the whole act, both for the voice and the instrument too. I confess I do admire it : but in recitativo
the sense much helps him, for there is but one proper
way of discoursing and giving the accents. Having
done our discourse, we all took coaches, my Lord's
and T. Killigrew's, and to Mrs. Knipp's chamber,
where this Italian is to teach her to sing her part.
And so we all thither, and there she did sing an
Italian song or two very fine, while he played the
bass upon a harpsicon there; and exceedingly taken
I am with her singing, and believe that she will do
miracles at that and acting. Her little girl is mighty
pretty and witty.

25th. Lay long in bed, talking with pleasure with
my poor wife, how she used to make coal fires, and
wash my foul clothes with her own hand for me, poor
wretch! in our little room at my Lord Sandwich's;
for which I ought for ever to love and admire her,
and do; and persuade myself she would do the same
thing again, if God should reduce us to it. At my
goldsmith's did observe the King's new medal, where,
in little, there is Mrs. Stewart's face as well done as
ever I saw anything in my whole life, I think; and
a pretty thing it is, that he should choose her face
to represent Britannia by.

March 1667

March 1st. In Mark Lane I do observe, it being
St. David's day, the picture of a man dressed like a
Welshman, hanging by the neck upon one of the
poles that stand out at the top of one of the merchants'

houses, in full proportion, and very handsomely done; which is one of the oddest sights I have seen a good while. Being returned home, I find Greeting, the flageolet-master, come, and teaching my wife; and I do think my wife will take pleasure in it, and it will be easy for her, and pleasant. So to the office, and then before dinner making my wife to sing. Poor wretch! her ear is so bad that it made me angry, till the poor wretch cried to see me so vexed at her, that I think I shall not discourage her so much again, but will endeavour to make her understand sounds, and do her good that way; for she hath a great mind to learn, only to please me. Tom Woodall, the known surgeon, is killed at Somerset House by a Frenchman.

2nd. After dinner with my wife to the King's house to see *The Maiden Queen*, a new play of Dryden's, mightily commended for the regularity of it, and the strain and wit; and the truth is, there is a comical part done by Nell which is Florimel, that I never can hope ever to see the like done again, by man or woman. The King and Duke of York were at the play. But so great performance of a comical part was never, I believe, in the world before as Nell do this, both as a mad girl, then most and best of all when she comes in like a young gallant; and hath the motions and carriage of a spark the most that ever I saw any man have. It makes me, I confess, admire her.

12th. Up, and to the office, where all the morning. At noon home, and there find Mr. Goodgroome, whose teaching of my wife only by singing over and over again to her, and letting her sing with him, not by herself, to correct her faults, I do not like at all, but was angry at it; but have this content, that I do think she will come to sing pretty well, and to trill in time, which pleases me well. This day a poor seaman, almost starved for want of food, lay in our yard a-dying. I sent him half-a-crown, and we ordered his ticket to be paid.

27th. Received from my brother the news of my mother's dying on Monday, about five or six o'clock in the afternoon, and that the last time she spoke of her children was on Friday last, and her last words were, " God bless my poor Sam ! " The reading hereof did set me a-weeping heartily. Found it necessary to go abroad with my wife to look after the providing mourning to send into the country—some tomorrow, and more against Sunday, for my family, being resolved to put myself and wife, and Barker and Jane, W. Hewer and Tom, in mourning, and my two under-maids, to give them hoods and scarfs and gloves. So to my tailor's, and up and down, and then home, and to bed, my heart sad, though my judgment at ease.

April 1667

April 11th. To Whitehall, thinking there to have seen the Duchess of Newcastle's coming this night to Court, to make a visit to the Queen, the King having been with her yesterday, to make her a visit since her coming to town. The whole story of this lady is a romance, and all she does is romantic. Her footmen in velvet coats, and herself in antique dress, as they say; and was the other day at her own play, *The Humorous Lovers*; the most ridiculous thing that ever was wrote, but yet she and her Lord mightily pleased with it; and she, at the end, made her respects to the players from her box, and did give them thanks. There is as much expectation of her coming to Court, that so people may come to see her, as if it were the Queen of Sheba : but I lost my labour, for she did not come this night. There have been two fires in the City within this week.

12th. Coming home, saw my door and hatch open, left so by Luce, our cookmaid, which so vexed me, that I did give her a kick in our entry, and offered a blow at her, and was seen doing so by Sir W. Pen's footboy, which did vex me to the heart, because I know he will be telling their family of it.

28th. (Lord's day.) After dinner, by water, the day being mighty pleasant, and the tide serving finely, reading in Boyle's book of colours, as high as Barn Elms, and there took one turn alone, and then back to Putney Church, where I saw the girls of the schools, few of which pretty; and there I came into a pew, and met with little James Pierce, which I was much pleased at, the little rogue being very glad to see me: his master, Reader to the Church. Here was a good sermon and much company, but I sleepy, and a little out of order, at my hat falling down through a hole beneath the pulpit, which, however, after sermon, by a stick, and the help of the clerk, I got up again. And so by water, the tide being with me again, down to Deptford.

May 1667

May 1st. To Westminster; in the way meeting many milkmaids with their garlands upon their pails, dancing with a fiddler before them; and saw pretty Nelly standing at her lodgings' door in Drury Lane in her smock sleeves and bodice, looking upon one; she seemed a mighty pretty creature.

7th. To St. James's; but there find Sir W. Coventry gone out betimes this morning, on horseback, with the King and Duke of York, to Putney Heath, to run some horses.

11th. My wife being dressed this day in fair hair did make me so mad, that I spoke not one word to her, though I was ready to burst with anger. After that, Creed and I into the Park, and walked, a most pleasant evening, and so took coach, and took up my wife, and in my way home discovered my trouble to my wife for her white locks, swearing several times, which I pray God forgive me for, and bending my fist, that I would not endure it. She, poor wretch, was surprised with it, and made me no answer all the way home; but there we parted, and I to the office late, and then home, and without supper to bed, vexed.

12th. (Lord's day.) Up, and to my chamber, to settle some accounts there, and by and by down comes my wife to me in her night-gown, and we began calmly, that, upon having money to lace her gown for second mourning, she would promise to wear white locks no more in my sight, which I, like a severe fool, thinking not enough, began to except against, and made her fly out to very high terms and cry, and in her heat, told me of keeping company with Mrs. Knipp, saying, that if I would promise never to see her more—of whom she hath more reason to suspect than I had heretofore of Pembleton—she would never wear white locks more. This vexed me, but I restrained myself from saying anything, but do think never to see this woman—at least, to have her here more: and so all very good friends as ever. My wife and I bethought ourselves to go to a French house to dinner, and so inquired out Monsieur Robins, my periwig-maker, who keeps an ordinary, and in an ugly street in Covent Garden, did find him at the door, and so we in; and in a moment almost had the table covered, and clean glasses, and all in the French manner, and a mess of potage first, and then a piece of bœuf-à-la-mode, all exceeding well seasoned, and to our great liking; at least it would have been any-where else but in this bad street, and in a periwig-maker's house; but to see the pleasant and ready attendance that we had, and all things so desirous to please, and ingenious in the people, did take me mightily. Our dinner cost us 6s. Walked over the fields to Kingsland, and back again; a walk, I think, I have not taken these twenty years; but puts me in mind of my boy's time, when I boarded at Kingsland, and used to shoot with my bow and arrows in these fields. A very pretty place it is; and little did any of my friends think I should come to walk in these fields in this condition and state that I am. Then took coach again, and home through Shoreditch; and at home my wife finds Barker to have been abroad, and telling her so many lies about it, that she struck her, and the wench said she would not stay with her; so I examined the wench, and found her in so many lies myself, that I was glad to be rid of her, and so resolved having her go away to-morrow.

26th. (Lord's day.) My wife and I to church, where several strangers of good condition came to our pew. After dinner I by water alone to West-minster to the parish church, and there did entertain myself with my perspective glass up and down the church, by which I had the great pleasure of seeing and gazing at a great many very fine women; and what with that, and sleeping, I passed away the time till sermon was done. I away to my boat, and, up with it as far as Barn Elms, reading of Mr. Evelyn's late new book against Solitude, in which I do not find much excess of good matter, though it be pretty for a bye discourse. I walked the length of the Elms, and with great pleasure saw some gallant ladies and people come with their bottles, and basket, and chairs, and form, to sup under the trees, by the waterside, which was mighty pleasant; so home. All our dis-course about Brampton, and my intentions to build there if I could be free of my engagement to my Uncle Thomas and his son, that they may not have what I have built, against my will, in case of me and my brothers being without heirs male; which is the true reason why I am against laying out money upon that place, together with my fear of some inconvenience by being so near Hinchingbroke; being obliged to be a servant to that family, and subject to what expense they shall cost me; and to have all that I shall buy, or do, esteemed as got by the death of my uncle, when indeed what I have from him is not worth naming.

27th. Abroad, and stopped at Bear Garden stairs, there to see a prize fought. But the house so full there was no getting in there, so forced to go through an ale-house into the pit, where the bears are baited; and upon a stool did see them fight, which they did very furiously, a butcher and a waterman. The former had the better all along, till by and by the latter dropped his sword out of his hand, and the butcher, whether not seeing his sword dropped I know not, but did give him a cut over the wrist, so as he was disabled to fight any longer. But, Lord! to see how in a minute the whole stage was full of watermen to revenge the foul play, and the butchers to defend their fellow, though most blamed him; and there they all fell to it to knocking down and cutting many on each side. It was pleasant to see, but that I stood in the pit, and feared that in the tumult I might get some hurt. At last the rabble broke up, and so I away.

31st. Late to supper, and with great quiet to bed; finding by the balance of my account that I am creditor £6900, for which the Lord of Heaven be praised!

June 1667

June 4th. Mr. Commander tells me, after all, that I cannot have a lease of the ground for my coach-house and stable, till a suit in law be ended. I am a little sorry, because I am pretty full in my mind of keeping a coach; but yet, when I think of it again, the Dutch and French both at sea, and we poor, and still out of order, I know not yet what turns there may be.

5th. To the Commissioners of the Treasury, and, after long waiting, I find them all sat; and, among the rest, Duncomb lolling, with his heels upon another chair, by that that he sat upon. Captain Perriman brings us word how the *Happy Return's* crew below in the Hope, ordered to carry the Portuguese Ambassador to Holland (and the Ambassador, I think, on board), refuse to go till paid; and by their example two or three more ships are in a mutiny; which is a sad consideration, while so many of the enemy's ships are at this day triumphing in the sea. Sir G. Carteret showed me a gentleman coming by in his coach, who hath been sent for up out of Lincolnshire, I think he says he is a justice of peace, that the Council have laid by the heels here, and here lies in a messenger's hands, for saying that a man and his wife are but one person, and so ought to pay but 12d. for both to the Poll Bill; by which others were led to do the like; and so here he lies prisoner.

10th. Up; and news brought us that the Dutch are come up as high as the Nore; and more pressing orders for fire-ships. W. Batten, W. Pen, and I to St. James's; where the Duke of York gone this morning betimes, to send away some men down to Chatham. So we three to Whitehall, and met Sir W. Coventry, who presses all that is possible for fire-ships. So we three to the office presently; and thither comes Sir Fretcheville Hollis, who is to command them all in some exploits he is to do with them on the enemy in the River. So we all down to Deptford, and pitched upon ships and set men at work:

but, Lord! to see how backwardly things move at this pinch, notwithstanding that, by the enemy's being now come up as high as almost the Hope, Sir J. Minnes, who was gone down to pay some ships there, hath sent up the money; and so we are possessed of money to do what we will with. Yet partly ourselves, being used to be idle and in despair, and partly people that have been used to be deceived by us as to money won't believe us; and we know not, though we have it, how almost to promise it; and our wants such, and men out of the way, that it is an admirable thing to consider how much the King suffers, and how necessary it is in a State to keep the King's service always in a good posture and credit.

11th. Brouncker came to us, who is just now going to Chatham upon a desire of Commissioner Pett's, who is very fearful of the Dutch, and desires help for God and the King and kingdom's sake. So Brouncker goes down, and Sir J. Minnes also, from Gravesend. This morning Pett writes us word that Sheerness is lost last night, after two or three hours' dispute. The enemy hath possessed himself of that place; which is very sad, and puts us into great fears of Chatham. After dinner, by W. Hewer's lucky advice, went to Mr. Fenn, and did get him to pay me about £400 of my wages, and W. Hewer received it for me, and brought it home this night. Home, and there to our business, hiring some fire-ships, and receiving, every hour almost, letters from Sir W. Coventry calling for more fire-ships: and an order from Council to enable us to take any man's ships; and Sir W. Coventry, in his letter to us, says he do not doubt but at this time, under an invasion, as he owns it to be, the King may, by law, take any man's goods. At this business late, and then home; where a great deal of serious talk with my wife about the sad state we are in, and especially from the beating up of drums this night for the trainbands upon

pain of death to appear in arms to-morrow morning
with bullet and powder, and money to supply themselves with victuals for a fortnight; which, considering
the soldiers drawn out to Chatham and elsewhere,
looks as if they had a design to ruin the City and give
it up to be undone; which, I hear, makes the sober
citizens to think very sadly of things.

12th. Up very betimes to our business at the office,
there hiring of more fire-ships; and at it close all the
morning. At noon home, and Sir W. Pen dined with
us. By and by, after dinner, my wife out by coach to
see her mother; and I in another, being afraid, at this
busy time, to be seen with a woman in a coach, as if
I were idle, towards The. Turner's; but met Sir W.
Coventry's boy; and there in a letter find that the
Dutch had made no motion since their taking Sheerness; and the Duke of Albemarle writes that all is
safe as to the great ships against any assault, the boom
and chain being so fortified; which put my heart into
great joy. When I come to Sir W. Coventry's
chamber, I find him abroad; but his clerk, Powell,
do tell me that ill news is come to Court of the Dutch
breaking the chain at Chatham; which struck me to
the heart. And to Whitehall to hear the truth of it;
and there, going up the stairs, I did hear some lackeys
speaking of sad news come to Court, saying, there is
hardly anybody in the Court but do look as if he cried.
I would not go into the house for fear of being seen,
but slunk out and got into a coach. I met Roger
Pepys, newly come out of the country. He and I
talked aside a little, he offering a match for Pall, one
Barnes, of whom we shall talk more the next time.
His father married a Pepys; in discourse, he told me
that his grandfather, my great grandfather, had £800
per annum, in Queen Elizabeth's time, in the very
town of Cottenham; and that we did certainly come
out of Scotland with the Abbot of Crowland. Home,

where all our hearts do now ache; for the news is true, that the Dutch have broke the chain and burned our ships, and particularly the *Royal Charles*: other particulars I know not, but it is said to be so. And, the truth is, I do fear so much that the whole kingdom is undone, that I do this night resolve to study with my father and my wife what to do with the little that I have in money by me, for I give up all the rest that I have in the King's hands, for Tangier, for lost. So God help us! and God knows what disorders we may fall into, and whether any violence on this office, or perhaps some severity on our persons, as being reckoned by the silly people, or perhaps may, by policy of State, be thought fit to be condemned by the King and Duke of York, and so put to trouble; though, God knows! I have, in my own person, done my full duty, I am sure. Home, and to bed with a heavy heart. The manner of my advising this night with my father was, I took him and my wife up to her chamber, and shut the door; and there told them the sad state of the times how we are like to be all undone; that I do fear some violence will be offered to this office, where all I have in the world is; and resolved upon sending it away—sometimes into the country— sometimes my father to lie in town, and have the gold with him at Sarah Giles's.

13th. No sooner up but hear the sad news confirmed of the *Royal Charles* being taken by them, and now in fitting by them—which Pett should have carried up higher by our several orders, and deserves, therefore, to be hanged for not doing it—and burning several others; and that another fleet is come up into the Hope. Upon which news the King and Duke of York have been below since four o'clock in the morning, to command the sinking of ships at Barking Creek, and other places, to stop their coming up higher; which put me into such a fear, that I presently

resolved of my father's and wife's going into the
country; and, at two hours' warning, they did go by
the coach this day, with about £1300 in gold in their
night-bag. Pray God give them good passage, and
good care to hide it when they come home! but my
heart is full of fear. They gone, I continued in fright
and fear what to do with the rest. W. Hewer hath
been at the banker's, and hath got £500 out of
Backewell's hands of his own money; but they are so
called upon that they will be all broke, hundreds
coming to them for money: and they answer him,
" It is payable at twenty days—when the days are out,
we will pay you "; and those that are not so, they
make tell over their money, and make their bags false,
on purpose to give cause to retell it, and so spend time.
I cannot have my 200 pieces of gold again for silver,
all being bought up last night that were to be had,
and sold for 24s. and 25s. apiece. So I must keep the
silver by me, which sometimes I think to fling into the
house of office, and then again know not how I shall
come by it, if we be made to leave the office. Every
minute some one or other calls for this or that order;
and so I forced to be at the office, most of the day,
about the fire-ships which are to be suddenly fitted
out: and it's a most strange thing that we hear
nothing from any of my brethren at Chatham; so
that we are wholly in the dark, various being the reports of what is done there; insomuch that I sent Mr.
Clapham express thither to see how matters go. I did,
about noon, resolve to send Mr. Gibson away after my
wife with another 1000 pieces, under colour of an
express to Sir Jeremy Smith; who is, as I hear, with
some ships at Newcastle; which I did really send to
him, and may, possibly, prove of good use to the King;
for it is possible, in the hurry of business, they may not
think of it at Court, and the charge of an express is
not considerable to the King. The King and Duke of

York up and down all the day here and there: some time on Tower Hill, where the City militia was; where the King did make a speech to them, that they should venture themselves no further than he would himself. I also sent, my mind being in pain, Saunders after my wife and father, to overtake them at their night's lodgings, to see how matters go with them. In the evening, I sent for my cousin Sarah and her husband, who came; and I did deliver them my chest of writings about Brampton, and my brother Tom's papers, and my journals, which I value much; and did send my two silver flagons to Kate Joyce's; that so, being scattered what I have, something might be saved. I have also made a girdle, by which, with some trouble, I do carry about me £300 in gold about my body, that I may not be without something in case I should be surprised; for I think, in any nation but our's, people that appear (for we are not indeed so) so faulty as we, would have their throats cut. In the evening comes Mr. Pelling, and several others, to the office, and tell me that never were people so dejected as they are in the City all over at this day; and do talk most loudly, even treason; as, that we are bought and sold—that we are betrayed by the Papists; and others, about the King, cry out that the office of the Ordnance hath been so backward as no powder to have been at Chatham nor Upnor Castle till such a time, and the carriages all broken; that Legg is a Papist; that Upnor, the old good castle built by Queen Elizabeth, should be lately slighted; that the ships at Chatham should not be carried up higher. They look upon us as lost, and remove their families and rich goods in the City; and do think verily that the French, being come down with his army to Dunkirk, it is to invade us, and that we shall be invaded. Mr. Clerke, the solicitor, comes to me about business, and tells me that he hears that the King hath

chosen Mr. Pierpont and Vaughan of the West, Privy
Councillors; that my Lord Chancellor was affronted
in the Hall this day, by people telling him of his
Dunkirk House; and that there are regiments ordered
to be got together, whereof to be commanders my
Lord Fairfax, Ingoldsby, Bethell, Norton, and Birch,
and other Presbyterians; and that Dr. Bates will
have liberty to preach. Now, whether this be true
or not, I know not; but do think that nothing but this
will unite us together. Late at night comes Mr.
Hudson, the cooper, my neighbour, and tells me that
he came from Chatham this evening at five o'clock,
and saw this afternoon the *Royal James*, *Oak*, and
London, burnt by the enemy with their fire-ships:
that two or three men-of-war came up with them,
and made no more of Upnor Castle's shooting than of
a fly; that those ships lay below Upnor Castle, but
therein, I conceive, he is in an error; that the Dutch
are fitting out the *Royal Charles*; that we shot so far
as from the Yard thither, so that the shot did no good,
for the bullets grazed on the water; that Upnor
played hard with their guns at first, but slowly afterwards, either from the men being beat off, or their
powder spent. But we hear that the fleet in the Hope
is not come up any higher the last flood; and Sir W.
Batten tells me that ships are provided to sink in the
River, about Woolwich, that will prevent their coming
up higher if they should attempt it. I made my will
also this day, and did give all I had equally between
my father and wife.

14th. Up, and to the office; where Mr. Fryer
comes and tells me that there are several Frenchmen and Flemish ships in the River, with passes
from the Duke of York for carrying of prisoners, that
ought to be parted from the rest of the ships, and
their powder taken, lest they do fire themselves when
the enemy comes, and so spoil us; which is good

advice, and I think I will give notice of it; and did so. But it is pretty odd to see how everybody, even at this high time of danger, puts business off of their own hands! He says that he told this to the Lieutenant of the Tower, to whom I, for the same reason, was directing him to go; and the Lieutenant of the Tower bade him come to us, for he had nothing to do with it; and yesterday comes Captain Crew, of one of the fire-ships, and told me that the officers of the Ordnance would deliver his gunner's materials, but not compound them, but that we must do it; whereupon I was forced to write to them about it; and one that like a great many came to me this morning by and by comes—Mr. Wilson, and, by direction of his, a man of Mr. Gauden's; who came from Chatham last night, and saw the three ships burnt, they lying all dry, and boats going from the men-of-war to fire them. But that, that he tells me of worst consequence is, that he himself, I think he said, did hear many Englishmen on board the Dutch ships speaking to one another in English; and that they did cry and say, " We did heretofore fight for tickets; now we fight for dollars!" and did ask how such and such a one did, and would commend themselves to them; which is a sad consideration. And Mr. Lewes, who was present at this fellow's discourse to me, did tell me, that he is told that when they took the *Royal Charles*, they said that they had their tickets signed, and showed some, and that now they came to have them paid, and would have them paid before they parted. And several seamen came this morning to me, to tell me that, if I would get their tickets paid, they would go and do all they could against the Dutch; but otherwise they would not venture being killed, and lose all they have already fought for; so that I was forced to try what I could do to get them paid. This man tells me that the ships burnt last night did lie above Upnor Castle, over against the Dock; and the boats came from the ships of war and burnt them; all which is very sad. And masters of ships, that we are lately taking up, do keep from their ships all their stores, or as much as they can, so that we can dispatch them, having not time to appraise them nor secure their payment; only some little money we have, which we are fain to pay the men we have with, every night, or they will not work. And indeed the hearts as well as affections of the seamen are turned away; and in the open streets in Wapping, and up and down, the wives have cried publicly, "This comes of your not paying our husbands; and now your work is undone, or done by hands that understand it not." And Sir W. Batten told me that he was himself affronted with a woman, in language of this kind, on Tower Hill publicly yesterday; and we are fain to bear it, and to keep one at the office door to let no idle people in, for fear of firing of the office and doing us mischief. The City is troubled at their being put upon duty: summoned one hour, and discharged two hours after; and then again summoned two hours after that; to their great charge as well as trouble. And Pelling, the apothecary, tells me the world says all over, that less charge than what the kingdom is put to, of one kind or other, by this business, would have set out all our great ships. It is said they did in open streets yesterday, at Westminster, cry, "A Parliament! a Parliament!" and I do believe it will cost blood to answer for these miscarriages. We do not hear that the Dutch are come to Gravesend; which is a wonder. But a wonderful thing it is that to this day we have not one word yet from Brouncker, or Peter Pett, or J. Minnes, of anything at Chatham. The people that come hither to hear how things go, make me ashamed to be found unable to answer them; for I am left alone here at the office; and the truth is, I am glad my station is to be here, near my own home and out of danger, yet in a place of doing the King good service. I have this morning good news from Gibson; three letters from three several stages, that he was safe last night as far as Royston, at between nine and ten at night. The dismay that is upon us all, in the business of the kingdom and Navy at this day, is not to be expressed otherwise than by the condition the citizens were in when the City was on fire, nobody knowing which way to turn themselves, while everything concurred to greaten the fire; as here the easterly gale and spring-tides for coming up both rivers, and enabling them to break the chain. D. Gauden did tell me yesterday, that the day before at the Council they were ready to fall together by the ears at the Council-table, arraigning one another of being guilty of the counsel that brought us into this misery, by laying up all the great ships. Mr. Hater tells me at noon that some rude people have been, as he hears, at my Lord Chancellor's, where they have cut down the trees before his house and broke his windows; and a gibbet either set up before or painted upon his gate, and these three words writ: " Three sights to be seen; Dunkirk, Tangier, and a barren Queen." It gives great matter of talk that it is said there is at this hour, in the Exchequer, as much money as is ready to break down the floor. This arises, I believe, from Sir G. Downing's late talk of the greatness of the sum lying there of people's money, that they would not fetch away, which he showed me and a great many others. Most people that I speak with are in doubt how we shall do to secure our seamen from running over to the Dutch; which is a sad but very true consideration at this day. At noon I am told that my Lord Duke of Albemarle is made

Lord High Constable; the meaning whereof at this time I know not, nor whether it be true or no. Dined, and Mr. Hater and W. Hewer with me; where they do speak very sorrowfully of the posture of the times, and how people do cry out in the streets of their being bought and sold; and both they, and everybody that come to me, do tell me that people make nothing of talking treason in the streets openly: as, that they are bought and sold, and governed by Papists, and that we are betrayed by people about the King, and shall be delivered up to the French, and I know not what. At dinner we discoursed of Tom of the Wood, a fellow that lives like a hermit near Woolwich, who, as they say, and Mr. Bodham, they tell me, affirms that he was by at the Justice's when some did accuse him there for it, did foretell the burning of the City, and now says that a greater desolation is at hand. Thence we read and laughed at Lilly's prophecies this month, in his *Almanac* this year. So to the office after dinner; and thither comes Mr. Pierce, who tells me his condition, how he cannot get his money, about £500 (which, he says, is a very great part of what he hath for his family and children), out of Viner's hand; and indeed it is to be feared that this will wholly undo the bankers. He says he knows nothing of the late affronts to my Lord Chancellor's house, as is said, nor hears of the Duke of Albemarle's being made High Constable; but says that they are in great distraction at Whitehall, and that everywhere people do speak high against Sir W. Coventry; but he agrees with me that he is the best Minister of State the King hath, and so from my heart I believe.

18th. To the office, and by and by word was brought me that Commissioner Pett is brought to the Tower, and there laid up close prisoner; which puts me into a fright, lest they may do the same with us as they do with him. Great news to-night of the blowing up of one of the Dutch greatest ships, while a Council of War was on board: the latter part, I doubt, is not so, it not being confirmed since; but the former, that they had a ship blown up, is said to be true.

19th. Comes an order from Sir R. Browne, commanding me this afternoon to attend the Council-board, with all my books and papers touching the Medway. I was ready to fear some mischief to myself, though it appears most reasonable that it is to inform them about Commissioner Pett. And so took coach and to the Council-chamber lobby, where I met Mr. Evelyn. While we were discoursing over our public misfortunes, I am called into a large Committee of the Council: present the Duke of Albemarle, Anglesey, Arlington, Ashly, Carteret, Duncomb, Coventry, Ingram, Clifford, Lauderdale, Morrice, Manchester, Craven, Carlisle, Bridgewater. And after Sir W. Coventry's telling them what orders His Royal Highness had made for the safety of the Medway, I told them to their full content what we had done, and showed them our letters. Then was Peter Pett called in, with the Lieutenant of the Tower. He is in his old clothes, and looked most sillily. His charge was chiefly the not carrying up of the great ships, and the using of the boats in carrying away his goods; to which he answered very sillily, though his faults to me seem only great omissions. Lord Arlington and Coventry very severe against him; the former saying that, if he was not guilty, the world would think them all guilty. The latter urged that there must be some faults, and that the Admiral must be found to have done his part. I did say an unhappy word, which I was sorry for, when he complained of want of oars for the boats; and there was, it seems, enough, and good enough, to carry away all the boats with from the King's occasions. He said he used never a boat till they were all gone but one; and that was to carry away things of great value, and these were his models of ships; which, when the Council, some of them, had said they wished that the Dutch had had them instead of the King's ships, he answered, he did believe the Dutch would have made more advantage of the models than of the ships, and that the King had had greater loss thereby; this they all laughed at. After having heard him for an hour or more, they bade him withdraw. He being gone, they caused Sir Richard Browne to read over his minutes; and then my Lord Arlington moved that they might be put into my hands to put into form, I being more acquainted with such business; that they were so. So I away back with my books and papers; and when I got out into the Court it was pretty to see how people gazed upon me, that I thought myself obliged to salute people and to smile, lest they should think I was a prisoner too; but afterwards I found that most did take me to be there to bear evidence against P. Pett; but my fear was such, at my going in, of the success of the day, that I did think fit to give T. Hater, whom I took with me, to wait the event, my closet-key and directions where to find £500 and more in silver and gold, and my tallies, to remove, in case of any misfortune to me. Home, and after being there a little, my wife came, and two of her fellow-travellers with her, with whom we drank: a couple of merchant-like men, I think, but have friends in our country. They being gone, my wife did give so bad an account of her and my father's method in burying of our gold, that made me mad; and she herself is not pleased with it, she believing that my sister knows of it. My father and she did it on Sunday, when they were gone to church, in open daylight, in the midst of the garden; where, for aught they knew, many eyes might see them; which put me into trouble, and I presently cast about, how to have it back again to secure it here, the times being a little better now.

21st. My wife shows me a letter from her father, who is going over sea, and this afternoon would take his leave of her. I sent him by her three Jacobuses in gold, having real pity for him and her. This day comes news from Harwich that the Dutch fleet are all in sight, near 100 sail great and small, they think, coming towards them; where, they think, they shall be able to oppose them; but do cry out of the falling back of the seamen, few standing by them, and those with much faintness. The like they write from Portsmouth, and their letters this post are worth reading. Sir H. Cholmely came to me this day, and tells me the Court is as mad as ever; and that the night the Dutch burned our ships the King did sup with my Lady Castlemaine, at the Duchess of Monmouth's, and there were all mad in hunting of a poor moth. All the Court afraid of a Parliament; but he thinks nothing can save us but the King's giving up all to a Parliament.

July 1667

July 12th. Sir Thomas Crew tells me how I am mightily in esteem with the Parliament; there being harangues made in the House to the Speaker, of Mr. Pepys's readiness and civility to show them everything.

13th. Mighty hot weather, I lying this night, which I have not done, I believe, since a boy, with only a rug and a sheet upon me.

14th. (Lord's day.) Up, and my wife, a little before four, and to make us ready; and by and by

Mrs. Turner came to us by agreement, and she and I stayed talking below while my wife dressed herself, which vexed me that she was so long about it, keeping us till past five o'clock before she was ready. She ready; and taking some bottles of wine, and beer, and some cold fowl with us into the coach, we took coach and four horses, which I had provided last night, and so away. A very fine day, and so towards Epsom, talking all the way pleasantly, and particularly of the pride and ignorance of Mrs. Lowther, in having of her train carried up. The country very fine, only the way very dusty. To Epsom, by eight o'clock, to the well; where much company, and I drank the water: they did not, but I did drink four pints. And to the town, to the King's Head; and hear that my Lord Buckhurst and Nelly are lodged at the next house, and Sir Charles Sedley with them; and keep a merry house. Poor girl! I pity her; but more the loss of her at the King's house. W. Hewer rode with us, and I left him and the women, and myself walked to the church, where few people to what I expected, and none I knew, but all the Houblons, brothers, and them after sermon I did salute, and walk with towards my inn. James did tell me that I was the only happy man of the Navy, of whom, he says, during all this freedom the people hath taken to speaking treason, he hath not heard one bad word of me, which is a great joy to me; for I hear the same of others, but do know that I have deserved as well as most. We parted to meet anon, and I to my women into a better room, which the people of the house borrowed for us, and there to a good dinner, and were merry, and Pembleton came to us, who happened to be in the house, and there talked and were merry. After dinner, he gone, we all lay down (the day being wonderful hot) to sleep, and each of us took a good nap, and then rose; and here Tom Wilson came to see me, and sat and talked an hour; and I perceive he hath been much acquainted with Dr. Fuller (Tom) and Dr. Pierson, and several of the great cavalier parsons during the late troubles; and I was glad to hear him talk of them, which he did very ingenuously, and very much of Dr. Fuller's art of memory, which he did tell me several instances of. By and by he parted, and we took coach and to take the air, there being a fine breeze abroad; and I carried them to the well, and there filled some bottles of water to carry home with me; and there I talked with the two women that farm the well, at £12 per annum, of the lord of the manor. Mr. Evelyn with his lady, and also my Lord George Barkeley's lady, and their fine daughter, that the King of France liked so well, and did dance so rich in jewels before the King at the ball I was at, at our Court, last winter, and also their son, a Knight of the Bath, were at church this morning. Here W. Hewer's horse broke loose, and we had the sport to see him taken again. Then I carried them to see my cousin Pepys's house, and 'light, and walked round about it, and they like it, as indeed it deserves, very well, and is a pretty place; and then I walked them to the wood hard by, and there got them in the thickets till they lost themselves, and I could not find the way into any of the walks in the wood, which indeed are very pleasant, if I could have found them. At last got out of the wood again; and I, by leaping down the little bank, coming out of the wood, did sprain my right foot, which brought me great pain, but presently, with walking, it went away for the present, and so the women and W. Hewer and I walked upon the Downes, where a flock of sheep was; and the most pleasant and innocent sight that ever I saw in my life. We found a shepherd and his little boy reading, far from

any houses or sight of people, the Bible to him; so
I made the boy read to me, which he did, with the
forced tone that children do usually read, that was
mighty pretty, and then I did give him something,
and went to the father, and talked with him; and I
find he had been a servant in my cousin Pepys's
house, and told me what was become of their old
servants. He did content himself mightily in my
liking his boy's reading, and did bless God for him,
the most like one of the old patriarchs that ever I
saw in my life, and it brought those thoughts of the
old age of the world in my mind for two or three
days after. We took notice of his woollen knit stockings of two colours mixed, and of his shoes shod with
iron, both at the toe and heels, and with great nails
in the soles of his feet, which was mighty pretty;
and, taking notice of them, "why," says the poor
man, "the Downs, you see, are full of stones, and
we are fain to shoe ourselves thus; and these," says
he, "will make the stones fly till they ring before
me." I did give the poor man something, for which
he was mighty thankful, and I tried to cast stones
with his horn crook. He values his dog mightily,
that would turn a sheep any way which he would
have him, when he goes to fold them: told me there
was about eighteen score sheep in his flock, and that
he hath four shillings a-week the year round for
keeping of them: and Mrs. Turner, in the common
fields here, did gather one of the prettiest nosegays
that I ever saw in my life. So to our coach, and
through Mrs. Minnes's wood, and looked upon Mr.
Evelyn's house; and so over the common, and
through Epsom town to our inn, in the way stopping
a poor woman with her milk-pail, and in one of my
gilt tumblers did drink our bellyfuls of milk, better
than any cream; and so to our inn, and there had
a dish of cream, but it was sour, and so had no

pleasure in it; and so paid our reckoning, and took coach, it being about seven at night, and passed and saw the people walking with their wives and children to take the air, and we set out for home, the sun by and by going down, and we in the cool of the evening all the way with much pleasure home, talking and pleasing ourselves with the pleasure of this day's work. Mrs. Turner mightily pleased with my resolution, which, I tell her, is never to keep a country-house, but to keep a coach, and with my wife on the Saturday to go sometimes for a day to this place, and then quit to another place; and there is more variety and as little charge, and no trouble, as there is in a country-house. Anon it grew dark, and we had the pleasure to see several glow-worms, which was mighty pretty, but my foot begins more and more to pain me, which Mrs. Turner, by keeping her warm hand upon it, did much ease; but so that when we came home, which was just at eleven at night, I was not able to walk from the lane's end to my house without being helped. So to bed, and there had a cere-cloth laid to my foot, but in great pain all night long.

22nd. Creed tells me of the fray between the Duke of Buckingham at the Duke's playhouse the last Saturday (and it is the first day I have heard that they have acted at either the King's or Duke's houses this month or six weeks) and Henry Killigrew, whom the Duke of Buckingham did soundly beat and take away his sword, and make a fool of, till the fellow prayed him to spare his life; and I am glad of it; for it seems in this business the Duke of Buckingham did carry himself very innocently and well, and I wish he had paid this fellow's coat well.

24th. About five o'clock down to Gravesend, all the way with extraordinary content reading of Boyle's Hydrostatics, which the more I read and understand, the more I admire, as a most excellent piece of philosophy.

29th. To Westminster Hall, where the Hall full of people to see the issue of the day, the King being to come to speak to the House to-day. One thing extraordinary was, this day a man, a Quaker, came naked through the Hall, only very civilly tied about the loins to avoid scandal, and with a chafing-dish of fire and brimstone burning upon his head, did pass through the Hall, crying, " Repent! repent! " Presently comes down the House of Commons, the King having made then a very short and no pleasing speech to them at all, not at all giving them thanks for their readiness to come up to town this busy time; but told them that he did think he should have had occasion for them, but had none, and therefore did dismiss them to look after their own occasions till October; and that he did wonder any should offer to bring in a suspicion that he intended to rule by an army, or otherwise than by the laws of the land, which he promised them he would do; and so bade them go home and settle the minds of the country in that particular; and only added, that he had made a peace which he did believe they would find reasonable, and a good peace, but did give them none of the particulars thereof. Thus they are dismissed again to their general great distaste.

August 1667

August 18th. There dined with me Mr. Turner and his daughter Betty. Betty is grown a fine young lady as to carriage and discourse. We had a good haunch of venison, powdered and boiled, and a good dinner. I walked towards Whitehall, but, being wearied, turned into St. Dunstan's Church, where I heard an able sermon of the minister of the place; and stood by a pretty, modest maid, whom I did labour to take by the hand; but she would not, but got further and further from me; and, at last, I could perceive her to take pins out of her pocket to prick me if I should touch her again—which seeing, I did forbear, and was glad I did spy her design. And then I fell to gaze upon another pretty maid in a pew close to me, and she on me; and I did go about to take her by the hand, which she suffered a little, and then withdrew. So the sermon ended, and the church broke up, and my amours ended also. Took coach and home, and there took up my wife, and to Islington. Between that and Kingsland, there happened an odd adventure: one of our coach-horses fell sick of the staggers, so as he was ready to fall down. The coachman was fain to 'light, and hold him up, and cut his tongue to make him bleed, and his tail; then he blew some tobacco in his nose, upon which the horse sneezed, and, by and by, grew well, and drew us all the rest of our way, as well as ever he did.

24th. (St. Bartholomew's day.) This morning was proclaimed the peace between us and the States of the United Provinces, and also the King of France and Denmark; and in the afternoon the Proclamations were printed and came out; and at night the bells rung; but no bonfires that I hear of anywhere, partly from the dearness of firing, but principally from the little content most people have in the peace.

26th. To the office, where we sat upon a particular business all the morning; and my Lord Anglesey with us; who, and my Lord Brouncker, do bring us news how my Lord Chancellor's seal is to be taken away from him to-day. The thing is so great and sudden to me, that it put me into a very great admiration what should be the meaning of it; and they do not own that they know what it should be: but this is certain, that the King did resolve it on Saturday, and did yesterday send the Duke of Albemarle, the only man fit for those works, to him for his purse; to which the Chancellor answered, that he received it from the King, and would deliver it to the King's own hand, and so civilly returned the Duke of Albemarle without it; and this morning my Lord Chancellor is to be with the King, to come to an end in the business. Dined at Sir W. Batten's, where Mr. Boreman was, who came from Whitehall; who tells us that he saw my Lord Chancellor come in his coach with some of his men, without his seal, to Whitehall to his chamber; and thither the King and Duke of York came and stayed together alone, an hour or more: and it is said that the King do say that he will have the Parliament meet, and that it will prevent much trouble by having of him out of their enmity, by his place being taken away; for that all their enmity will be at him. It is said also that my Lord Chancellor answers that he desires he may be brought to his trial, if he have done anything to lose his office; and that he will be willing, and is most desirous, to lose that, and his head both together. Upon what terms they parted nobody knows; but the Chancellor looked sad, he says. Then in comes Sir Richard Ford, and says he hears that there is nobody more presses to reconcile the King and Chancellor than the Duke of Albemarle and Duke of Buckingham; the latter of which is very strange, not only that he who was so lately his enemy should do it, but that this man, that but the other day was in danger of losing his own head, should so soon come to be a mediator for others; it shows a wise Government. They all say that he is but a poor man, not worth above £3000 a-year in land; but this I cannot believe: and all do blame him for having built so great a house, till he had got a better estate.

27th. To Whitehall, and there hear how it is like

to go well enough with my Lord Chancellor; that he is like to keep his seal, desiring that he may stand his trial in Parliament, if they will accuse him of anything. Here Sir J. Minnes and I looking upon the pictures; and Mr. Cheffins, being by, did take us, of his own accord, into the King's closet, to show us some pictures, which, indeed, is a very noble place, and exceeding great variety of brave pictures, and the best hands. I could have spent three or four hours there well, and we had great liberty to look; and Cheffins seemed to take pleasure to show us, and commend the pictures. I to visit Colonel Fitzgerald, who hath been sick at Woolwich, where most of the officers and soldiers quartered there, since the Dutch being in the river, have died or been sick, and he among the rest; and, by the growth of his beard and gray hairs, I did not know him. This day, Mr. Pierce, the surgeon, was with me; and tells me how this business of my Lord Chancellor's was certainly designed in my Lady Castlemaine's chamber; and that, when he went from the King on Monday morning, she was in bed, though about twelve o'clock, and ran out in her smock into her aviary looking into Whitehall garden; and thither her woman brought her her nightgown; and stood joying herself at the old man's going away: and several of the gallants of Whitehall, of which there were many staying to see the Chancellor's return, did talk to her in her bird-cage; among others, Blancford, telling her she was the bird of paradise.

28th. I hear to-night that Mr. Brouncker is turned away yesterday by the Duke of York, for some bold words he was heard by Colonel Werden to say in the garden, the day the Chancellor was with the King—that he believed the King would be hectored out of everything. For this the Duke of York, who all say hath been very strong for his father-in-law at this trial, hath turned him away;

and everybody, I think, is glad of it; for he was a pestilent rogue, an atheist, that would have sold his King and country for 6d. almost, so covetous and wicked a rogue he is, by all men's report. But one observed to me, that there never was the occasion of men's holding their tongues at Court and everywhere else as there is at this day, for nobody knows which side will be uppermost.

31st. At the office all the morning; where by Sir W. Pen I do hear that the seal was fetched away to the King yesterday from the Lord Chancellor by Secretary Morrice; which puts me into a great horror. My Lord Brouncker tells me that he hath of late discoursed about this business with Sir W. Coventry, who he finds is the great man in the doing this business of the Chancellor's, and that he do persevere in it, though against the Duke of York's opinion, to which he says that the Duke of York was once of the same mind, and if he had thought fit since, for any reason, to alter his mind, he hath not found any to alter his own, and so desires to be excused, for it is for the King's and kingdom's good. And it seems that the Duke of York himself was the first man that did speak to the King of this, though he hath since altered his mind; and W. Coventry did tell the Duke of York that he was not fit to serve a Prince that did not know how to retire, and live a private life; and that he was ready for that, if it be his and the King's pleasure. In the evening Mr. Ball of the Excise-office tells me that the seal is delivered to Sir Orlando Bridgman; the man of the whole nation that is the best spoken of, and will please most people; and therefore I am mighty glad of it. He was then at my Lord Arlington's, whither I went, expecting to see him come out; but stayed so long, and Sir W. Coventry coming there, whom I had not a mind should see me there idle upon a post-night, I went home without seeing him; but he is there with his seal in his hand. This day, being dissatisfied with my wife's learning so few songs of Goodgroome, I did come to a new bargain with him to teach her songs at so much, viz., 10s. a song, which he accepts of, and will teach her.

September 1667

September 2nd. I went to see a great match at tennis, between Prince Rupert and one Captain Cooke, against Bab. May and the elder Chichly; where the King was, and Court; and it seems they are the best players at tennis in the nation. But this puts me in mind of what I observed in the morning, that the King, playing at tennis, had a steelyard carried to him, and I was told it was to weigh him after he had done playing; and at noon Mr. Ashburnham told me that it is only the King's curiosity, which he usually hath of weighing himself before and after his play, to see how much he loses in weight by playing: and this day he lost $4\frac{1}{2}$ lbs. I to Sir W. Batten and Sir W. Pen, and there discoursed of Sir W. Coventry's leaving the Duke of York, and Mr. Wren's succeeding him. They told me both seriously, that they had long cut me out for Secretary to the Duke of York, if ever Sir W. Coventry left him; which, agreeing with what I have heard from other hands heretofore, do make me not only think that something of that kind hath been thought on, but do comfort me to see that the world hath such an esteem of my qualities as to think me fit for any such thing; though I am glad, with all my heart, that I am not so; for it would never please me to be forced to the attendance that that would require, and leave my wife and family to themselves, as I must do in such a case; thinking myself now in the best place that ever man was in to please his own mind in, and, therefore, I will take care to preserve it.

27th. Anon comes Pelling, and he and I to Gray's Inn Fields, thinking to have heard Mrs. Knight sing at her lodgings, by a friend's means of his; but we came too late; so must try another time.

October 1667

October 4th. To see Sir W. Batten. He is asleep; and so I could not see him; but in an hour after, word is brought me that he is so ill, that it is believed he cannot live till to-morrow, which troubles me and my wife mightily, partly out of kindness, he being a good neighbour—and partly because of the money he owes me, upon our bargain of the late prize.

8th. Up pretty betimes, though not so soon as we intended, by reason of Murford's not rising, and then not knowing how to open our door, which, and some other pleasant simplicities of the fellow, did give occasion to us to call him Sir Martin Mar-all, and W. Hewer being his helper and counsellor we did call him, all this journey, Mr. Warner, which did give us good occasion of mirth now and then. At last, rose, and up, and broke our fast, and then took coach, and away, and at Newport did call on Mr. Lowther, and he and his friend, and the master of the house, their friend, where they were, a gentleman, did presently get a-horseback, and went with us to Audley End, and did go along with us all over the house and garden; and mighty merry we were. The house indeed do appear very fine, but not so fine as it hath heretofore to me; particularly the ceilings are not so good as I always took them to be, being nothing so well wrought as my Lord Chancellor's are; and though the figure of the house without be very extraordinary good, yet the staircase is exceeding poor; and a great many

pictures, and not one good one in the house but one
of Harry the Eighth, done by Holbein; and not one
good suit of hangings in all the house, but all most
ancient things, such as I would not give the hanging-up
of in my house; and the other furniture, beds and
other things, accordingly. Only the gallery is good,
and, above all things, the cellars, where we went
down and drank of much good liquor; and indeed the
cellars are fine: and here my wife and I did sing to
my great content. And then to the garden, and there
ate many grapes, and took some with us; and so away
thence, exceeding well satisfied, though not to that
degree that, by my old esteem of the house, I ought
and did expect to have done, the situation of it not
pleasing me. Here we parted with Lowther and his
friends, and away to Cambridge, it being foul rainy
weather, and there did take up at the Rose, for the
sake of Mrs. Dorothy Drawwater, the vintner's
daughter, which is mentioned in the play of *Sir
Martin Mar-all*. Here we had a good chamber, and
bespoke a good supper; and then I took my wife, and
W. Hewer, and Willet, it holding up a little, and showed
them Trinity College and St. John's Library, and went
to King's College Chapel, to see the outside of it
only; and so to our inn, and with much pleasure did
this, they walking in their pretty morning gowns,
very handsome, and I proud to find myself in condition to do this; and so home to our lodging, and
there, by and by, to supper, with much good sport,
talking with the drawers concerning matters of the
town, and persons whom I remember, and so, after
supper, to cards; and then to bed, lying, I in one
bed, and my wife and girl in another, in the same
room, and very merry talking together, and mightily
pleased both of us with the girl. Saunders, the only
violin in my time, is, I hear, dead of the plague in the
late plague there.

9th. Up, and got ready, and ate our breakfast; and then took coach; and the poor, as they did yesterday, did stand at the coach to have something given them, as they do to all great persons; and I did give them something: and the town music did also come and play; but Lord! what sad music they made! So through the town, and observed at our College of Magdalene the posts new painted, and understand that the Vice-Chancellor is there this year. And so away for Huntingdon; and came to Brampton at about noon, and there find my father and sister and brother all well: and up and down to see the garden with my father, and the house, and do altogether find it very pretty; especially the little parlour and the summer-houses in the garden, only the wall do want greens upon it, and the house is too low-roofed; but that is only because of my coming from a house with higher ceilings. But altogether is very pretty; and I bless God that I am like to have such a pretty place to retire to. After dinner, I walked up to Hinchingbroke, where my Lady expected me; and there spent all the afternoon with her: the same most excellent, good, discreet lady that ever she was; and, among other things, is mightily pleased with the lady that is like to be her son Hinchingbroke's wife. By and by my wife comes with Willet, my wife in her velvet vest, which is mighty fine, and becomes her exceedingly. I am pleased with my Lady Paulina and Anne, who both are grown very proper ladies, and handsome enough. But a thousand questions my Lady asked me, till she could think of no more almost, but walked up and down the house with me. But I do find, by her, that they are reduced to great straits for money, having been forced to sell her plate, £800 or £900 worth; and she is now going to sell a suit of her best hangings, of which I could almost wish to buy a piece or two, if the pieces will be broke.

But the house is most excellently furnished, and brave rooms and good pictures, so that it do please me infinitely beyond Audley End. Home, and there Mr. Shepley stayed with us and supped. Supper done, we all to bed, only I a little troubled that my father tells me that he is troubled that my wife shows my sister no countenance, and him but very little, but is as a stranger in the house; and I do observe she do carry herself very high; but I perceive there was some great falling out when she was here last, but the reason I have no mind to inquire after, for vexing myself, being desirous to pass my time with as much mirth as I can while I am abroad. My wife and I in the high bed in our chamber, and Willet in the trundle bed, which she desired to lie in, by us.

10th. Up, to walk up and down the garden with my father, to talk of all our concernments: about a husband for my sister, whereof there is at present no appearance; but we must endeavour to find her one now, for she grows old and ugly: then for my brother; and resolve he shall stay here this winter, and then I will either send him to Cambridge for a year, till I get him some church promotion, or send him to sea as a chaplain, where he may study, and earn his living. Then walked round about our Green, to see whether, in case I cannot buy out my uncle Thomas and his son's right in this house, that I can buy another place as good thereabouts to build on, and I do not see that I can. But this, with new building, may be made an excellent pretty thing, and I resolve to look after it as soon as I can, and Goody Gorum dies. By coach round the town of Brampton, to observe any other place as good as ours, and find none; and so back with great pleasure; and thence went all of us, my sister and brother, and W. Hewer, to dinner to Hinchingbroke, where we had a good plain country dinner, but most kindly used; and

239

here dined the minister of Brampton and his wife,
who is reported a very good, but poor, man. Here
I spent alone with my Lady, after dinner, the most
of the afternoon, and anon the two twins were sent
for from school, at Mr. Taylor's, to come to see me,
and I took them into the garden, and there, in one
of the summer-houses, did examine them, and do find
them so well advanced in their learning, that I am
amazed at it; they repeating a whole ode without
book out of Horace, and did give me a very good
account of anything almost, and did make me very
readily very good Latin, and did give me good
account of their Greek grammar, beyond all possible
expectation; and so grave and manly as I never
saw, I confess, nor could have believed; so that they
will be fit to go to Cambridge in two years at most.
They are both little, but very like one another, and
well-looked children. Took leave for a great while
again, but with extraordinary kindness from my
Lady, who looks upon me like one of her own family
and interest. Thence I walked over the park with
Mr. Shepley, and through the grove, which is mighty
pretty, as is imaginable, and so over their drawbridge
to Nun's Bridge, and so to my father's, and there sat
and drank, and talked a little, and then parted.
And he being gone, and what company there was,
my father and I with a dark lantern, it being now
night, into the garden with my wife, and there went
about our great work to dig up my gold. But, Lord!
what a toss I was for some time in, that they could
not justly tell where it was; that I began heartily
to sweat, and be angry, that they should not agree
better upon the place, and at last to fear that it was
gone: but by and by poking with a spit, we found
it, and then began with a spud to lift up the ground.
But, good God! to see how sillily they did it, not
half a foot under ground, and in the sight of the

world from a hundred places, if anybody by accident were near hand, and within sight of a neighbour's window; only my father says that he saw them all gone to church before he began the work, when he laid the money. But I was out of my wits almost, and the more from that, upon my lifting up the earth with the spud, I did discern that I had scattered the pieces of gold round about the ground among the grass and loose earth; and taking up the iron head-pieces wherein they were put, I perceived the earth was got among the gold, and wet, so that the bags were all rotten, and all the notes, that I could not tell what in the world to say to it, not knowing how to judge what was wanting, or what had been lost by Gibson in his coming down; which, all put together, did make me mad; and at last I was forced to take up the head-pieces, dirt and all, and as many of the scattered pieces as I could with the dirt discern by candle-light, and carry them up into my brother's chamber, and there lock them up till I had eaten a little supper; and then, all people going to bed, W. Hewer and I did all alone, with several pails of water and basins, at last wash the dirt off the pieces, and parted the pieces and the dirt, and then began to tell them, by a note which I had of the value of the whole in my pocket; and do find that there was short above a hundred pieces, which did make me mad; and considering that the neighbour's house was so near that we could not possibly speak one to another in the garden at that place where the gold lay—especially my father being deaf—but they must know what we had been doing, I feared that they might in the night come and gather some pieces and prevent us the next morning; so W. Hewer and I out again about midnight, for it was now grown so late, and there by candle-light did make shift to gather forty-five pieces more. And so

in, and to cleanse them; and by this time it was
past two in the morning; and so to bed, with my
mind pretty quiet to think that I have recovered so
many. I lay in the trundle bed, the girl being gone
to bed to my wife, and there lay in some disquiet
all night, telling of the clock till it was daylight.

11th. And then W. Hewer and I, with pails and
a sieve, did lock ourselves into the garden, and there
gather all the earth about the place into pails, and
then sift those pails in one of the summer-houses,
just as they do for diamonds in other parts of the
world; and 'there, to our great content, did by nine
o'clock make the last night's forty-five up seventy-
nine; so that we are come to about twenty or thirty
of what I think the true number should be; and
perhaps within less; and of them I may reasonably
think that Mr. Gibson might lose some; so that I
am pretty well satisfied that my loss is not great,
and do bless God that it is so well. So do leave my
father to make a second examination of the dirt; and
my mind at rest in it, being but an accident; and so
gives me some kind of content to remember how
painful it is sometimes to keep money, as well as to
get it, and how doubtful I was to keep it all night,
and how to secure it to London; so got all my gold
put up in bags. We to breakfast, and about ten
o'clock took coach, my wife and I, and Willet, and
W. Hewer, and Murford, and Bowles (whom my Lady
lent me to go along with me my journey, not telling
her the reason, that it was only to secure my gold),
and my brother John on horseback; and with these
four I thought myself pretty safe. But, before we
went out, the Huntingdon music came to me and
played, and it was better than that of Cambridge.
Here I took leave of my father, and did give my sister
20s. She cried at my going; but whether it was at
her unwillingness for my going, or any unkindness of

my wife's, or no, I know not; but, God forgive me!
I take her to be so cunning and ill-natured, that I
have no great love for her; but only [she] is my
sister, and must be provided for. My gold I put into
a basket, and set under one of the seats; and so my
work every quarter of an hour was to look to see
whether all was well; and I did ride in great fear
all the day. Mr. Shepley saw me beyond St. Neots,
and there parted, and we straight to Stevenage,
through Bald Lanes, which are already very bad;
and at Stevenage we came well before night, and all
sat, and there with great care I got the gold up to
my chamber, my wife carrying one bag, and the girl
another, and W. Hewer the rest in a basket, and
set it all under a bed in our chamber, and then sat
down to talk, and were very pleasant, satisfying myself, among other things, from John Bowles, in some
terms of hunting, and about deer, bucks, and does.
Brecocke alive still, and the best host I know almost.

12th. Up, and ate our breakfast, and set out
about nine o'clock, and so to Barnett, where we
baited. By five o'clock got home, where I find all
well; and did bring my gold, to my heart's content,
very safe, having not this day carried it in a basket,
but in our hands; the girl took care of one, and my
wife another bag, and I the rest, I being afraid of
the bottom of the coach, lest it should break. At
home we find that Sir W. Batten's body was to-day
carried from hence, with a hundred or two of coaches,
to Walthamstow, and there buried. The Parliament
met on Thursday last, and adjourned to Monday
next. The King did make them a very kind speech,
promising them to leave all to them to do, and call
to account what and whom they pleased; and
declared by my Lord Keeper how many (thirty-six)
acts he had done since he saw them; among others,
disbanding the army, and putting all Papists out of

employment, and displacing persons that had managed their business ill. The Parliament is mightily pleased with the King's speech, and voted giving him thanks for what he said and hath done; and, among things, would by name thank him for displacing my Lord Chancellor, for which a great many did speak in the House, but it was opposed by some, and particularly Harry Coventry, who got that it should be put to a Committee to consider what particulars to mention in their thanks to the King, saying that it was too soon to give thanks for the displacing of a man, before they knew or had examined what was the cause of his displacing. And so it rested; but this do show that they are and will be very high; and Mr. Pierce do tell me that he fears, and do hear, that it hath been said among them, that they will move for the calling my Lord Sandwich home, to bring him to account; which do trouble me mightily; but I trust it will not be so. Anon comes home Sir W. Pen from the burial; and he says that Lady Batten and her children-in-law are all broke in pieces, and that there is but £800 found in the world, of money; and it is in great doubt what we shall do towards doing ourselves right with them, about the prize-money. With Sir W. Pen to my Lady Batten, whom I had not seen since she was a widow, which she took unkindly, but I did excuse it; and the house being full of company, and of several factions, she against the children, and they against one another and her, I away.

November 1667

November 29th. Waked about seven o'clock this morning with a noise I supposed I heard, near our chamber, of knocking, which, by and by, increased; and I, more awake, could distinguish it better. I then waked my wife, and both of us wondered at it, and lay so a great while, while that increased, and at last heard it plainer, knocking, as if it were breaking down a window for people to get out; and then removing of stools and chairs; and plainly, by and by, going up and down our stairs. We lay, both of us, afraid; yet I would have rose, but my wife would not let me. Besides, I could not do it without making noise; and we did both conclude that thieves were in the house, but wondered what our people did, whom we thought either killed, or afraid, as we were. Thus we lay till the clock struck eight, and high day. At last, I removed my gown and slippers safely to the other side of the bed over my wife; and there safely rose, and put on my gown and breeches, and then, with a firebrand in my hand, safely opened the door, and saw nor heard anything. Then, with fear, I confess, went to the maid's chamber-door, and all quiet and safe. Called Jane up, and went down safely, and opened my chamber-door, where all well. Then more freely about, and to the kitchen, where the cook-maid up, and all safe. So up again, and when Jane came, and we demanded whether she heard no noise, she said, " yes, but was afraid," but rose with the other maid, and found nothing; but heard a noise in the great stack of chimneys that goes from Sir J. Minnes through our house; and so we sent, and their chimneys have been swept this morning, and the noise was that, and nothing else. It is one of the most extraordinary accidents in my life, and gives ground to think of Don Quixote's adventures how people may be surprised, and the more from an accident last night, that our young gib-cat did leap down our stairs from top to bottom, at two leaps, and frighted us, that we could not tell well whether it was the cat or a spirit, and do sometimes think this morning that the house might be haunted.

30th. To Arundel House, to the election of Officers for the next year; where I was near being chosen of the Council, but am glad I was not, for I could not have attended, though, above all things, I could wish it; and do take it as a mighty respect to have been named there. My Lord Anglesey told me this day that he did believe the House of Commons would, the next week, yield to the Lords; but, speaking with others this day, they conclude they will not, but that rather the King will accommodate it by committing my Lord Clarendon himself. I remember what Mr. Evelyn said, that he did believe we should soon see ourselves fall into a Commonwealth again.

December 1667

December 3rd. To Sir W. Coventry's, the first time I have seen him at his new house since he came to lodge there. The main business I went about was about Gilsthrop, Sir W. Batten's clerk; who, being upon his death-bed, and now dead, hath offered to make discoveries of the disorders of the Navy and of £65,000 damage to the King; which made mighty noise in the Commons' House; and members appointed to go to him, which they did; but nothing to the purpose got from him, but complaints of false musters, and ships being refitted with victuals and stores at Plymouth, after they came fitted from other ports; but all this to no purpose, nor more than we know, and will own. But the best is, that this loggerhead should say this, that understands nothing of the Navy, nor ever would; and hath particularly blemished his master by name among us. I told Sir W. Coventry of my letter to Sir R. Brookes, and his answer to me. He advises me in what I write to him to be as short as I can, and obscure, saving in things fully plain; for all that he do is to make mischief; and that the greatest wisdom in dealing with the Parliament in the world is to say little, and let them get out what they can by force; which I shall observe. He declared to me much of his mind to be ruled by his own measures, and not to go so far as many would have him to the ruin of my Lord Chancellor, and for which they do endeavour to do what they can against Sir W. Coventry. "But," says he, "I have done my do in helping to get him out of the administration of things, for which he is not fit; but for his life or estate I will have nothing to say to it; besides that my duty to my master the Duke of York is such that I will perish before I will do anything to displease or disoblige him, where the very necessity of the kingdom do not in my judgement call me." Home; and there met W. Batelier, who tells me the first great news that my Lord Chancellor is fled this day, and left a paper behind him for the House of Lords, telling them the reason of his retiring, complaining of a design for his ruin.

4th. I hear that the House of Lords did send down the paper which my Lord Clarendon left behind him, directed to the Lords, to be seditious and scandalous; and the Commons have voted that it be burned by the hands of the hangman, and that the King be desired to agree to it. I do hear, also, that they have desired the King to use means to stop his escape out of the nation. This day Gilsthrop is buried, who hath made all the late discourse of the great discovery of £65,000, of which the King hath been wronged.

5th. This day, not for want, but for good husbandry, I sent my father, by his desire, six pair of my old shoes, which fit him, and are good; yet, methought, it was a thing against my mind to have him wear my old things.

21st. The Nonconformists are mighty high, and

their meetings frequented and connived at; and they do expect to have their day now soon; for my Lord of Buckingham is a declared friend to them, and even to the Quakers, who had very good words the other day from the King himself; and, what is more, the Archbishop of Canterbury is called no more to the Cabal, nor, by the way, Sir W. Coventry; which I am sorry for the Cabal at present being, as he says, the King, and Duke of Buckingham, and Lord Keeper, the Duke of Albemarle, and Privy Seal. The Bishops, differing from the King in the late business in the House of Lords, have caused this and what is likely to follow, for everybody is encouraged nowadays to speak, and even to preach, as I have heard one of them, as bad things against them as ever in the year 1640; which is a strange change. Home to sit with my wife, who is a little better, and her cheek assuaged. I read to her out of *The History of Algiers*, which is mighty pretty reading, and did discourse alone about my sister Pall's match, which is now on foot with one Jackson, another nephew of Mr. Phillips's, to whom he hath left his estate.

27th. A Committee of Tangier met; the Duke of York there; and there I did discourse over to them their condition as to money, which they were all mightily, as I could desire, satisfied with, but the Duke of Albemarle, who takes the part of the Guards against us in our supplies of money, which is an odd consideration for a dull heavy blockhead as he is, understanding no more of either than a goose; but the ability and integrity of Sir W. Coventry, in all the King's concernments, I do and must admire.

January 1668

January 1st. Dined with my Lord Crew, with whom was Mr. Browne, Clerk of the House of Lords, and Mr. John Crew. Here was mighty good discourse, as there is always; and among other things my Lord Crew did turn to a place in the *Life of Sir Philip Sidney*, wrote by Sir Fulke Greville, which do foretell the present condition of this nation, in relation to the Dutch, to the very degree of a prophecy; and is so remarkable that I am resolved to buy one of them, it being, quite throughout, a good discourse. Here they did talk much of the present cheapness of corn, even to a miracle; so as their farmers can pay no rent, but do fling up their lands; and would pay in corn; but, which I did observe to my Lord, and he liked well of it, our gentry are grown so ignorant in everything of good husbandry, that they know not how to bestow this corn; which, did they understand but a little trade, they would be able to join together, and know what markets there are abroad, and send it thither, and thereby ease their tenants and be able to pay themselves. They did talk much of the disgrace the Archbishop is fallen under with the King, and the rest of the Bishops also. Thence I after dinner to the Duke of York's playhouse, and there saw *Sir Martin Mar-all*; which I have seen so often, and yet am mightily pleased with it, and think it mighty witty, and the fullest of proper matter for mirth that ever was writ; and I do clearly see that they do improve in their acting of it. Here a mighty company of citizens, 'prentices, and others; and it makes me observe, that when I began first to be able to bestow a play on myself, I do not remember that I saw so many by half of the ordinary 'prentices and mean people in the pit at 2s. 6d. apiece as now; I going for several years no higher than the 12d. and then the 18d. places, though I strained hard to go in when I did; so much the vanity and prodigality of the age is to be observed in this particular. Thence I to Whitehall, and there walked up and down the house a while, and do hear nothing of anything done further in this business of the change of Privy Councillors; only I hear that Sir G. Savile, one of the Parliament Committee of nine for examining the Accounts, is by the King made a Lord, the Lord Halifax, which, I believe, will displease the Parliament. By and by I met with Mr. Brisband; and having it in my mind this Christmas to do what I never can remember that I did, go to see the gaming at the groom-porter's, I having in my coming from the playhouse stepped into the two Temple halls, and there saw the dirty 'prentices and idle people playing; wherein I was mistaken in thinking to have seen gentlemen of quality playing there, as I think it was when I was a little child, that one of my father's servants, John Bassum, I think, carried me in his arms thither. I did tell Brisband of it, and he did lead me thither, where, after staying an hour, they began to play at about eight at night, where to see how differently one man took his losing from another, one cursing and swearing, and another only muttering and grumbling to himself, a third without any apparent discontent at all; to see how the dice will run good luck in one hand, for half an hour together, and another have no good luck at all; to see how easily here, where they play nothing but guineas, a £100 is won or lost; to see two or three gentlemen come in there drunk, and putting their stock of gold together, one 22 pieces, the second 4, and the third 5 pieces; and these to play one with another, and forget how much each of them brought, but he that brought the 22 thinks that he brought no more than the rest; to see the different humours of gamesters to change their luck, when it is bad, how ceremonious they are to call for new dice, to shift their places, to alter their manner of throwing, and that with great industry, as if there was anything in it; to see how

some old gamesters, that have no money now to
spend as formerly, do come and sit and look on, and
among others, Sir Lewis Dives, who was here, and
hath been a great gamester in his time; to hear their
cursing and damning to no purpose, as one man
being to throw a seven if he could, and, failing to do
it after a great many throws, cried he would be
damned if ever he flung seven more while he lived,
his despair of throwing it being so great, while
others did it as their luck served almost every throw;
to see how persons of the best quality do here sit
down, and play with people of any, though meaner;
and to see how people in ordinary clothes shall come
hither, and play away 100, or 200 or 300 guineas,
without any kind of difficulty; and, lastly, to see the
formality of the groom-porter, who is their judge of
all disputes in play and all quarrels that may arise
therein, and how his under-officers are here to
observe true play at each table, and to give new
dice, is a consideration I never could have thought
had been in the world, had I not now seen it. And
mighty glad I am that I did see it, and it may be
will find another evening, before Christmas be over,
to see it again, when I may stay later, for their heat
of play begins not till about eleven or twelve o'clock;
which did give me another pretty observation of a
man, that did win mighty fast when I was there.
I think he won £100 at single pieces in a little time.
While all the rest envied him his good fortune, he
cursed it, saying, "It comes so early upon me, for
this fortune two hours hence would be worth something to me, but then I shall have no such luck."
This kind of profane mad entertainment they give
themselves. And so I, having enough for once, refusing to venture, though Brisband pressed me hard,
and tempted me with saying that no man was ever
known to lose the first time, the devil being too

cunning to discourage a gamester; and he offered
me also to lend me ten pieces to venture; but I did
refuse, and so went away.

14th. To my bookseller, Martin, and there did
receive my book I expected of China, a most excellent
book with rare cuts; and there fell into discourse
with him about the burning of Paul's when the City
was burned, his house being in the churchyard.
And he tells me that it took fire first upon the end of
a board that, among others, was laid upon the roof
instead of lead, the lead being broke off, and thence
down lower and lower; but that the burning of the
goods under St. Faith's arose from the goods taking
fire in the churchyard, and so got into St. Faith's
Church; and that they first took fire from the
Draper's side, by some timber of the houses that were
burned falling into the church. He says that one
warehouse of books was saved under Paul's; and
there were several dogs found burned among the
goods in the churchyard, and but one man, which
was an old man, that said he would go and save a
blanket which he had in the church, and, being
weak, the fire overcame him.

21st. Comes news from Kate Joyce that if I would
see her husband alive, I must come presently. So
I to him, and find his breath rattled in his throat;
and they did lay pigeons to his feet, and all despair
of him. It seems on Thursday last he went, sober
and quiet, to Islington, and behind one of the inns,
the White Lion, did fling himself into a pond; was
spied by a poor woman, and got out by some people,
and set on his head and got to life; and so his wife
and friends sent for. He confessed his doing the thing,
being led by the Devil; and do declare his reason to
be his trouble in having forgot to serve God as he
ought, since he came to his new employment; and I
believe that, and the sense of his great loss by the fire,

did bring him to it; for he grew sick, and worse and worse to this day. The friends that were there, being now in fear that the goods and estate would be seized on (though he lived all this while) because of his endeavouring to drown himself, my cousin did endeavour to remove what she could of plate out of the house, and desired me to take my flagons; which I did, but in great fear all the way of being seized; though there was no reason for it, he not being dead. So, with D. Gauden, to Guildhall, to advise with the Town-Clerk about the practice of the City and nation in this case; and he thinks that it cannot be found self-murder; but if it be, it will fall, all the estate, to the King. So I to my cousin's again; where I no sooner come but find her husband was departed. So, at their entreaty, I presently to Whitehall, and there find Sir W. Coventry; and he carried me to the King, the Duke of York being with him, and there told my story which I had told him; and the King, without more ado, granted that, if it was found, the estate should be to the widow and children. I presently to each Secretary's office, and there left caveats, and so away back to my cousin's, leaving a chimney on fire at Whitehall, in the King's closet, but no danger. And so, when I came thither, I find her all in sorrow, but she and the rest mightily pleased with my doing this for them; and which, indeed, was a very great courtesy, for people are looking out for the estate.

February 1668

February 1st. To the office till past two o'clock; where at the Board some high words passed between Sir W. Pen and I, begun by me, and yielded to by him, I being in the right in finding fault with him for his neglect of duty. Home, my head mighty full of business now on my hands, viz., of finishing my

Tangier accounts; of auditing my last year's accounts; of preparing answers to the Commissioners of Accounts; of drawing up several important letters to the Duke of York and the Commissioners of the Treasury; the marrying of my sister; the building of a coach and stables against summer, and the setting many things in the Office right; and the drawing up a new form of contract with the Victualler of the Navy, and several other things, which pains, however, will go through with.

2nd. (Lord's day.) All the morning setting my books in order in my presses, for the following year, this number being much increased since the last, so as I am fain to lay by several books to make room for better, being resolved to keep no more than just my presses will contain. A very good dinner we had, of a powdered leg of pork and a loin of lamb roasted.

7th. Met my cousin, Roger Pepys, the Parliament meeting yesterday and adjourned to Monday next; and here he tells me that Mr. Jackson, my sister's servant, is come to town, and hath this day suffered a recovery on his estate, in order to the making her a settlement. There is a great trial between my Lord Gerard and Carr to-day, who is indicted for his life at the King's Bench, for running from his colours; but all do say that my Lord Gerard, though he designs the ruining of this man, will not get anything by it. To the Commissioners of Accounts, and there presented my books, and was made to sit down, and used with much respect, otherwise than the other day, when I came to them as a criminal about the business of prizes. I sat here with them a great while, while my books were inventoried. I find these gentlemen to sit all day, and only eat a bit of bread at noon, and a glass of wine; and are resolved to go through their business with great severity and method. Met my cousin Roger again, and Mr. Jackson, who is a plain young man, handsome enough for Pall, one of no education nor discourse, but of few words, and one altogether that, I think, will please me well enough. My cousin had got me to give the odd sixth £100 presently, which I intended to keep to the birth of the first child; and let it go—I shall be eased of the care. So there parted, my mind pretty well satisfied with this plain fellow for my sister, though I shall, I see, have no pleasure nor content in him, as if he had been a man of reading and parts, like Cumberland. Lord Brouncker, and W. Pen, and I, and with us Sir Arnold Breames, to the King's playhouse, and there saw a piece of *Love in a Maze*, a dull, silly play, I think; and after the play, home with W. Pen and his son Lowther, whom we met there.

8th. Cousin Roger and Jackson by appointment came to dine with me, and Creed, and very merry, only Jackson hath few words, and I like him never the worse for it. The great talk is of Carr's coming off in all his trials, to the disgrace of my Lord Gerard, to that degree, and the ripping up of so many notorious rogueries and cheats of my Lord's, that my Lord, it is thought, will be ruined; and, above all, do show the madness of the House of Commons, who rejected the petition of this poor man by a combination of a few in the House; and, much more, the base proceedings (just the epitome of all our public managements in this age) of the House of Lords, that ordered him to stand in the pillory for those very things, without hearing and examining what he hath now, by the seeking of my Lord Gerard himself, cleared himself of, in open Court, to the gaining himself the pity of all the world, and shame for ever to my Lord Gerard. To the Strand, to my bookseller's, and there bought an idle roguish French book, which I have bought in plain binding, avoiding the buying of it better bound, because I resolve, as soon as I have read it, to burn it, that it may not stand in the list of books, nor among them, to disgrace them if it should be found. My wife well pleased with my sister's match, and designing how to be merry at their marriage.

27th. With my wife to the King's House, to see *The Virgin Martyr*, the first time it hath been acted a great while; and it is mighty pleasant; not that the play is worth much, but it is finely acted by Beck Marshall. But that which did please me beyond anything in the whole world was the wind-music when the angel comes down, which is so sweet that it ravished me, and indeed, in a word, did wrap up my soul so that it made me really sick, just as I have formerly been when in love with my wife; that neither then, nor all the evening going home, and at home, I was able to think of anything, but remained all night transported, so as I could not believe that ever any music hath that real command over the soul of a man as this did upon me; and makes me resolve to practise wind-music, and to make my wife do the like.

March 1668

March 1st. (Lord's day.) Up very betimes, and by coach to Sir W. Coventry's; and there, largely carrying with me all my notes and papers, did run over our whole defence in the business of tickets, in order to the answering the House on Thursday next; and I do think, unless they be set without reason to ruin us, we shall make a good defence. I find him in great anxiety, though he will not discover it, in the business of the proceedings of Parliament; and would as little as is possible have his name mentioned in our discourse to them; and particularly the business of selling places is now upon his hand to

defend himself in; wherein I did help him in his
defence about the flag-maker's place, which is named
in the House. We did here do the like about the
complaint of want of victuals in the fleet in the year
1666, which will lie upon me to defend also. In
lieu of a coach this year I have got my wife to be
contented with her closet being made up this summer,
and going into the country this summer for a month
or two, to my father's, and there Mercer and Deb.
and Jane shall go with her, which I the rather do
for the entertaining my wife, and preventing of
fallings out between her and my father or Deb. To
Mrs. Martin's, and here I was mightily taken with a
starling which she hath, that was the King's, which
he kept in his bedchamber; and do whistle and talk
the most and best that ever I heard anything in my
life. Spent the evening talking with W. Hewer
about business of the House, and declaring my
expectation of all our being turned out.

2nd. Mr. Moore was with me, and do tell me,
and so W. Hewer tells me, he hears this morning
that all the town is full of the discourse that the
Officers of the Navy shall be all turned out, but
honest Sir John Minnes, who, God knows, is fitter
to have been turned out himself than any of us,
doing the King more hurt by his dotage and folly
than all the rest can do by their knavery, if they had
a mind to it. This day I have the news that my
sister was married on Thursday last to Mr. Jackson;
so that work is, I hope, well over.

3rd. Up betimes to work again, and then met at
the office, where to our great business of this answer
to the Parliament; where to my great vexation I
find my Lord Brouncker prepared only to excuse
himself, while I, that have least reason to trouble
myself, am preparing with great pains to defend
them all; and more, I perceive, he would lodge the

beginning of discharging ships by ticket upon me; but I care not, for I believe I shall get more honour by it when the Parliament, against my will, shall see how the whole business of the office was done by me. I with my clerks to dinner, and thence presently down with Lord Brouncker, W. Pen, T. Harvy, T. Middleton, and Mr. Tippets, who first took his place this day at the table, as a Commissioner, in the room of Commissioner Pett. Down by water to Deptford, where the King, Queen, and Court are to see launched the new ship built by Mr. Shish, called the *Charles*. God send her better luck than the former! Here some of our brethren, who went in a boat a little before my boat, did by appointment take opportunity of asking the King's leave that we might make full use of the want of money, in our excuse to the Parliament for the business of tickets, and other things they will lay to our charge, all which arise from nothing else; and this the King did readily agree to, and did give us leave to make our full use of it. The ship being well launched, I back again by boat.

4th. Vexed and sickish to bed, and there slept about three hours, and then waked, and never in so much trouble in all my life of mind, thinking of the task I have upon me, and upon what dissatisfactory grounds, and what the issue of it may be to me.

5th. With these thoughts I lay troubling myself till six o'clock, restless, and at last getting my wife to talk to me to comfort me, which she at last did, and made me resolve to quit my hands of this office, and endure the trouble no longer than I can clear myself of it. So with great trouble, but yet with some ease, from the discourse with my wife, I up, and at my office, whither came my clerks, and I did huddle the best I could some more notes for my discourse to-day, and by nine o'clock was ready, and did go down to the Old Swan, and there by boat, with T. Hater and W. Hewer with me, to Westminster, where I found myself come time enough, and my brethren all ready. But I full of thoughts and trouble touching the issue of this day; and, to comfort myself, did go to the Dog and drink half-a-pint of mulled sack, and in the Hall did drink a dram of brandy at Mrs. Hewlett's; and with the warmth of this did find myself in better order as to courage, truly. So we all up to the lobby; and between eleven and twelve o'clock were called in, with the mace before us, into the House, where a mighty full House; and we stood at the Bar, namely, Brouncker, Sir J. Minnes, Sir T. Harvey, and myself, W. Pen being in the House, as a Member. I perceive the whole House was full of expectation of our defence what it would be, and with great prejudice. After the Speaker had told us the dissatisfaction of the House, and read the Report of the Committee, I began our defence most acceptably and smoothly, and continued at it without any hesitation or loss, but with full scope, and all my reason free about me, as if it had been at my own table, from that time till past three in the afternoon; and so ended, without any interruption from the Speaker; but we withdrew. And there all my fellow-officers, and all the world that was within hearing, did congratulate me, and cry up my speech as the best thing they ever heard; and my fellow-officers were overjoyed in it: we were called in again by and by to answer only one question, touching our paying tickets to ticket-mongers; and so out; and we were in hopes to have had a vote this day in our favour, and so the generality of the House was; but my speech, being so long, many had gone out to dinner and come in again half drunk; and then there are two or three that are professed enemies to us and everybody else; among others, Sir T. Littleton, Sir Thomas Lee, Mr. Wiles, the coxcomb whom I saw heretofore at the cock-fighting, and a few others; I say, these did rise up and speak against the coming to a vote now, the House not being full, by reason of several being at dinner, but most because that the House was to attend the King this afternoon about the business of religion, wherein they pray him to put in force all the laws against Nonconformists and Papists; and this prevented it, so that they put it off to to-morrow come se'nnight. However, it is plain we have got great ground; and everybody says I have got the most honour that any could have had opportunity of getting; and so, our hearts mightily overjoyed at this success, we all to dinner to my Lord Brouncker's —that is to say, myself, T. Harvey, and W. Pen, and there dined; and thence with Sir Anthony Morgan, who is an acquaintance of Brouncker's, a very wise man, we after dinner to the King's house, and there saw part of *The Discontented Colonel*. To my wife, whom W. Hewer had told of my success, and she overjoyed; and, after talking awhile, I betimes to bed, having had no quiet rest a good while.

6th. Up betimes, and with Sir D. Gauden to Sir W. Coventry's chamber: where the first words he said to me was, " Good-morrow, Mr. Pepys, that must be Speaker of the Parliament House "; and did protest I had got honour for ever in Parliament. He said that his brother, that sat by him, admires me; and another gentleman said that I could not get less than £1000 a-year if I would put on a gown and plead at the Chancery Bar; but, what pleases me most, he tells me that the Solicitor-General did protest that he thought I spoke the best of any man in England. After several talks with him alone, touching his own businesses, he carried me to White-hall, and there parted; and I to the Duke of York's lodgings, and find him going to the Park, it being a very fine morning, and I after him; and, as soon as he saw me, he told me, with great satisfaction, that I had converted a great many yesterday, and did, with great praise of me, go on with the discourse with me. And, by and by, overtaking the King, the King and Duke of York came to me both; and he said, " Mr. Pepys, I am very glad of your success yesterday "; and fell to talk of my well speaking; and many of the Lords there. My Lord Barkeley did cry me up for what they had heard of it; and others, Parliament-men there, about the King, did say that they never heard such a speech in their lives delivered in that manner. Progers, of the Bedchamber, swore to me afterwards before Brouncker, in the afternoon, that he did tell the King that he thought I might teach the Solicitor-General. Everybody that saw me almost came to me, as Joseph Williamson and others, with such eulogies as cannot be expressed. From thence I went to Westminster Hall, where I met Mr. G. Montagu, who came to me and kissed me, and told me that he had often heretofore kissed my hands, but now he would kiss my lips; protesting that I was another Cicero, and said all the world said the same of me. Mr. Ashburnham, and every creature I met there of the Parliament, or that knew anything of the Parliament's actings, did salute me with this honour; Mr. Godolphin; Mr. Sands, who swore he would go twenty miles, at any time, to hear the like again, and that he never saw so many sit four hours together to hear any man in his life, as there did to hear me; Mr. Chichly; Sir John Duncomb; and everybody do say that the kingdom will ring of my abilities, and that I have done myself right for my whole life; and so Captain Cocke and others of my friends say that no man had ever such an opportunity of making his abilities known; and, that I may cite all at once, Mr. Lieutenant of the Tower did tell me that Mr. Vaughan did protest to him, and that in his hearing, he said so to the Duke of Albemarle, and afterwards to Sir W. Coventry, that he had sat twenty-six years in Parliament and never heard such a speech there before; for which the Lord God make me thankful! and that I may make use of it not to pride and vain-glory, but that, now I have this esteem, I may do nothing that may lessen it.

26th. To the Duke of York's house, to see the new play, called *The Man is the Master*, where the house was, it being not one o'clock, very full. But my wife and Deb. being there before, with Mrs. Pierce and Corbet and Betty Turner, whom my wife carried with her, they made me room; and there I sat, it costing me 8s. upon them in oranges, at 6d. apiece. By and by the King came; and we sat just under him, so that I durst not turn my back all the play. The play is a translation out of French, and the plot Spanish, but not anything extraordinary at all in it, though translated by Sir W. Davenant, and so I found the King and his company did think meanly of it, though there was here and there some-thing pretty; but the most of the mirth was sorry poor stuff, of eating of sack-posset and slabbering them-selves, and mirth fit for clowns; the prologue but poor, and the epilogue little in it but the extra-ordinariness of it, being sung by Harris and another in the form of a ballad. Thence, by agreement, we all of us to the Blue Balls hard by, whither Mr. Pierce also goes with us, who met us at the play, and anon comes Manuel, and his wife, and Knipp, and Harris, who brings with him Mr. Banister, the great master of music; and after much difficulty in getting of music, we to dancing, and then to a supper of French dishes, which yet did not please me, and then to dance and sing; and mighty merry we were till about eleven or twelve at night, with mighty great content in all my company, and I did, as I love to do, enjoy myself. My wife extraordinary fine to-day, in her flower tabby suit, bought a year and more ago, before my mother's death put her into mourning, and so not worn till this day; and everybody in love with it; and indeed she is very fine and handsome in it. I having paid the reckoning, which came to almost £4, we parted; my company and William Batelier, who was also with us, home in a coach, round by the Wall, where we met so many stops by the watches, that it cost us much time and some trouble, and more money, to every watch, to them to drink; this being increased by the trouble the 'prentices did lately give the City, so that the Militia and watches are very strict at this time; and we had like to have met with a stop for all night at the constable's watch, at Moorgate, by a pragmatical constable; but we came well home at about two in the morning. This afternoon at the play Sir Fr. Hollis spoke to me as a secret and matter of confidence in me, and friendship to Sir W. Pen, who is now out of town, that it were well he were made acquainted that he finds in the House of Commons, which met this day, several motions made for the calling strictly again upon the Miscarriages, and particularly in the business of the Prizes, and the not prosecuting of the first victory, only to give an affront to Sir W. Pen, whose going to sea this year does give them matter of great dislike.

April 1668

April 2nd. With Lord Brouncker to the Royal Society, where they had just done; but there I was forced to subscribe, to the building of a College, and did give £40; and several others did subscribe, some greater and some less sums; but several I saw hang off; and I doubt it will spoil the Society, for it breeds faction and ill-will, and becomes burdensome to some that cannot, or would not, do it. Here, to my great content, I did try the use of the Otacousticon, which was only a great glass bottle broke at the bottom, putting the neck to my ear, and there I did plainly hear the dancing of the oars of the boats in the Thames to Arundel gallery window, which, without it, I could not in the least do, and may, I believe, be improved to a great height, which I am mighty glad of.

May 1668

May 22nd. Comes Mr. Martin, the purser, and brings me his wife's starling, which was formerly the King's, which I am mighty proud of. To the Duke of York's house, and saw *Sir Martin Mar-all*. The house full; and though I have seen it, I think, ten times, yet the pleasure I have is yet as great as ever. I fitted myself for my journey to Brampton to-morrow, which I fear will not be pleasant, because of the wet weather, it raining very hard all this day; but the less it troubles me because the King and Duke of York and Court are at this day at Newmarket, at a great horse-race, and proposed great pleasure for two or three days, but are in the same wet.

25th. The first fair day that we have had some time. So up, and to walk with my father again in the garden, consulting what to do with him and this house when Pall and her husband go away; and I think it will be to let it, and he go live with her, though I am against letting the house for any long time, because of having it to retire to, ourselves. After dinner took horse, there going with me and my boy, my two brothers, and one Browne, whom they call in mirth Colonel, for our guide, and also Mr. Shepley, to the end of Huntingdon, and another gentleman who accidentally came thither, one Mr. Castle; and I made them drink at the Chequers, where I observed the same tapster, Tom, that was there when I was a little boy; and so, at the end of the town, took leave of Shepley and the other gentleman, and away to Cambridge, the waters not being now so high as before. Here 'lighting, I took my boy and two brothers, and walked to Magdalene College: and there into the butteries, as a stranger, and there drank of their beer, which pleased me, as the best I ever drank; and hear by the butler's man, who was son to Goody Mulliner over against the College, that we used to buy stewed prunes of, concerning the College and persons in it; and find very few, only Mr. Hollins and Pechell, I think, that were of my time. Thence, giving the fellow something, away walked to Chesterton, to see our old walk, and there into the Church, the bells ringing, and saw the place I used to sit in, and so to the ferry, and ferried over to the other side, and walked with great pleasure, the river being mighty high by Barnewell Abbey; and so by Jesus College to the town, and so to our quarter, and to supper.

June 1668

June 29th. To Dr. Turberville's, and there did receive a direction for some physic, and also a glass of something to drop into my eyes; he gives me hopes that I may do well.

August 1668

August 2nd. (Lord's day.) Up, and at home all the morning, hanging and removing of some pictures in my study and house. After dinner I and Tom, my boy, by water up to Putney, and there heard a sermon, and many fine people in the church. Thence walked to Barn Elms, and there, and going and coming, did make the boy read to me several things, being nowadays unable to read myself anything, for above two lines together, but my eyes grow weary.

19th. This week my people wash, over the water, and so I little company at home. Being busy above, a great cry I hear, and go down; and what should it be but Jane, in a fit of direct raving, which lasted half an hour. It was beyond four or five of our strength to keep her down; and, when all come to all, a fit of jealousy about Tom, with whom she is in love. So at night, I, and my wife, and W. Hewer called them to us, and there I did examine all the thing, and them, in league. She in love, and he hath got her to promise him to marry, and he is now cold in it, so that I must rid my hands of them, which troubles me.

September 1668

September 4th. This night Knipp tells us that there is a Spanish woman lately come over, that pretends to sing as well as Mrs. Knight; both of whom I must endeavour to hear.

16th. Walking it to the Temple, and in my way observe that the Stocks are now pulled quite down; and it will make the coming into Cornhill and Lombard Street mighty noble. I stopped, too, at Paul's, and there did go into St. Faith's Church, and also in the body of the west part of the Church; and do see a hideous sight of the walls of the Church ready to fall, that I was in fear as long as I was in it; and here I saw the great vaults underneath the body of the Church. No hurt, I hear, is done yet, since

their going to pull down the Church and steeple;
but one man, one Mound, this week fell from the top
of the roof, of the east end that stands next the steeple,
and there broke himself all to pieces. It is pretty
here to see how the late Church was but a case
wrought over the old Church; for you may see the
very old pillars standing whole within the wall of
this.

January 1669

January 23rd. To the office till noon, when word
brought me that my Lord Sandwich was come; so
I presently rose, and there I found my Lords Sandwich, Peterborough, and Sir Charles Harbord; and
presently after them comes my Lord Hinchingbroke,
Mr. Sidney, and Sir William Godolphin. And after
greeting them, and some time spent in talk, dinner
was brought up, one dish after another, but a dish
at a time, but all so good; but, above all things, the
variety of wines, and excellent of their kind, I had
for them, and all in so good order, that they were
mightily pleased, and myself full of content at it;
and indeed it was, of a dinner of about six or eight
dishes, as noble as any man need to have, I think;
at least, all was done in the noblest manner that ever
I had any, and I have rarely seen in my life better
anywhere else, even at the Court. After dinner, my
Lords to cards, and the rest of us sitting about them
and talking, and looking on my books and pictures,
and my wife's drawings, which they commended
mightily; and mighty merry all day long, with
exceeding great content, and so till seven at night;
and so took their leaves, it being dark and foul
weather. Thus was this entertainment over, the
best of its kind, and the fullest of honour and content
to me, that ever I had in my life; and I shall not

easily have so good again. The truth is I have some
fear that I am more behindhand in the world for
these last two years, since I have not, or for some time
could not, look after my accounts, which do a little
allay my pleasure. But I do trust in God that I am
pretty well yet, and resolve, in a very little time, to
look into my accounts, and see how they stand.

February 1669

February 18th. Expecting to have this day seen
Bab. and Betty Pepys here, but they came not; and so
after dinner my wife and I to the Duke of York's
house to a play, and there saw *The Mad Lover*, which
do not please me so well as it used to do, only Betterton's part still pleases me. But here who should
have come to us but Bab. and Betty and Talbot, the
first play they were yet at; and going to see us, and
hearing by my boy, whom I sent to them, that we
were here, they came to us hither, and happened all
of us to sit by my cousin Turner and The. We
carried them home first, and then took Bab. and
Betty to our house, where they lay and supped, and
pretty merry, and very fine with their new clothes,
and good comely girls they are enough, and very
glad I am of their being with us, though I would
very well have been contented to be without the
charge. So they to bed.

March 1669

March 9th. Up, and to the Tower; and there
find Sir W. Coventry alone, writing down his Journal,
which, he tells me, he now keeps of the material
things; upon which I told him, and he is the only
man I ever told it to, I think, that I kept it most
strictly these eight or ten years; and I am sorry almost

that I told it him, it not being necessary, nor may be convenient, to have it known.

23rd.   I took coach with Commissioner Middleton, Captain Tinker, and Mr. Huchinson, and out towards Chatham, and dined at Dartford, where we stayed an hour or two, it being a cold day; and so on, and got to Chatham just at night, with very good discourse by the way, but mostly of matters of religion, wherein Huchinson his vein lies. After supper we fell to talk of spirits and apparitions, whereupon many pretty particular stories were told, so as to make me almost afraid to lie alone, but for shame I could not help it; and so to bed; and, being sleepy, fell soon to rest, and so rested well.

May 1669

May 31st.   Up very betimes, and continued all the morning with W. Hewer, upon examining and stating my accounts, in order to the fitting myself to go abroad beyond sea, which the ill condition of my eyes, and my neglect for a year or two, hath kept me behindhand in, and so as to render it very difficult now, and troublesome to my mind to do it; but I this day made a satisfactory entrance therein.   Had another meeting with the Duke of York at Whitehall on yesterday's work, and made a good advance; and so, being called by my wife, we to the Park, Mary Batelier, and a Dutch gentleman, a friend of hers, being with us.   Thence to The World's End, a drinking-house by the Park; and there merry, and so home late.

And thus ends all that I doubt I shall ever be able to do with my own eyes in the keeping of my Journal, I being not able to do it any longer, having done now so long as to undo my eyes almost every time that I take a pen in my hand; and, therefore, whatever comes of it, I must forbear; and, therefore, resolve, from this time forward, to have it kept by my people in longhand, and must be contented to set down no more than is fit for them and all the world to know; or, if there be anything, I must endeavour to keep a margin in my book open, to add, here and there, a note in shorthand with my own hand.

And so I betake myself to that course, which is almost as much as to see myself go into my grave; for which, and all the discomforts that will accompany my being blind, the good God prepare me!

S. P.

May 31, 1669.

NOTES

1659

P. 1, l. 3. *My old pain :* Pepys had undergone an operation for the stone (a growth in the kidneys or bladder) on March 26th, 1658. He always celebrated its success at each anniversary by giving a dinner to Mrs. Turner, at whose house in Salisbury Court the operation had been carried out.

l. 4. *Axe Yard :* in Westminster.

l. 7. *The condition of the State :* Amidst the anarchy which followed the death of Cromwell in 1658 a conscious desire among the people for a Restoration was slowly forming. The rule of the army officers, prominent among whom were Lambert, Fairfax, and Monk, had collapsed, and in the City there had arisen a general demand for a free Parliament. Monk eventually declared himself in favour of a Restoration, and made the first overtures to Charles.

l. 10. *Lawson lies still in the river :* John Lawson was Commander of the Fleet in 1659.

l. 15. *High :* pretentiously, arrogantly. Elsewhere in the Diary this word is used to express extremity of religious or political opinion.

P. 2, l. 22. Jan. 2nd. *Mr. Crewe's :* Mr. Crewe was Sir Edward Montagu's father-in-law.

1660

P. 3, l. 10. 19th. *The Council :* i.e. the Privy Council.
Stumbled : perplexed.

l. 15. 26th. *My Lord's lodgings :* " my Lord " is Sir Edward Montagu, later Earl of Sandwich, Pepys's patron and cousin, to whom he usually refers thus. So Lady Sandwich is " my Lady."

l. 19. *A neat's tongue :* an ox-tongue.

l. 22. *Mr. Pierce :* a surgeon in the army, and later the King's surgeon.

P. 3, l. 23. *My brother Tom :* Tom is frequently mentioned in the Diary. At this time he was working under his father in the tailor's shop, and when his father retired took over the management of it. His death on March 15th, 1664, is recorded in the Diary. He was then thirty.

l. 31. 30th. *" Great, good, and just " :* the opening lines of Montrose's verses on the execution of Charles I.

P. 4, l. 8. Feb. 3rd. *Mrs. Turner :* née Jane Pepys, a cousin of Samuel's.

Joyce : William Joyce, uncle Fenner's son-in-law (see Jan. 26th).

l. 34. 21st. *Pursell :* Henry Purcell, father of the composer.

P. 5, l. 4. *Canon:* a musical composition in which the different parts (here the eight voices) take up the same subject one after another in strict imitation.

l. 12. 22nd. *To Cambridge :* Pepys was preparing to go to Cambridge to arrange for his brother John's admission to Christ's College.

l. 28. 24th. *Hinchingbroke :* Hinchingbroke House, near Huntingdon, which had formerly been the residence of Cromwell, now occupied by Montagu.

ll. 31, 32. *Messrs. Hill, Zanchy, Burton,* etc.: Fellows of Magdalene.

l. 34. *The Three Tuns :* this inn still stands, on Castle Hill, a few hundred yards from the College.

P. 6, l. 10. 26th. *St. Botolph's Church :* in Trumpington Street.

l. 12. *Tripos :* the person chosen by the Senior Proctor to make the disputation on Ash Wednesday.

l. 16. *Lost his journey :* " had his journey for nothing."

l. 18. *Put to a stand :* surprised, perplexed.

l. 30. 27th. *Flageolet:* a small wind-instrument with a mouthpiece and six principal holes.

P. 7, l. 8. 28th. *By the same token:* moreover, " which reminds me that . . ." etc.

l. 16. 29th. *Metheglin :* a sweet mixed drink brewed from honey.

l. 20. Mar. 2nd. *Mr. Prin :* William Prynne, the famous Puritan persecuted by Laud.

l. 27. 5th. *The Covenant :* the Solemn League and Covenant with Scotland, accepted by the English Parliament in 1643. It was an agreement to establish Presbyterianism in both countries.

NOTES

P. 8, l. 14. 6th. *Purser's place :* a purser was a commissioned officer who had charge of the provisions, money, etc. of a ship.

l. 16. *Knights of Windsor :* the body of military pensioners residing within the precincts of Windsor Castle.

l. 22. *Tag, rag, and bobtail :* riff-raff.

l. 33. *The Protector :* Richard Cromwell, Oliver's son, who had always been a political nonentity.

P. 9, l. 4. *The twelve Halls :* those of the twelve great Merchant Companies of London.

l. 11. 9th. *The Painted Chamber :* a room in the old Palace of Westminster, so called from its mural paintings, sometimes used as the meeting-place of Parliament. It was destroyed by fire in 1834.

l. 17. 12th. *Mr. Bowyer's :* Mr. Bowyer was Mrs. Pepys's stepfather.

l. 18. *Huntsmore :* in Buckinghamshire.

P. 10, l. 33. 16th. *The Great Exchange :* so called during the Commonwealth.

The inscription : "Exit tyrannus, Regum ultimus, anno libertatis Angliæ, anno Domini 1648 Januarii XXX."

P. 11, l. 12. 24th. *Mr. Creed :* Deputy Treasurer to the Fleet, and always a colleague of Pepys.

On board : Pepys had embarked on the *Swiftsure* the previous day.

l. 23. 25th. *The Cinque Ports :* originally five fortified ports on the South Coast: Dover, Hastings, Hythe, Romney, and Sandwich. Rye and Winchelsea were added.

P. 12, l. 5. 29th. *A letter :* accompanying the Declaration of Breda.

l. 21. May 2nd. *Act of Oblivion :* a statutory free pardon.

l. 22. *Confirming of the sales :* many Cavaliers had been forced to sell their lands during the Commonwealth period by the burden of punitive fines. It was a problem at the Restoration whether or not they should receive compensation.

P. 13, l. 19. 3rd. *Twelfth year of his reign :* assuming him to have reigned since 1649.

l. 26. *Coach :* a room in the stern of a man-of-war, by the captain's cabin.

P. 14, l. 26. *Jack Cole :* an old crony of Pepys's.

P. 15, l. 32. 14th. *Queen of Bohemia :* Elizabeth, daughter of James I and widow of Frederick, Elector Palatine; she returned to England at the Restoration.

P. 16, l. 1. *Prince of Orange :* afterwards William III.

l. 14. *Governor :* tutor.

l. 26. *Sallet :* salad.

l. 28. *Press bed :* a bed constructed to fold up, when not in use, into a recess closed by a door.

P. 17, l. 1. 16th. *Princess Royal :* Mary, daughter of Charles I and mother of the Prince of Orange.

l. 20. 17th. *The club :* the bill.

l. 29. *The Lord Chancellor :* Edward Hyde, afterwards the Earl of Clarendon, the chief adviser and friend of the King in his exile.

P. 18, ll. 27, 28. 22nd. *Dukes of York and Gloucester :* James and Henry Stuart, Charles II's brothers.

l. 36. *Mr. Coventry :* afterwards Sir William Coventry, Secretary to the Duke of York. He was the only one of Pepys's colleagues on the Navy Board whom Pepys admired for his ability. Later he became one of Charles's ministers.

P. 22, l. 1. 23rd. *The priest's hole :* a secret recess in the wainscoting of some great country houses, used as a refuge for Roman Catholic priests subject to the penal laws.

l. 3. *Lords Commissioners :* at the Restoration the ancient form of naval administration was revived. It consisted of a Lord High Admiral (the Duke of York) and the Navy Board (four " principal officers " and three Lords Commissioners).

l. 7. 24th. *Canons* (or canions): ornamental rolls worn round the lower end of the legs of breeches.

P. 23, l. 15. 25th. *Sir W. Batten :* the Surveyor, and a naval officer of experience and ability, whom later Pepys as Clerk of the Acts came to dislike. Their wives did not get on well together.

l. 33. 27th. *Congees :* bows.

P. 25, l. 15. June 1st. *For Weymouth :* M.P. for Weymouth.

P. 26, l. 20. 23rd. *The King's evil :* scrofula, a disease which it was believed the mystical power of kingship could cure. Children were especially subject to scrofula, and Dr. Johnson, who had it as a child, was one of the last to be touched—by Queen Anne.

P. 27, l. 2. 29th. *Mr. Barlow :* a former Clerk of the Acts who claimed that he still had a right to the office.

P. 27, l. 13. July 1st. *Camlet:* originally a beautiful Oriental fabric made of the hair of goats and kids, especially of the Angora goat. The same name was applied also to imitations.

P. 28, l. 29. 8th. *Roger Pepys:* son of Talbot Pepys, a barrister of Impington. Roger was M.P. for Cambridge in 1661.

l. 36. 13th. *Nightgown:* dressing-gown.

P. 29, l. 3. " *Recipe* ": or *recepi* (Latin).

l. 4. *Docket:* an abstract of a proposed letter-patent from the King.

l. 15. *My house:* in Seething Lane, Westminster.

l. 26. 17th. *Will:* William Hewer, Pepys's chief clerk. He afterwards became a Commissioner of the Navy and Treasurer for Tangier, and was the constant companion of Pepys, who died in his house at Clapham.

P. 30, l. 7. Aug. 2nd. *Sir W. Pen:* a distinguished seaman and colleague of Pepys on the Navy Board, the father of the famous Quaker who founded Pennsylvania. Pepys afterwards came to hate him " for his base treacherous tricks " (see July 5, 1662).

P. 31, l. 1. 10th. *Privy Seal:* Pepys had been sworn in as a Clerk of the Privy Seal on July 23rd.

l. 24. 18th. *The Cockpit:* a theatre in Drury Lane.

l. 25. *The Loyal Subject:* by John Fletcher.

l. 26. *Kinaston:* one of the last actors who played female parts.

l. 36. 19th. *Mr. Mills:* Rector of St. Olave's Church, Hart St.

P. 32, l. 29. Sept. 16th. *The Pell-Mell:* the promenade in St. James's Park, which got its name from the early form of croquet called Pell-Mell which was played there.

l. 30. *Making a river through the Park:* the canal. " The Park " always means St. James's Park.

l. 34. 21st. *Corpse of the Duke of Gloucester:* he had died of small-pox.

P. 33, l. 13. *Samphire* (Fr. *l'herbe de Saint Pierre*) : a fleshy European plant growing along the seashore, which was used to make a favourite pickle of that time.

l. 14. *Mardyke Fort:* four miles E. of Dunkirk.

P. 34, l. 6. Oct. 3rd. *The Duke:* James, Duke of York, afterwards James II.

l. 29. 11th. *The Moor of Venice:* Shakespeare's *Othello.*

l. 35. 13th. *Major-General Harrison:* one of the regicides.

P. 35, l. 11. 21st. *Cooke's head :* John Cook, the barrister ordered by Parliament to conduct the prosecution of Charles I.

l. 19. 29th. *Lord Mayor's Day :* Old Style—Nov. 9th, after the reform of the calendar in 1752.

P. 37, l. 1. Nov. 2nd. *Kirton's :* Pepys's bookseller's.

l. 7. *The Queen's coming :* the Infanta Catherine of Braganza.

l. 10. 4th. *Our own church :* St. Olave's, Hart Street.

l. 26. *Black patch :* a small piece of black silk worn on the face to show off the complexion by contrast.

l. 27. 12th. *The Comptroller's house :* Sir Robert Slingsby, Comptroller of the Navy. He died on Oct. 27th, 1661.

l. 30. *My sister :* Paulina Pepys (Pall), a refractory girl. But she was the only one of Pepys's family to have children. Her son John Jackson became Pepys's heir and is the ancestor of the present Pepys-Cockerell family.

P. 38, l. 5. 15th. *And others of good quality :* female servants at this time were often the daughters of quite well-to-do merchants.

l. 12. 20th. *Beggar's Bush :* by Beaumont and Fletcher.

l. 26. 21st. *Lignum vitæ :* a very hard, dark, close-grained wood from the West Indies or S. America.

l. 28. *Moyre :* mohair.

P. 39, l. 3. 22nd. *Whisk :* a kind of collar.

l. 15. *Princess Henrietta :* Charles II's favourite sister, afterwards Duchess of Orleans.

l. 30. 27th. *Which do like me well :* an instance of the archaic impersonal use of the verb " to like," " me " being dative = which I like very much, or which suits me admirably.

P. 40, l. 7. Dec. 4th. *Moiety :* half.

l. 9. *Oliver, Ireton, Bradshaw,* etc.: as regicides.

l. 13. *A man of so great courage as he was :* Cromwell. Pepys had been a Cromwellian in his day.

l. 21. 12th. *My mother Bowyer :* his mother-in-law.

P. 41, l. 1. 21st. *Young Jermyn :* nephew of the Earl of St. Albans.

l. 2. *The Duke of York's marrying the Chancellor's daughter :* the marriage between James and Anne Hyde was extremely unpopular.

1661

P. 43, l. 11. Jan. 1st. *Carboned :* burnt, singed.

NOTES

P. 44, l. 4. 2nd. *Trinity House :* a Corporation of English mariners, dating from the early sixteenth century, with headquarters at Deptford. It had been dissolved in 1647 and was now being reconstituted by Royal Charter. *Duke of Albemarle :* General Monk's new title.

l. 20. 7th. *Great stir . . . by the Fanatics :* the "rebellion" of Fifth-Monarchy men. Their leader, Thomas Venner, a cooper, was executed on January 19th.

l. 25. *The Silent Woman*—by Ben Jonson.

P. 45, l. 7. 9th. *Train-bands :* the militia.

P. 46, l. 17. 22nd. *Dr. Thomas Fuller :* author of *Worthies of England*, published 1662 (see Feb. 10th of that year).

P. 47, l. 8. Feb. 4th. *Some sports :* "Questions and Commands," a game referred to in the *Tatler* and the *Spectator*, and also in Wycherley and Fielding.

P. 48, l. 6. 14th. *Who the King is like to have for his Queen :* Charles did not marry Catherine of Braganza until May 21st, 1662.

l. 22. 18th. *Lutestring :* a plain, stout, lustrous silk.

P. 49, l. 7. April 2nd. *Pelemele :* a variant spelling of Pell-Mell (see note Sept. 16th, 1660).

l. 19. *Betwit :* upbraid.

P. 52, l. 25. 22nd. *Mum :* a kind of ale brewed with wheat.

P. 53, l. 13. 23rd. *Mond :* orb.

P. 55, l. 28. *The leads :* a familiar term for a flat roof which may be treated as a floor.

P. 56, ll. 21, 26. *Serjeant Glynne, Maynard :* old Cromwellians.

P. 57, l. 4. 24th. *Chambers :* small pieces without a carriage used for salutes.

l. 35. May 23rd. *Dr. Bates :* a Puritan divine.

P. 58, l. 7. *In procession with their broom-staffs :* for the beating of bounds on Holy Thursday.

l. 17. June 5th. *Botargo :* dried roe of mullet (*i.e.* a species of caviare), which was eaten with bread and butter to excite thirst.

l. 32. 11th. *Sir G. Carteret :* Treasurer of the Navy. Pepys had a characteristically low opinion of his abilities.

P. 59, l. 12. 18th. *Harpsichon :* harpsichord, an early keyboard instrument like the spinet.

l. 28. 29th. *Hooker's Ecclesiastical Polity :* Richard Hooker (1553–1600). The *Laws of Ecclesiastical Polity* was published in 1593.

l. 36. 30th *Trillo :* the shake.

P. 61, l. 3. July 8th. *A caveat :* notice given by an interested person to stay proceedings until a party is heard in opposition, *e.g.* a caveat entered in a probate court to stop the proving of a will.

l. 23. 23rd. *Mrs. Palmer :* afterwards Lady Castlemaine.

l. 30. 24th. *The Wardrobe :* the building in which the officers charged with the care of the royal wardrobe conducted their business.

P. 63, l. 23. Aug. 31st. *Benevolence :* a voluntary contribution made by the subjects to their sovereign.

P. 64, l. 23. Sept. 7th. *Bartholomew Fair :* by Ben Jonson.

P. 65, l. 6. 11th. *Balty :* Balthazar St. Michel, Mrs. Pepys's brother.

l. 9. *Servant :* suitor.
Trepan : ensnare.

P. 66, l. 1. Oct. 19th. *Rule for a gentleman :* the popular *Advice to a Son*, by Francis Osborne.

P. 67, l. 12. Dec. 13th. *Dead colour :* pale complexion.

1662

P. 69, l. 3. Jan. 13th. *Chemical glasses :* " Prince Rupert drops," formed by the dropping of molten glass into a cold fluid.

l. 7. *Gleek :* a game for three persons. Forty-four cards were used, twelve being dealt to each player, while the remaining eight formed a common " stock." The object was to collect sets of three cards of equal rank, so the game must have resembled closely our " rummy."

l. 9. 14th. *Vellum :* a fine clear white parchment.

l. 17. 16th. *Gambo :* Gambia.

P. 70, l. 9. Feb. 3rd. *Tearing the ribbons :* an old custom at marriage festivities.

l. 30. 9th. *God forgive me ! :* for breaking the Sabbath. There was more than one strain of the Puritan in Pepys (cf. his views on dancing, Nov. 11th, 1661).

P. 71, l. 14. 15th. *Sasse :* lock or sluice.

P. 72, l. 17. March 1st. *My little picture :* his miniature.

P. 73, l. 10. 26th. *Jowl :* cheek.

l. 11. *Tanzy :* a sweet dish of eggs, cream, and sack, etc.

l. 24. April 1st. *The great cheese-cake house :* Islington was famous for its cheese-cakes and custards. Cf. the old " Maids of Honour " Teashop at Richmond which still exists, dating from the time of Anne Boleyn, when its cheese-cakes were first relished by Henry VIII.

P. 74, l. 13. 30th. *The town :* Pepys is at Portsmouth on business.

l. 28. May 3rd. *The lions :* cf. references to the lions in the Tower in Cowper's letters and *passim*.

P. 75, l. 31. June 14th. *Sir Henry Vane :* executed as a regicide.

P. 76 l. 1. *Those that writ after him :* those who reported his words.

P. 77, l. 19. 30th. *Fanatics :* in the latter half of the seventeenth century " Fanatic " was an opprobious term for an English Nonconformist.

l. 23. *Chimney-money :* hearth-money, a duty of 2*s.* a year on each hearth, imposed during this reign, repealed 1689.

P. 78, l. 17. July 5th. *Umbles :* the liver, kidneys, etc. of deer. Hence the phrase " to eat humble pie."

P. 80, l. 5. Aug. 20th. *Guyland :* a Moorish usurper who was threatening Tangier, which had been handed over to England by Portugal as part of Catherine of Braganza's dowry.

P. 82, l. 23. Sept. 3rd. *When the candle is going out :* " Sale by an inch of candle " was an old form of auction in which bidding continued until the piece of candle burned out.

P. 83, l. 1. 7th. *What ministers are flung out that will not conform :* the Act of Uniformity, imposing the Prayer Book, the oath of non-resistance, and the renunciation of the Covenant on clergymen of every rank, was passed on May 19th, 1662, and on Aug. 24th about 1200 " Nonconformist " ministers who refused to comply were ejected from their livings. (This was part of the famous Clarendon Code.)

l. 11. *Mr. Crofts :* later Duke of Monmouth, and called Crofts after his guardian, Lord Crofts.

P. 84, l. 33. Oct. 10th. *Vexed me to the blood :* rubbed the skin off. Cf. the somewhat similar phrase, " cut to the quick."

P. 85, l. 10. *Proctor :* an officer who enforces order and obedience to the laws and ordinances of the University.

l: 11. *Regent House :* now called the Senate House.

l. 18. *Taxor :* or Taxer, one of the two officers in Cambridge formerly chosen yearly to regulate the assize of bread and to see that the true gauge of weights and measures was observed.

P. 85, l. 30. 14th. *My father and I admitted to all the lands.* A lawsuit had arisen over the will of Pepys's uncle Robert, who had left the Brampton estate to Samuel's father. It was awarded in their favour.

P. 86, l. 26. Nov. 27th. *Quarrefowr :* a place where four roads meet (Fr. *carrefour*).

Gracious Street : Gracechurch St.

P. 87, l. 5. Dec. 1st. *Skates :* skating is said to have been made fashionable by the Cavaliers in exile with Charles II in Holland.

l. 20. 25th. *Bullen :* Boulogne.

l. 32. *Groom-porter :* an officer in the royal household who attended to the furnishing of the King's lodgings. Every Christmas he conducted gambling in the Temple Halls, and later Pepys attended one of these meetings (see Jan. 1st, 1668).

P. 88, l. 17. 26th. *Hudibras :* by Samuel Butler.

1663

P. 90, l. 11. Jan. 6th. *Dr. Calamy :* a Puritan Nonconformist preacher.

l. 12. *Sunday was sennight,* i.e. last Sunday week.

l. 31. 8th. *The Adventures of Five Hours :* based on a play by the contemporary Spanish dramatist Calderon.

P. 91, l. 30. 13th. *Sack posset :* a beverage of hot milk curdled by wine and spiced.

P. 92, l. 2. Feb. 4th. *Apposition-Day :* Speech-Day.

l. 13. *Stephanus :* Stephens's *Thesaurus Græcæ Linguæ,* which Pepys bought on Dec. 24th, 1662, for £4 10s. and presented to St. Paul's.

l. 14. *Colet :* John Colet the Humanist, friend of Sir Thomas More, who founded St. Paul's School early in the sixteenth century.

l. 20. March 18th. *Triangle :* more fully triangle virginal, an early kind of keyboard instrument. Obviously not the percussion instrument to which the name refers to-day.

l. 21. *Ashwell :* a new servant.

P. 93, l. 2. April 4th. *A few days ago :* Mar. 26th.

l. 8. *lamprey :* a sort of eel.

l. 17. 30th. *The lions :* in the Tower, one of the " sights of London " at that time.

l. 23. May 1st. *Good husbandry :* economy.

NOTES

P. 94, l. 3. *Jade :* a mean, vicious, or worn-out horse.

l. 4. *Stone-horse :* stallion.

l. 26. *Morris-dancing :* a Moorish dance, naturally forbidden during the Cromwellian period.

P. 95, l. 7. 4th. *Coranto :* a dance characterised by a running or gliding step (Fr. *courante*).

P. 96, l. 25. June 2nd. *Tierce :* a cask whose content is one-third of a pipe, or 42 gallons.

P. 98, l. 32. July 10th. *My Lord Chancellor :* already in 1663 Clarendon was very unpopular in the country, but his fall from power did not come till 1667.

P. 99, l. 19. *A cap :* a Cardinal's hat.

P. 101, l. 2. 13th. *Mrs. Stewart :* another of the King's mistresses.

P. 102, l. 18. 26th. *The Wells :* the medicinal Wells at Epsom were just becoming fashionable at this time.

l. 35. 27th. *Fox Hall :* Vauxhall.

P. 103, l. 14. *Subsidies :* originally extraordinary taxation granted by Parliament, had come to be granted annually or for fixed periods, and consisted of a tax of 4s. in the £ on the yearly value of land and 2s. 8d. in the £ on the yearly value of goods. The assessments in the Subsidy Book were continually becoming obsolete.

P. 106, l. 8. *A little bait :* a little food.

l. 22. Sept. 14th. *Hanger :* a short and slightly curved sword used by seamen.

P. 108, l. 2. Oct. 19th. *Sir J. Minnes :* successor of Sir Robert Slingsby, who had died on Oct. 27th, 1661, to the office of Comptroller of the Navy. He, too, according to Pepys, was thoroughly incapable.

l. 24. *Pigeons put to her feet :* this was a charm which was believed sometimes to save a person's life. Compare it with Pepys's hare's foot as a preventive of the colic.

P. 109, l. 6. *Hambrough :* Hamburg.

l. 37. Oct. 29th. *Hypocras :* a drink made of wine flavoured with spices.

P. 112, l. 10. Nov. 15th. *Which methinks is a poor thing to be forced to be commanded :* Queen Catherine was never very popular in England, especially since she was childless.

l. 15. 18th. *Letter of reproof :* Pepys had heard tales about Lord Sandwich's behaviour and his growing unpopularity at Court, and had resolved to warn him of the danger to his reputation.

NOTES

P. 114, l. 25. 19th. *Mr. Gauden :* Victualler of the Navy.

P. 119, l. 1. Dec. 10th. *Link :* a torch made of tow and pitch.

1664

P. 121, l. 3. Feb. 1st. *The wall :* the inner side of a pavement or sidewalk, next to the wall, and away from the filth of the kennel, or gutter.

   l. 8. *Laughing at Sir W. Petty about his boat :* Sir W. Petty had invented a new kind of sailing-boat " upon two keels," as Pepys tells us elsewhere.

   l. 10. *Gresham College :* in 1645 a scientific society had begun to meet here, calling itself the " Invisible College." It was revived at the Restoration and was formally incorporated by a Charter as the Royal Society of London on July 15th, 1662.

P. 122, l. 12. Mar. 18th. *Against anon :* quickly.

   l. 13. *To church :* St. Bride's.

P. 124, l. 27. April 25th. *Bednal Green :* Bethnal Green.

P. 126, l. 5. June 4th. *Prince Rupert* (1619–1682) : cousin to the King and son of Elizabeth, Queen of Bohemia. He was a dashing commander both on land and on sea.

   l. 20. *Opiniastrément :* obstinately.

P. 128, l. 17. July 11th. *The Wells :* the mineral springs near Barnet.

P. 129, l. 25. 14th. *Clarendon Park :* near Salisbury.

   l. 34. *Nose :* insult.

P. 133, l. 35. Aug. 27th. *Impertinently :* improperly, awkwardly; *not* saucily.

P. 135, l. 8. Nov. 15th. *A Committee of Tangier :* Pepys had been nominated on the newly-appointed Commission for the Affairs of Tangier in November 1662.

P. 136, l. 19. Dec. 15th. *Comet :* this comet was visible for three months. See Dryden's *Annus Mirabilis.*

   l. 34. 24th. *Our defeat at Guinea :* an English merchant fleet had been " beaten to dirt " by De Ruyter off the Guinea Coast. England and Holland were not then officially at war, but such collisions on the high seas were frequent even in time of peace.

P. 138, l. 4. 31st. *My hare's foot :* a charm against the colic. But Pepys lost faith in this particular hare's foot when it was pointed out to him that it lacked the joint, which was essential.

1665

P. 140, l. 7. Feb. 9th. *Mr. Barlow :* see June 29th, 1660, and note.

l. 16. 15th. *Mr. Povy :* Treasurer for Tangier.

l. 19. *Lord Brouncker :* another colleague of Pepys's at the Navy Office, and first President of the Royal Society.

P. 145, l. 24. June 17th. *A thrush :* an ulceration.

l. 26. 21st. *Our tallies :* this seems to mean receipts given in acknowledgment of debt.

P. 146, l. 2. 30th. *Shot the bridge :* before the erection of the present London Bridge, the fall of water at ebb-tide was very great, and to pass at that time was called " shooting the bridge," because it was dangerous for small boats.

l. 6. *Thus this book of two years ends :* this marks the conclusion of the third volume of the shorthand manuscript.

l. 25. July 7th. *Sack :* a dry Spanish wine (L. *siccus*). *Malaga :* coming from Malaga, near Gibraltar. *Tent :* a Spanish red wine.

P. 147, l. 5. 15th. *Mr. Carteret :* son of Sir G. Carteret and suitor to Lady Jemimah Montagu, daughter of the Earl of Sandwich.

P. 149, l. 31. 26th. *Her painting :* Mrs. Pepys had taken to painting a little while before. Apparently she met with more success in this than in her music, for on Jan. 23rd, 1669, we find Pepys's guests admiring her work.

P. 153, l. 32. Aug. 15th. *Bringing :* being brought. As often, the active used for the passive participle.

P. 156, l. 20. Sept. 3rd. *The same man :* Mr. Browne (see Aug. 28, just before).

P. 157, l. 33. 10th. *Mr. Evelyn :* the other famous diarist of the seventeenth century. This anecdote of Pepys's reveals a very different Evelyn from the sedate, cultured artist of his own pages.

P. 158, l. 27. Oct. 7th. *Transire* (from the Latin): a customs document, describing the cargo of a ship and its consignees, etc.

P. 160, l. 5. 11th. *A very rash act :* this, and his failure in an attack on Bergen in the previous August, were the chief reasons for the fall of Sandwich. For his being made Spanish Ambassador did not conceal the disgrace of being dismissed from the position of Admiral of the Fleet.

P. 160, l. 20. 15th. *A duo of counterpoint :* a piece of music consisting of two melodies, one forming an accompaniment to the other.

P. 162, l. 23. Nov. 5th. *Gardenage :* " The Gard'ner's Almanac," published in 1666.

l. 35. *Grate :* cage.

P. 164, l. 35. 24th. *He did present me with it :* this, and other old manuscripts borrowed from Evelyn, Pepys never returned, but kept in his library.

P. 165, l. 26. Dec. 6th. *Solyman's words to Roxalana :* in Sir William Davenant's *Siege of Rhodes.* They began:

> " Beauty, retire ! Thou dost my pity move.
> Believe my pity, and then trust my love.
>
> > *(Exit* Roxalana.)
>
> At first I thought her by our Prophet sent,
> As a reward for valour's toils,
> More worth than all my father's spoils,
> And now she is become my punishment.
> But thou art just, O Power Divine !
> With new and painful arts
> Of studied war I break the hearts
> Of half the world, and she breaks mine."

P. 166, l. 26. 31st. *Melancholy because of the great plague :* there were almost 70,000 deaths in 1665 out of a population in London of less than half a million.

l. 36. *A new Act :* the country was on the verge of a financial breakdown. In December 1664 a " Royal Aid " of $2\frac{1}{2}$ millions, to be raised by a monthly assessment, had been voted; in October 1665 an additional $1\frac{1}{4}$ millions had been voted, and a proviso had been introduced in the Act requiring that the money raised should be applicable only to the purposes of the war. Parliament, by thus claiming the right of appropriation of supplies, hoped, as Pepys says, " to bring credit to the Exchequer."

1666

P. 171, l. 18. June 13th. *Sir Christopher Mings :* a distinguished naval commander, who had died from the wounds he received in the victorious fight with the Dutch on June 3rd (of which Pepys gives a long account in the full Diary).

P. 173, l. 3. 29th. *Callice :* Calais.

P. 174, l. 33. July 6th. *Lombard Street :* where the goldsmiths, forerunners of modern bankers, conducted their business.

P. 174, l. 37. *Bab Allen :* Mrs. Knipp, the actress (see Jan. 6th, 1666).

P. 175, l. 30. 28th. *Dr. Charleton :* the King's physician.

P. 178, l. 25. Sept. 2nd. *Pudding Lane :* between Eastcheap and Lower Thames Street.

P. 180, l. 27. *Likely :* in the obsolete sense of " promising," " agreeable."

P. 181, l. 24. *Buttulph's Wharf :* Botolph's Wharf, Billingsgate.

l. 30. *A pair of virginals :* an oblong spinet. " Pair " here signifies gradation or sequence, as nowadays " a pair of stairs " (Grove, *Hist. of Music*).

P. 184, l. 14. 4th. *The Iron gate :* Irongate Stairs, Lower Thames Street.

l. 19. *Kennels* (and below, Sept. 6th, *cannels*) *:* gutters.

l. 28. *Parmesan cheese :* a pressed cheese of rich flavour made from skim-milk.

P. 186, l. 4. 5th. *Our lane :* Seething Lane.

P. 187, l. 21. *Buckled . . . like parchment :* bent, crinkled.

P. 188, l. 23. 6th. *Nonsuch :* Nonsuch House, near Epsom.

P. 189, l. 15. 7th. *St. Faith's :* St. Faith-under-Paul's, a four-aisled crypt beneath the choir of the old church in St. Paul's.

l. 37. *St. Ellen's :* St. Helen's, in the Isle of Wight.

P. 190, l. 3. *The General :* the Duke of Albemarle.

P. 191, l. 34. 8th. *Low spirits :* " poor spirit," *i.e.* contemptible conduct.

P. 192, l. 33. 9th. *Decimo-tertio :* a thirteenth.

P. 193, l. 8. 15th. *Houses lost by this fire :* the Fire is said to have destroyed 13,200 houses and to have reduced two-thirds of the capital to ruins.

l. 22. *An express :* a dispatch conveyed by a special messenger.

l. 28. *The Vice-chamberlain :* Sir G. Carteret.

P. 194, l. 30. 26th. *Blind :* dark.

P. 195, l. 28. *Hotspurs :* used generically of any hot-headed, impetuous man. Prototype Sir Henry Hotspur of *King Henry IV, Part I.*

P. 196, l. 12. Oct. 7th. *Current :* fluent.

P. 197, l. 35. *Taken this order :* John Pepys had taken holy orders and his M.A. degree in the summer of 1666, but afterwards abandoned the clerical career and became

Clerk to the Corporation of Trinity House in 1670 through his brother's influence.

P. 198, l. 13. Nov. 10th. *Discourse of 666 : An Interpretation of the Number 666* (1642) by Francis Potter—a piece of mathematical mysticism, probably inspired by the similar elaborations of early mediæval theologians.

P. 199, l. 9. Dec. 17th. *Alphabet :* catalogue.

l. 12. 19th. *Many of the music :* many of the musical profession.

P. 200, l. 23. 25th. " *It is decreed* " : another of Pepys's songs, of which the words were from Catiline's opening speech in Jonson's *Catiline :*

" It is decreed—nor shall thy fate, O Rome!
Resist my vow, though hills were set on hills."

1667

P. 201, l. 12. Jan. 23rd. *King's House :* the King's Theatre.

Humorous Lieutenant : by John Fletcher.

l. 19. *Nelly :* Nell Gwyn.

ll. 27, 28. Feb. 2nd. *A poem . . . of Dryden's—Annus Mirabilis.*

P. 202, l. 23. 7th. *Dead :* unconscious.

P. 203, l. 14. 12th. *Italian Signor Baptista :* organist to Queen Catherine.

l. 23. *Recitativo :* a kind of musical recitation, characterised by freedom from strict form in its tonal and metrical structure, being rhetorical rather than melodic in its phrasing.

P. 204, l. 1. *Actor :* actress.

P. 206, l. 14. March 1st. *Known :* well-known, famous.

l. 20. 2nd. *Florimel :* a maid of honour.

P. 207, l. 2. 12th. *His ticket to be paid :* owing to lack of money sailors were given writs on the Exchequer for the amount of wages due to them. These could not be cashed on demand, and so tended to depreciate from their face value, to the disadvantage of the sailor. (Cf. June 5, June 14th, 1667, below.)

P. 208, l. 9. April 28th. *Boyle's book of colours : Experiments and Considerations touching Colours* (1664).

Barn Elms : where the Ranelagh Club grounds are now, between Putney and Hammersmith, on the Surrey side of the river.

NOTES

P. 209, l. 21. May 12th. *Pembleton :* the dancing-master,
about whom there had been a violent quarrel between
Pepys and his wife in May 1663.

l. 28. *An ordinary :* a tavern or eating-house where
table d'hôte meals were served.

l. 32. *Potage :* soup.

P. 210, l. 20. 26th. *The parish church :* St. Margaret's.

l. 28. *New book against Solitude :* " My little book in
answer to Sir Geo. Mackenzie was now published,
entitled ' Public Employment and an Active Life,
with its Appanages, preferred to Solitude '."—Evelyn's
Diary, Feb. 15th, 1667.

P. 213, l. 12. June 10th. *An admirable thing to consider :*
i.e. causes amazement to consider, but the reverse of
admirable in the modern sense.

P. 215, l. 34. 13th. *Below :* below London Bridge.

P. 216, l. 9. *Backewell :* a goldsmith of Lombard Street.

P. 217, l. 10. *Writings :* documents.

P. 218, l. 4. *Dunkirk House :* Clarendon House on the
north side of Piccadilly, opposite St. James's Palace
(cf. Feb. 20th, 1665). Clarendon was popularly
accused of having been bribed to sell Dunkirk to the
French.

P. 219, l. 11. 14th. *Compound them :* mix them to form
gunpowder.

P. 221, l. 26. " *Dunkirk, Tangier, and a barren Queen* " :
another popular charge against Clarendon was that
he had purposely married Charles II to a Queen whom
he knew to be incapable of bearing children, in return
for the port of Tangier as dowry. It was later found
impossible to hold Tangier, and it was evacuated in
1683.

P. 223, l. 7. 19th. *Sir Richard Browne :* Clerk of the
Council.

P. 225, l. 8. 21st. *Jacobuses :* gold coins of value 25s.
sterling, struck in the reign of James I.

P. 229, l. 22. July 14th. *Cere-cloth :* a poultice.

P. 230, l. 24. 29th. *A peace :* Peace with the Dutch was
formally signed at Breda on July 31st.

P. 231, l. 33. Aug. 26th. *Lord Chancellor's seal :* Clarendon
fell on Aug. 27th, 1667.

l. 35. *Admiration :* wonder.

P. 232, l. 33. *He :* Clarendon.

P. 233, l. 28. 27th. *Bird-cage :* aviary.

l. 37. 28th. *Father-in-law :* the Duchess of York was

Clarendon's daughter, Anne Hyde. Indeed this marriage was one of the causes of his unpopularity and downfall.

P. 235, l. 14. Sept. 2nd. *Steelyard :* a lever balance.

l. 24. *Secretary to the Duke of York :* Pepys did not become Secretary to James until he came to the throne in 1685. But in 1673, when James resigned the office of Lord High Admiral, Pepys was promoted to the equivalent post of Secretary to the new Admiralty Commission.

P. 236, l. 3. 27th. Around this entry, together with that of Sept. 4th, 1668, the plot of " And So to Bed," J. B. Fagan's play about Pepys, was woven.

l. 21. Oct. 8. *Mr. Warner :* Sir Martin's serving-man in the play by Dryden.

l. 30. *Heretofore :* see Feb. 27th, 1660.

P. 238, l. 26. 9th. *Willet :* Deb. Willet, Pepys's new servant-girl.

P. 239, l. 15. *Trundle-bed :* a low bed on small wheels, trundled under another bed in the day-time.

P. 240, l. 4. 10th. *Twins :* Oliver and John Montagu, sons of Lady Sandwich.

l. 34. *A spit :* a slender pointed iron rod for roasting meat over a fire. Similarly, *spud* below.

P. 243, l. 21. 12th. *Where we baited :* to bait = to stop for food and drink on a journey.

l. 28. *Sir W. Batten's body :* he had died on Oct. 5th.

P. 245, l. 34. Nov. 29th. *Gib-cat :* tom-cat.

P. 246, l. 1. 30th. *Arundel House :* where the Royal Society was now sitting.

1668

P. 249, l. 10. Jan. 1st. *Farmers :* an Act of 1689 granting farmers a bounty on export when the price of corn fell below 80s. a quarter eventually solved this problem.

l. 20. *The Archbishop :* Gilbert Sheldon, Archbishop of Canterbury.

P. 252, l. 24. 21st. *Kate Joyce :* Pepys's cousin's wife.

l. 32. *Set on his head :* old-fashioned first-aid to the drowning.

l. 36. *His new employment :* as a tavern-keeper.

P. 253, l. 22. *Caveats :* see July 8th, 1661, note.

P. 254, l. 1. Feb. 1st. *My Tangier accounts :* Pepys had been Treasurer for Tangier since March 1665.

P. 254, l. 12. 2nd. *My presses :* large bookcase (cf. the " clothes-press ").

l. 15. *Being resolved to keep no more than just my presses will contain :* Pepys kept this resolution, and there are exactly 3000 volumes in the Pepysian Library.

l. 21. 7th. *Servant :* suitor.

P. 256, l. 7. 27th. *The Virgin Martyr :* by Massinger and Dekker.

l. 27. March 1st. *The business of tickets :* a ticket was a certificate issued to a sailor from the officers of his ship containing particulars of his service. Countersigned by the Navy Board, it was converted into a warrant on the Treasury for the amount of wages due to him. But as these tickets could not be cashed without protracted delay, they formed a virtual paper currency which depreciated from its face value as the credit of the Treasury grew more and more unsound. There were " ticket-mongers " who made a profit by buying up the tickets of needy sailors at far less than their actual worth. The " business of tickets " thus constituted the chief abuse in naval administration, and the only defence which Pepys could have put forward was sheer necessity through lack of money.

l. 28. *Answering the House :* a Parliamentary inquiry into the conduct of the Navy Office had been set on foot as a consequence of the fiasco of the Dutch war.

P. 258, l. 12. 3rd. *The former :* see June 12th, 1667.

P. 259, l. 7. 5th. *Mulled sack :* heated, sweetened, and spiced.

The Hall : Westminster Hall.

P. 261, l. 7. *He :* the King.

P. 263, l. 5. 26th. *Tabby :* " watered silk."

l. 19. *Pragmatical :* officious.

P. 264, l. 6. April 2nd. *Otacousticon :* ear-trumpet.

l. 30. May 25th. *In the garden :* Pepys is at Brampton.

P. 265, l. 1. *Two brothers :* John Pepys and John Jackson, his brother-in-law.

P. 266, l. 27. Sept. 16th. *Stocks :* the Stocks Market.

1669

P. 268, l. 10. Feb. 18th. *Bab. and Betty Pepys . . .* and *Talbot :* the children of Roger Pepys of Impington, Pepys's cousin.

l. 12. *The Mad Lover :* by John Fletcher.

l. 28. March 9th. *To the Tower :* Sir. W Coventry

had been imprisoned in the Tower on March 4th on a charge brought against him by the Duke of Buckingham, with whom he had quarrelled.

P. 270, l. 4. May 31st. *In longhand :* this Diary in longhand was never begun.

l. 12. *My being blind :* Pepys never actually became blind, nor was he ever in danger of becoming so, according to Sir D'Arcy Power, who considers that the trouble was " hypermetropia with some degree of astigmatism." But optical science was not then sufficiently advanced to afford him the relief which would have enabled him to continue the Diary.

INDEX

INDEX

INDEX

Palmer, Mrs. *See* Castlemaine, Lady.

Papists, the, scare of a plot, 198, 222

Parliament, 1, 2, 4, 7, 10, 12, 17, 25, 42, 97, 102, 104, 195, 199, 230, 243–4, 247, 254, 259 ,260, and *passim*

Pell-Mell, 32 n., 49, 100, 104

Pen, Sir W., 26, 29 n., 30, 31, 35, 41, 47–8, 49, 51, 58–9, 66, 77, 78, 87, 145, 173, 184, 190, 195, 197, 214, 234, 253, 263, and *passim*

Pepys, John (brother), 6, 11, 57, 86, 192, 197 n., 202, 239

Pepys, John (father), 6, 9, 11, 37, 40, 60–63, 93, 138, 171, 216, 224–25

Pepys, Margaret (mother), 11, 207

Pepys, Mrs., 31, 37, 39, 67, 98, 106, 134, 149, 206, 209, 216, 263, and *passim*

Pepys, Paulina (sister), 37 n., 43, 61, 63, 85, 214, 242, 254, 264

Pepys, Robert (uncle), 60

Pepys, Thomas (brother), 3 n., 27, 42, 68, 75, 81, 93, 122–23

Periwigs, 111, 156

Pett, Mr., Commissioner for the Navy, 47, 215, 222 seq., etc.

Pierce, Mr., surgeon, 3 n., 5, 6, 26, 83, 91, 96, 116, 124–5, 127, 194, 222 seq., and *passim*

Pierce, Mrs., 43, 165, 201, 262

Plague, the Great, 117, 125, 144, 151 seq., 166 n.

Plays : "Hamlet," 62, 135
"Midsummer Night's Dream," 83
"Othello," 34
"Romeo and Juliet," 72
"Twelfth Night," 65, 90

Plays: Others, 90, 91, 95, 96, 133, 262, and *passim*

Portraits, 67, 169–71

Portsmouth, Pepys a burgess of, 74

Povy, Mr., 140 n., 142, 154, etc.

Princess Royal, 17 n., 20, 40

Prize-fighting, 124

Queen, the, Catherine of Braganza, 49, 68, 75, 80–3, 87, 98, 100–101, 108–9, 111–12, 127, 132, 150

"Royal Charles, The," 78, 215, 218, 219, 258

Royal Society, the, 263, and *see* Gresham College, Arundel House.

Rupert, Prince, 126 n., 139–40, 196–7, 235

St. James's Park, 34, 49, 87, 127, and *passim*

St. Michel, Balthazar, 65 n.

St. Paul's Cathedral, 185, 189, 252, 266

St. Paul's School, 67, 92, 189

Sandwich, Earl of, 3 n., 5 seq., 37, 43, 54, 63, 79, 82, 84, 89, 97, 101, 104, 112 seq., 129, 134, 144, 154, 157, 160–61, 165–6, 168–9, 197, 267, and *passim*

Sandwich, Lady, 34–5, 61, 74, 146, 238

Skating, 87 n.

Songs, 3, 5, 71, 165, 200

Stewart, Mrs., 101, 135, 205

Tangier, affairs of, 79, 88, 92, 135 n., 142, 146, 156, 166, 248, and *passim*

Tea, a China drink, 33

Tennis, 235

Tower, the, 74, 178, 185, etc.

Townshend, Mr., 49

Treasurer, Lord, 114–15, 135

INDEX

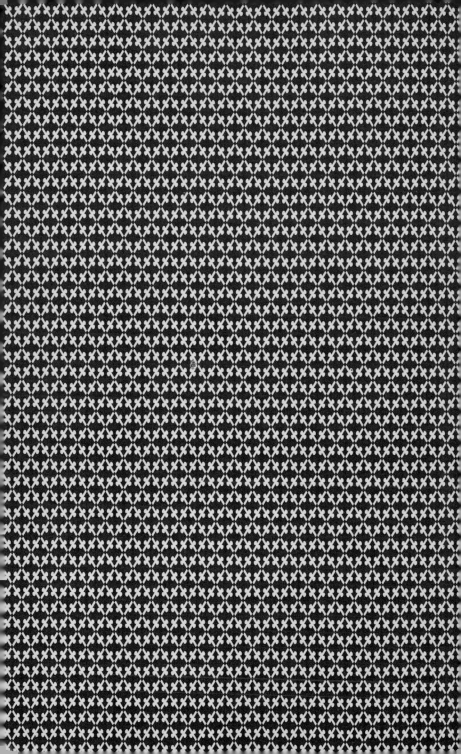